The Open University

Science Short Course

Human genetics and health issues

Mark Hirst and Judith Metcalfe

This publication forms part of the Open University course SK195 *Human genetics and health issues* (a revision of the first edition, S195 *An Introduction to the Human Genome*). Details of this and other Open University courses can be obtained from the Student Registration and Enquiry Service, The Open University, PO Box 197, Milton Keynes MK7 6BJ, United Kingdom (tel. +44 (0)845 300 60 90; email general-enquiries@open.ac.uk).

Alternatively, you may visit the Open University website at www.open.ac.uk where you can learn more about the wide range of courses and packs offered at all levels by The Open University.

To purchase a selection of Open University course materials visit www.ouw.co.uk, or contact Open University Worldwide, Walton Hall, Milton Keynes MK7 6AA, United Kingdom for a brochure (tel. +44 (0)1908 858793; fax +44 (0)1908 858787; email ouw-customer-services@open.ac.uk).

The Open University
Walton Hall, Milton Keynes
MK7 6AA

First published 2001. Second edition 2005. Third edition 2009.

Copyright © 2001, 2005, 2009 The Open University

Edited and designed by The Open University.

Typeset by SR Nova Pvt Ltd, Bangalore, India.

Printed and bound in the United Kingdom by Halstan Printing Group, Amersham.

The paper used in this publication is procured from forests independently certified to the level of Forest Stewardship Council (FSC) principles and criteria. Chain of custody certification allows the tracing of this paper back to specific forest-management units (see www.fsc.org).

ISBN 978 1 84873 280 3
3.1

The paper used in this publication contains pulp sourced from forests independently certified to the Forest Stewardship Council (FSC) principles and criteria. Chain of custody certification allows the pulp from these forests to be tracked to the end use (see www.fsc-uk.org).

Contents

Chapter 1   Human genetics and health issues: an overview   1

Chapter 2   The biology of the cell   7

2.1   The cell   7

2.2   The cell cycle   9

2.3   Summary of Chapter 2   13

Chapter 3   The human genome: chromosomes and genes   14

3.1   The chromosomes that constitute the human genome   14

3.2   Phenotype and genotype   16

3.3   Summary of Chapter 3   18

Chapter 4   Transmission of the genetic material   19

4.1   The formation of sperm and eggs   19

4.2   Fertilisation   24

4.3   Chromosome mixing during meiosis   26

4.4   To know or not to know the sex of an unborn baby   30

4.5   Summary of Chapter 4   31

Chapter 5   The inheritance of genes   32

5.1   A family history   32

5.2   Patterns of single-gene inheritance: dominant and recessive alleles   33

5.3   X-linked characters: colour blindness   36

5.4   Multiple alleles: the ABO system   38

5.5   Summary of Chapter 5   40

Chapter 6   The inheritance of genetic disorders   41

6.1   Pedigree charts   42

6.2   Huntington's disease: a dominant disorder   42

6.3   Cystic fibrosis: a recessive disorder   46

6.4   Summary of Chapter 6   52

Chapter 7   The influence of the environment on the phenotype   53

7.1   Environmental factors   53

7.2   A multifactorial character: height   54

7.3	Distinguishing between genotype and environment	56
7.4	Height around the world	59
7.5	Summary of Chapter 7	61

Chapter 8	Genetic disorders with multifactorial inheritance	62
8.1	The environment within the uterus	62
8.2	Coronary heart disease	63
8.3	The continuum of human disease	66
8.4	Summary of Chapter 8	67

Chapter 9	Introducing the substances of life	68
9.1	The components of cells	68
9.2	Proteins	69
9.3	The structure of proteins	71
9.4	Summary of Chapter 9	73

Chapter 10	What is your genome made of?	74
10.1	The chemical structure of DNA	74
10.2	DNA replication	77
10.3	Summary of Chapter 10	80

Chapter 11	Using information stored in DNA	81
11.1	One gene–one protein	81
11.2	The flow of information from DNA to RNA to protein	82
11.3	From DNA to RNA: transcription	82
11.4	From RNA to protein: translation	85
11.5	Where do transcription and translation occur in the cell?	88
11.6	The genetic code	89
11.7	Genes, proteins and cells	91
11.8	Summary of Chapter 11	92

Chapter 12	Mutation	93
12.1	Gene mutation	93
12.2	From gene mutation to protein structure	95
12.3	The rate of DNA mutation	97
12.4	Chromosome mutations	98
12.5	Summary of Chapter 12	100

Chapter 13   From protein to phenotype   101

13.1   Cystic fibrosis   101

13.2   Huntington's disease   106

13.3   Summary of Chapter 13   109

Chapter 14   Sequencing and interpreting the human genome   110

14.1   Deciphering the human genome sequence   110

14.2   DNA roles and genome organisation   113

14.3   Beyond whole genome sequencing: identifying genetic variation in
        the human genome   116

14.4   Other genome projects   117

14.5   Summary of Chapter 14   120

Chapter 15   Analysis of the human genome sequence   121

15.1   The genetic organisation of chromosome 21   122

15.2   A snapshot of the genetic organisation of the human genome   125

15.3   Sequence variation across the human genome and its effects   128

15.4   Identifying the genes that cause genetic diseases   130

15.5   Duplicated regions in the human genome   131

15.6   Summary of Chapter 15   133

Chapter 16   Cancer: somatic mutation and cellular disease   134

16.1   Somatic mutations   134

16.2   Genetic change and cancer   136

16.3   Environmental factors   141

16.4   Summary of Chapter 16   143

Chapter 17   Genes and populations   144

17.1   Differences between populations   144

17.2   Natural selection in action   146

17.3   Chance or random events   150

17.4   Human genome diversity   151

17.5   Summary of Chapter 17   153

Chapter 18   What will a knowledge of the sequence of the
human genome do for us?   154

Chapter 19   Genetic testing   156

19.1 Genetic counselling   157

19.2 Prenatal diagnosis   158

19.3 Genetic testing of children   161

19.4 Genetic testing of adults   162

19.5 Commercial interest and genetic testing   164

19.6 Summary of Chapter 19   167

Chapter 20   Genetic medicine: dreams and realities   168

20.1 Gene therapy   168

20.2 Saviour siblings and designer babies?   173

20.3 Designer drugs: pharmacogenetics and pharmacogenomics   174

20.4 'Personal' genomics   178

20.5 Expectations and prospects of genetics   179

20.6 Summary of Chapter 20   182

Chapter 21   Genetics, public health and health policy   183

21.1 Predictive medicine?   183

21.2 Population screening for genetic disease: the precedents   184

21.3 Scaling up   188

21.4 An example of genetic health care provision: the UK   191

21.5 Summary of Chapter 21   194

Questions: answers and comments   195

Appendix 1 How the human genome was sequenced:
molecular cloning and the technique of DNA sequencing   202

Acknowledgements   208

Index   209

SK195 Course Team

Chair:	Mark Hirst
Authors:	Mark Hirst, Judith Metcalfe
Consultant authors (Chapters 18–21):	Adam Hedgecoe, Jon Turney
Consultant author (Appendix):	Robert Saunders
Consultant:	Jane Anderson
Science Short Course Awards Director:	Elizabeth Whitelegg
Course Managers:	Isla McTaggart, Kat Hull
Course Coordinator:	Nick Adams
Course Team Assistant:	Jenny Hudson
Editors:	Dick Sharp, Margaret Swithenby, Matthew Driver, Stephen Jones
Graphic Artists:	Sue Dobson, Sara Hack
Graphic Design:	Jenny Nockles, Sarah Hofton, Sara Hack, Chris Hough
Picture Researchers:	Lydia Eaton, Martin Keeling
External Assessor:	Prof. Janet Bainbridge, OBE

Chapter 1
Human genetics and health issues: an overview

Imagine you have found some old family photograph albums which span many generations. What are the distinctive family features, or characters, that demonstrate the relatedness of individuals? In other words, what characters do they have in common? For example, they might have brown eyes, a white forelock in their hair, ears that are closely attached to the head, that is, without lobes. But you will also notice the striking differences between related individuals. For example, they may differ in height or hair texture. Some similarities and differences extend to characters that are not visible. For example, individuals may share the same blood group, or they may differ in the amount of cholesterol (a type of fat) circulating in the blood.

Working back through the albums, consider those individuals who have passed away and the reasons for their deaths, such as cancer or heart disease. All these visible and invisible characters of an individual and also their medical histories are governed by their genes and the environments in which they have lived.

Genes are units of inheritance. Our characters — the structure and appearance of an individual, such as blue or brown eye colour — depend on the functions of genes. Genes also contribute to a person's behaviour and health, including susceptibility to certain diseases, such as heart disease. How do genes influence our individual characters and the type of disease each of us might develop? How are genes transmitted from generation to generation? Where are genes located? These are some of the questions that this course sets out to answer.

You have selected this course almost certainly because you are interested in learning more about human genetics — the study of genes — and thus you may already be familiar with some of the scientific terms used in this chapter. (If you are not, then don't worry — they are fully explained in later chapters. For now, just appreciate the overview of the course that this chapter provides.) One of our aims in writing this course is to put you in a stronger position when you read about the science of genetics and listen to informed debates about modern techniques of manipulating genes, by increasing your understanding of the concepts and issues involved.

Many thousands of genes have been discovered, including many that have roles in disease. These genes are scattered throughout the human genome. But what is the human genome? The physical appearance of the bulk of the human genome is 46 long, thin structures known as chromosomes. The genome of all individuals (with a few exceptions) looks like that in Figure 1.1. It is along the length of each chromosome that the genes are located. The term genome is a combination of the two words 'gene' and 'chromosome'.

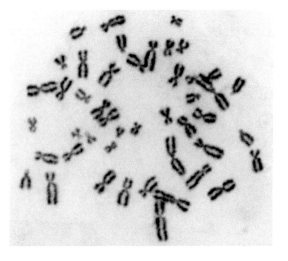

Figure 1.1   The human genome: 46 long, thin chromosomes, made conspicuous by the use of dyes. This photograph shows chromosomes in a white blood cell, magnified approximately 1000 times.

Chromosomes are built up from a remarkable substance called DNA (which stands for <u>d</u>eoxyribo<u>n</u>ucleic <u>a</u>cid). DNA is breathtakingly simple in structure and yet capable of directing the way we grow, reproduce and survive; hence it is often referred to as the genetic blueprint — the plan — of human life. Since genes are part of chromosomes they too are composed of DNA, which is why DNA is referred to as the *genetic material*.

Where, within the human body, are the chromosomes located? We, like many different types of organism, are composed of many millions of millions of cells; indeed, the cell is often referred to as the 'unit of life'. Cells are too small to be seen with the naked eye, but if you were to take a scraping from the inside of your cheek and look at it under a microscope you would see some cells, like the one in Figure 1.2. The important feature about cells for the human genome is the large structure called the nucleus, because it is inside the nucleus that the chromosomes are found. Within the nucleus of every cell in the human body (with a few exceptions) is a copy of the human genome. This adds up to a huge amount of DNA within any single individual.

In order to understand more about genes and the rest of the genome, in 1991 a formal programme, the Human Genome Project (HGP), was established to discover all the genes along each chromosome and to sequence the entire length of the human genome. On Monday 26 June 2000, scientists announced world-wide that they had completed a rough or first draft of the sequence of the human genome. The powerful headlines shown at the top of Figure 1.3 were the way that some British newspapers captured the attention of their readers, on or around that date. Was the HGP 'the breakthrough that changes everything' (Figure 1.3), and, if it was, *how* will it? Does the draft sequence really have implications for 'every person on the planet', just for scientists and doctors or just for those in high-income countries? Later in the course, we will explore how the HGP led to the sequence of the genome and look at the implications for the future that arises from our knowledge about our genes.

What do the words 'sequence of the human genome' actually mean? DNA contains information in a code that can be written in a four-letter language, A, C, G and T, in which each letter represents a different chemical (<u>a</u>denine, <u>c</u>ytosine, <u>g</u>uanine and <u>t</u>hymine). Like all codes, the one in DNA carries information or instructions; in this case, ones that direct the growth and survival of each individual. Like every letter in each word in this sentence, to be meaningful, the letters A, C, G and T have to be in the correct order or sequence in each gene. The HGP involved identifying each of these letters in the correct sequence for each chromosome in turn for the whole genome.

Before we go any further, we should try to gain some appreciation of the immense scale of *one copy* of the human genome and hence the phenomenal scope of the task that faced the scientists engaged in the HGP. The human genome comprises approximately six billion, 6 000 000 000, letters (chemicals) of A, C, G and T, joined together in pairs, i.e. 3 000 000 000 pairs, in a linear sequence along the length of the chromosomes. In order to appreciate the scale of this, consider the following data. The typeface of this book enables approximately 5000 letters to be printed on one page. Thus the sequence of the human genome would take a total of 600 000 pages and fill about 3000 books the

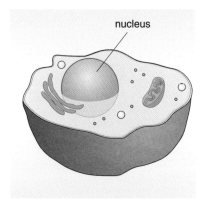

Figure 1.2 A drawing of a typical cell cut in two to reveal the nucleus. Note that about 20 such cells laid side by side would measure 1 mm on a ruler.

nucleus

Figure 1.3   A collage of newspaper headlines, published on or around
26 June 2000 (top), announcing the publication of the first draft sequence of
the human genome, and published since 2000 (bottom), showing the continued
media attention given to 'breakthroughs' in understanding the human genome.

size of this one! The project was made possible only by a large number of staff
working in a substantial number of laboratories and, importantly, by database
technology on computers. By June 2000, the HGP had determined about 85%
of the sequence of the four letters with about 99.9% accuracy. The figure of
85% was chosen as the point at which the genome would have scientific and
medical value; hence the announcement on 26 June 2000 of the rough draft.
Since these initial publications, further sequencing produced a more complete
and accurate sequence, so that by 2003 very few gaps and errors remained in
the then published sequence. Since the early years of the HGP, the technology

we use to obtain a DNA sequence has improved significantly. What used to take several years in the 1990s can now be achieved in a few weeks; so much so that obtaining the complete DNA sequence of many different individuals is now realistic. Breakthroughs and landmark achievements continue to reach the media, as the headlines in some newspapers on the bottom of Figure 1.3 show: decoding the genomes of cancer cells, DNA from extinct Neanderthals and the discovery of many millions of DNA base differences between individuals. The ultimate goal of the scientists who first started the HGP still remains, however: to understand and interpret fully all the details of the human genome sequence including the genes it contains.

Let's return to June 2000. Our understanding of the human genome did not begin on this date; in fact, we had been learning about it, bit by bit, throughout the whole of the 20th century. The study of genes began in 1900 when it was shown that genes govern inheritance in many different creatures. In 1907 it was shown that the same patterns of inheritance could account for the transmission of eye colour in humans. However, not until 1953 was the structure of DNA deduced by Watson and Crick. Hence, most of this course will consider aspects of genetics and the genome that were understood long before the publication of the first draft of the human genome.

Human genetics is a huge topic. It would be possible to write a course that focused on just one aspect of it. However, our goal in this course is to introduce not only the science, but also some of the health issues generated by the study of genes and to offer a view of the differences in how genetics impacts upon health care across the globe. The science deals with the structure and function of the genome within each individual and the medical aspects such as disease genes and gene therapy. Although there are thousands of genes, some with very complicated names and functions, we discuss only a few straightforward but representative examples in order to demonstrate the basic principles.

The health issues include, for example, DNA testing for the presence of genes related to specific diseases. An issue is a topic that can always be considered from more than one point of view or perspective. For example, if the fetus of an expectant mother tested positive for a debilitating genetic disease, she might be confronted with the choice of a termination or having an affected child. The expectant mother's point of view and her partner's might be very different from that of the medical profession or society in general. Hence, health issues, in turn, raise social and ethical issues. Issues emerging from the study of genes are mainly dealt with towards the end of the course.

Since the course has a broad coverage, it cannot cover any topic in depth. Both the scope and content of the course are illustrated in outline in Figure 1.4. The left-hand side shows the different perspectives from which the genome can be considered, and the right-hand side describes the content of the course in relation to each perspective. Any given chapter in this book may focus on just one perspective, or consider two or more of these perspectives by relating them to one another. The course can be roughly divided into three sections: the first looks at genes and patterns of inheritance (Chapters 2–8), the second focuses on DNA (Chapters 9–17), and the third considers health, social and ethical issues (Chapters 18–21).

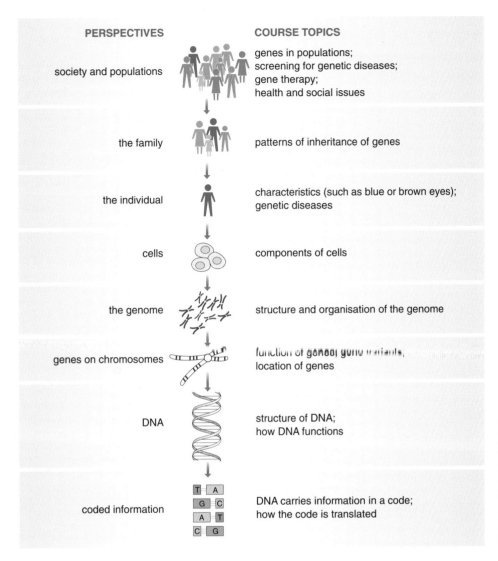

PERSPECTIVES		COURSE TOPICS
society and populations		genes in populations; screening for genetic diseases; gene therapy; health and social issues
the family		patterns of inheritance of genes
the individual		characteristics (such as blue or brown eyes); genetic diseases
cells		components of cells
the genome		structure and organisation of the genome
genes on chromosomes		function of genes, gene variants, location of genes
DNA		structure of DNA; how DNA functions
coded information		DNA carries information in a code; how the code is translated

Figure 1.4   The different perspectives from which genes can be considered and the topics included in the course in relation to each perspective. You will find it helpful to refer back to this diagram as you progress through the course.

The Study Guide

Have you read Part I of the Study Guide for the course, which gives a summary of the structure and content of this book along with information to guide your study? If not, then you should do so now.

Activities such as the one below, expand and illustrate what you have been reading in this book. They are in Part II of the Study Guide. These activities are designed to help you become actively involved in your own learning process, and develop the skills and understanding, i.e. the learning outcomes (see Section 1.4 of the Study Guide), you require for tackling the end-of-course assessment (ECA).

Activity 1.1   Genes in the news

By the end of the course you should be able to extract relevant information and discuss the science both in the course book and in news articles. This activity gets you started. Now go to the Study Guide and complete this activity.

Chapter 2
The biology of the cell

We begin this course with a description of the cell, because the genome is housed within the cell nucleus. Another important property of cells is that they can reproduce themselves, and we explore what happens to the genome during this process.

The basic biological concepts introduced in this chapter provide a framework for understanding the genome and how it functions; later chapters will refer back to and build on these ideas.

2.1   The cell

Humans consist of many millions of millions of cells. A single human **cell** is a complex entity that, to some extent, is self-sufficient; many processes go on within it independently of what is happening in other cells. Each cell has many components, only some of which are considered in this chapter; these are shown in Figure 2.1.

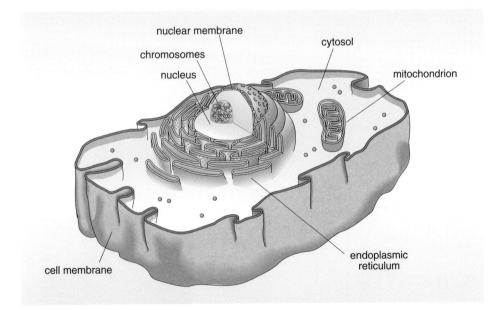

Figure 2.1   Schematic drawing of a cell in cross-section, showing some of the features that are found in most human cells.

In science it is often useful, when dealing with complex ideas, to think of an *analogy*. One analogy for the appearance of the cell in Figure 2.1 is a polythene bag filled with colourless minestrone soup. Both have an outer boundary that contains a fluid material in which are suspended a number of substances and diversely-shaped objects but, beyond that, the analogy is a poor one. In the cell, the outer layer, the **cell membrane**, is not simply a bag that keeps the contents of the cell in one place. The cell membrane is a highly complex structure that has a number of important properties. It is true that its main function is to constrain the chemical substances inside it, allowing them to interact with each other, but it is also an active structure: it carries out a variety of functions that are vital to the life of the cell. Most importantly, unlike a polythene bag, it is not completely impermeable so certain substances, but not others, can pass through it.

Various objects are contained inside the cell (Figure 2.1). The largest of these is the **nucleus**, which is surrounded by the *nuclear membrane* and contains the cell's genetic material, the **chromosomes** (Figure 1.1). The cell is filled with a watery fluid that surrounds all the various objects except the nucleus, called the **cytosol**. In addition to water, the cytosol contains a lot of chemical substances and some very small objects. Unlike the nucleus, of which there is only one in a cell, the other objects occur in varying numbers. For example, there may be a few or many thousands of *mitochondria* (singular: mitochondrion) which in cross-section appear sausage-shaped. Their function is to produce the energy that fuels all the other processes that go on inside the cell. Within the cytosol is a complex, three-dimensional, lace-like system of membranes called the *endoplasmic reticulum*. This has a structure similar to that of the cell membrane and forms a kind of 'scaffolding' within the cell.

There is no cell in the human body that looks remotely like the one shown in Figure 2.1, because that cell illustrates only features that are common to many types of cell. Although almost all of the cells in the body conform to a basic structure, there is a great deal of variation. Figure 2.2 gives an idea of how they differ in shape, size and content, according to their particular function in the body. Thus skin cells (Figure 2.2a) form a protective layer over the body surface, nerve cells (Figure 2.2c) help you to sense your surroundings, and muscle cells (Figure 2.2e) enable you to move. Red blood cells (Figure 2.2f) are packed with the substance *haemoglobin*, which carries oxygen around the body. Digestive cells lining the gut (Figure 2.2d) absorb the products of the digestion of food. Each sperm cell (Figure 2.2b) has a long tail that enables it to swim and so make contact with an egg cell.

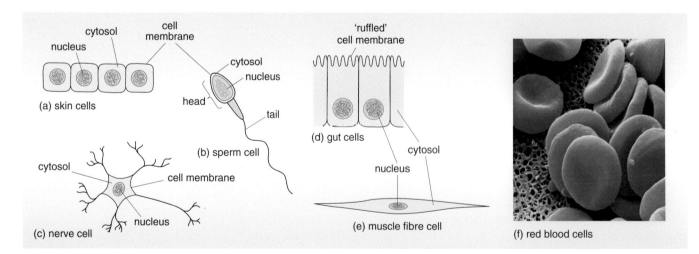

Figure 2.2   The diversity of cells in a human is revealed in the drawings (a)–(e). These are not drawn to the same scale. (f) is a photograph of red blood cells, which contain no nucleus.

■ What features are common to all of the cells in Figure 2.2a to e?

☐ Each cell contains a nucleus and is bounded by a cell membrane. Outside the nucleus, but contained within the cell membrane, is the cytosol.

The cell membrane gives a particular cell its shape. The exact shape of a cell is determined partly by the mechanical properties of the membrane, and partly by the presence of other cells adjacent to it. Nerve cells, for example, typically have an elongated tortuous shape (Figure 2.2c) because they have grown through the spaces between other, tightly packed cells. Red blood cells, on the other hand, have a characteristic flattened-disc shape (Figure 2.2f).

The different types of cell carry out different tasks. Each type does a few things very well, and we call this *specialisation*. Note that the structure of each specialised type of cell is closely related to the functions that it carries out.

The close relationship between structure and function is a fundamental characteristic of biological material.

Although some particular types of cell, notably blood cells, move about the body to some degree independently of one another, most cells are clustered together with others to form a tissue. Many tissues consist almost entirely of one cell type — muscle, for example, is made up almost exclusively of many millions of muscle fibre cells (Figure 2.2e). Other tissues are composed of two or more cell types, such as the gut, which is lined with gut cells (Figure 2.2d) but also contains muscle cells as well as having a rich supply of blood cells, provided by small capillaries (fine tubes at the end of arteries).

2.2   The cell cycle

A fundamental and very important property of most cells is their capacity to reproduce themselves. All of the cells in your body are descendants of a *fertilised egg*, i.e. a cell composed of an egg cell and the nucleus of a sperm cell, shown at the left-hand end of Figure 2.3. Every cell (with a few exceptions) of an individual contains exactly the same genetic material, regardless of what type of cell it is. To explain how this comes about, we need to consider the *cell cycle* in some detail.

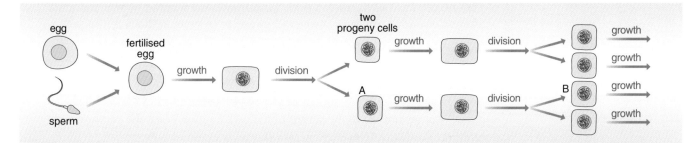

Figure 2.3   A sequence of cell divisions. All of the cells in the body are descendants of a fertilised egg. This cell produces two progeny cells when it divides, and so on. The letter A represents the start, and the letter B the finish, of one cell cycle.

In essence, a cell enlarges and makes copies of everything it contains; it then divides to give two progeny cells, each of which receives a complete set of all of the substances and objects that the 'parent' cell contained. The original parent cell itself effectively disappears, leaving only the two progeny cells. The new cells grow before the cycle starts again. The sequence of cell growth followed by cell division repeats again and again, as shown in Figure 2.3.

During the phase of *cell growth,* the chromosomes within the nucleus exist as very long thin threads, and at this stage cannot be seen under a microscope. It is during this phase that each chromosome is copied along its length, to produce an identical copy. Somewhere along their length, the original chromosome and its copy are joined together. The point of attachment is called the **centromere**, and the original chromosome and its copy are called **chromatids** (Figure 2.4). (Note that the pair of chromatids, when joined together at the centromere, is also referred to as a chromosome.) Because chromosomes are composed of DNA (and other substances) this involves copying the DNA, a process called *DNA replication.*

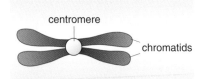

Figure 2.4 Two chromatids joined at the centromere.

The other phase of the cell cycle, **cell division** (which we consider in detail in the next section), involves two events. In the first, called nuclear division, one copy of each chromosome is distributed to each end of the parent cell. In the second, the parent cell divides to create two progeny cells, each with genetic material identical with that of the parent cell.

2.2.1   Cell division: sharing out the genome

Each progeny cell must have a complete set of the parent cell's chromosomes so that each has a copy of the genetic material. The process by which the contents of the nucleus are divided into two is called **mitosis**. For simplicity, mitosis is described here for a cell with just four chromosomes, but the same principles apply when there are 46 chromosomes, as in the case of the human genome. Mitosis begins when each long thin chromosome condenses into a coil, which condenses again into a supercoiled structure recognisable as a chromosome under a microscope (Figure 2.5).

Look back at the chromosomes in Figure 1.1, photographed during mitosis, and you will see that each chromosome is much more condensed and more distinct than in Figure 2.5. This is because Figure 1.1 illustrates a later stage of mitosis than Figure 2.5. Notice that in both these figures each chromosome is double along its length, with each chromatid joined to its copy at the centromere.

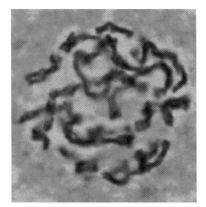

Figure 2.5 The chromosomes become conspicuous at the beginning of mitosis, particularly when special dyes are used to make them stand out from the background. The photograph shows chromosomes in a white blood cell, magnified approximately 1000 times.

Once started, mitosis is a continuous process, as shown in Figure 2.6. During an early stage of mitosis, the nuclear membrane disappears (Figure 2.6a) so that the cell no longer has a nucleus. The loss of the nuclear membrane is necessary to allow unrestrained movement of the chromosomes within the cell. The chromosomes line up in the centre of the cell (Figure 2.6b), the centromeres split and the chromatids then separate, so that each becomes a chromosome in its own right. One member of each former pair of chromatids migrates to one end of the cell, while its partner migrates to the other end (Figure 2.6c). There is now a set of four chromosomes clustered at one end of the cell and an identical set of four chromosomes clustered at the other end (Figure 2.6d). The chromosomes gradually uncoil and elongate again and in so doing become indistinguishable (Figure 2.6e and f), and eventually invisible again. At the same time, a nuclear membrane forms around each chromosome cluster so that the cell temporarily has two nuclei (Figure 2.6e). Mitosis is complete.

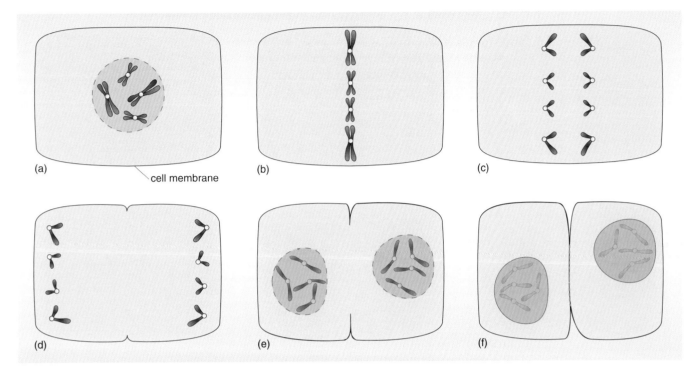

(a)

cell membrane

(b)

(c)

(d)

(e)

(f)

Figure 2.6 The essential features of cell division by mitosis. (a) The nuclear membrane begins to disappear. The four chromosomes each consist of two chromatids attached at a centromere. (b) The four chromosomes are aligned across the centre of the cell. (c) The pairs of chromatids separate in each of the four chromosomes, giving rise to eight separate chromosomes each with its own centromere. One member of each former pair of chromatids migrates to opposite ends of the cell. (d) Four chromosomes arrive at one end of the cell, and an identical set of four arrives at the other end. (e) A nuclear membrane forms around each set of four chromosomes, and each chromosome uncoils and begins to elongate again. (f) Division of the cytosol between the two progeny cells is achieved by constriction of the cell membrane.

Unlike the chromosomes in Figure 2.6d, each chromosome in Figure 2.6a consists of two chromatids. However, in both diagrams each chromosome has a single centromere. Once the centromere splits, each chromatid becomes a chromosome with its own centromere. (A chromosome can be single or double, but always has one centromere.)

To complete cell division, the cell must divide into two. This is achieved by constriction of the membrane across the middle of the cell, dividing it and its contents equally into two (Figure 2.6f). One cell has become two.

■ What is the essential outcome of cell division by mitosis?

☐ Two cells are formed, each with an exactly identical copy of the genetic material in the original cell.

Each progeny cell contains an identical copy of the genetic material in the original cell.

The new cells enter into a phase of growth, during which time the chromosomes are again replicated and then cell division can begin again; hence the term cell cycle (Figure 2.3).

Activity 2.1   Sharing out the genome: cell division

Now would be a good time to view the video sequence on this topic, which shows the separation of the pairs of chromatids particularly clearly.

2.2.2   Cell division and growth of the individual

Cell division leads to an increase in the number of cells and thus to the growth of an embryo from a fertilised egg, as shown in Figure 2.7. During the growth of the embryo cells become specialised. Cell division is obviously important during the growth of a fetus and child, but even when the individual has reached adult size, some cells continue to divide with new cells replacing those that die (Figure 2.7). This process occurs at different rates in different parts of the body. Cells in the lining of the gut are replaced every few hours; those in the kidney and liver live for weeks.

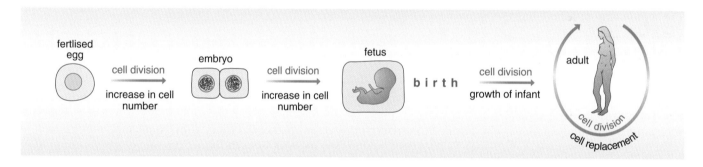

Figure 2.7   The growth of an individual from a fertilised egg involves an increase in cell number by cell division. In the adult some cells divide to produce replacement cells.

There are, in fact, two quite different forms of nuclear division. Mitosis, which occurs in most tissues, involves replication of the DNA content and exact duplication of cells. A quite different nuclear division takes place in the cells of the sex organs that give rise to egg cells in females and sperm cells in males. This will be described in Chapter 4, after we have examined the physical structure of the genome.

Question 2.1

Which of the following statements is incorrect?

(a) The cell nucleus contains DNA.

(b) The cytosol is found in the nucleus.

(c) The cell membrane forms the outer layer of the cell.

(d) Each type of cell is specialised to carry out particular functions.

Question 2.2

(a) At what phase of the cell cycle — cell growth or cell division — do the following events occur: (i) chromosomes replicate; (ii) a nuclear membrane is formed; (iii) identical copies of chromosomes separate from each other?

(b) Starting with (i), put the three events (i) to (iii) into the order in which they would occur.

Question 2.3

An effective way to check and reinforce your understanding of a key concept in the text is to write down a summary or definition of it. Try this now by writing down a summary of the key concept of 'cell division'.

2.3   Summary of Chapter 2

The cell is the basic unit of life. The cell is surrounded by a cell membrane, which contains the cytosol and various objects. The largest object in the cell is the nucleus, which is surrounded by the nuclear membrane and which contains the chromosomes.

There are many different types of cell in the human body, each of which is specialised to carry out particular functions.

The cell cycle is composed of a phase of cell growth and a phase of cell division. The latter involves mitosis, in which chromosomes, copied during the phase of cell growth, are shared equally between the two progeny cells so that each has an identical copy of genetic material.

The growth of an individual from a fertilised egg involves an increase in cell number by cell division. In the adult some cells continue to divide to produce replacement cells.

Chapter 3
The human genome: chromosomes and genes

Almost all of the different types of cell in an individual contain the same genetic material in the chromosomes, as a consequence of mitosis. You had a glimpse of the appearance of the 46 human chromosomes in Figure 1.1, and in this chapter we examine their size, shape and genetic composition.

Chromosomes can be regarded as strings of genes arranged along their length, rather like beads on a thread. Each gene consists of a short section of the DNA (described in Chapter 1) that runs the full length of each chromosome. Genes direct our characters, such as eye colour, and also the processes that go on inside us, from the small-scale processes of cell division to the large-scale processes of development and reproduction.

We will build on the concepts introduced in this chapter later in the course, and particularly in Chapters 4 to 6.

3.1   The chromosomes that constitute the human genome

Laboratory techniques are available to aid in the preparation and staining of the chromosomes from a single cell, so that they are readily distinguished and can be photographed under the microscope. Recall from Chapter 2 that, during mitosis, the chromosomes become visible (because they have condensed) and it is during mitosis that chromosome number, size and shape can be most easily studied. Every *species* has a particular number of chromosomes, each with a characteristic size and shape. For example, chimpanzee cells have 48 chromosomes, turkey cells have 82, and the cells of some species of ferns have over 1000 chromosomes!

Figure 3.1 shows the chromosomes of a human female, arranged to reveal their features. This distinctive pattern is described as the human female **karyotype**,

Figure 3.1   Photograph of the stained chromosomes of a human female, arranged as a karyotype (photographed through a microscope, magnified approximately 1000 times). The chromosome images are cut from a photograph of a spread of chromosomes at mitosis (such as the one shown in Figure 1.1). The pairs of chromosomes have been arranged in a conventional sequence and are numbered 1 to 22, with one pair of X chromosomes. Each chromosome has duplicated before mitosis begins, and so consists of two chromatids about to separate.

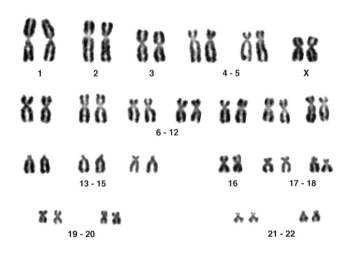

that is, the pattern of chromosomes that is unique to human females. The same term, karyotype, is used for the standard chromosome set of an individual, as in 'human female karyotype', or of a species, as in 'human karyotype'. (Each chromosome in Figure 3.1, like the chromosomes in Figures 2.6a and 2.6b, consists of two chromatids about to separate, one into each of two new cells.)

■ What is the most striking feature of the human chromosomes shown in Figure 3.1?

☐ The 46 chromosomes are present as 23 pairs of various sizes; the members of each pair look the same.

The chromosomes in 22 of the pairs have been given a number starting with the largest and progressing to the smallest. Thus, there is a pair of chromosome 1, a pair of chromosome 2, etc. Members of a pair are said to be *homologous*, which means 'having a similar structure', thus there are 22 **homologous** pairs of chromosomes. Although the chromosomes of some homologous pairs are longer or shorter than others, it is still difficult to distinguish between several pairs of chromosomes on this criterion alone. For example, look at the pairs of chromosomes numbered 6 to 12 in Figure 3.1: if those chromosomes were mixed up it would be difficult to separate them into pairs again on the basis of visual appearance alone. This difficulty was overcome in the 1970s by the discovery of special staining techniques that produce distinctive patterns of bands on chromosomes (Figure 3.2).

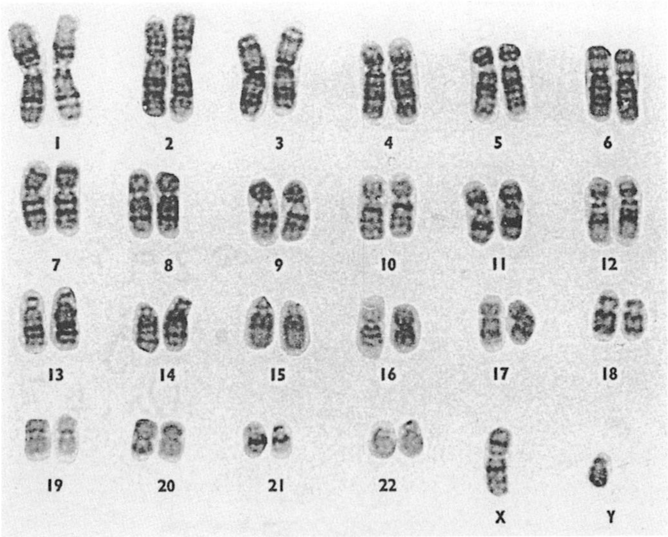

Figure 3.2   Photograph of the chromosomes of a human male, arranged as a karyotype and stained to reveal their characteristic banding pattern (photographed through a light microscope, magnified approximately 1000 times).

Such techniques have made it possible to define the differences between the members of one pair and those of another, as shown in Figure 3.2. The chromosomes of a human male, arranged as a karyotype, could be from any cell in the body (with a few exceptions).

■ How does the human female karyotype (Figure 3.1) differ from the human male karyotype (Figure 3.2)?

☐ The female karyotype has two X chromosomes whereas the male has one X chromosome and a small Y chromosome.

The X and Y chromosomes are called **sex chromosomes** because they play an important role in sex determination: females with a pair of homologous X chromosomes are described as XX, and males are described as XY. (We look at this in more detail in the next chapter.) Apart from these sex chromosomes, both males and females contain similar sets of 22 homologous pairs of non-sex chromosomes, or *autosomes*.

■ In Figure 3.2, what does the banding pattern of the homologous pairs of chromosomes numbered 6–12 reveal?

☐ First, each pair can be distinguished from all other pairs, and second, each chromosome appears to have an identical banding pattern with its partner.

The two observations that you have just made about chromosomes reveal important information about inheritance. We will look at the implications of each of these observations in turn.

Each of the 24 *different* kinds of chromosome that may occur in a human cell (that is, chromosomes 1 to 22, plus X and Y) carries different *genes*; each has particular genes arranged in a specific order along its length. However, both partners in a pair of homologous chromosomes, for example the pair of chromosome 1, carry the *same* genes in the *same* order. This means that each gene along the 22 autosomes, and the X chromosomes in females, is present twice in the nucleus of almost all cells, a feature that has important consequences for inheritance. Furthermore, the set of genes is the same in all humans.

> Different chromosomes contain different genes, but the partners in a pair of homologous chromosomes carry the same genes in the same order along their lengths.

Figure 3.3 shows that the two sex chromosomes look quite different from each other. They also carry different genes and, given the small size of the Y chromosome, you may not be surprised to learn that it contains very few genes, the most important of which is the gene that carries instructional information for the development of *testes* (male reproductive glands; singular testis) rather than *ovaries* (female reproductive glands; singular ovary).

3.2   Phenotype and genotype

By examining collections of family photographs spanning several generations, it is possible to follow the growth of individuals from birth, through to the teenage years and into adulthood. Brothers and sisters may share features that they also share with their biological parents, but in addition they have their own particular combination of characters that make them recognisable as individuals. You can detect visible features or **characters**: whether the hair is curly or straight; whether

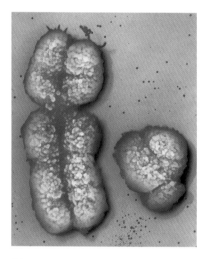

Figure 3.3   A pair of male sex chromosomes: the X chromosome (on the left) and the Y chromosome (on the right). Each chromosome consists of two chromatids attached at the centromere. This photograph was taken with the aid of a scanning electron microscope which has much greater magnification than a light microscope. The chromosomes here are magnified approximately 10 000 times.

the ears are 'unattached', that is, they are with lobes, or 'attached', without lobes (see Figure 3.4); how tall a person is or the colour of their skin. But what we can see is only a very small fraction of the differences between individuals. For example, we cannot see their blood group and blood pressure. The sum of all the characters that an individual possesses, including their morphology (the shape and structure of their body), their speed of movement and co-ordination as well as their temperament and personality, is described as the **phenotype**.

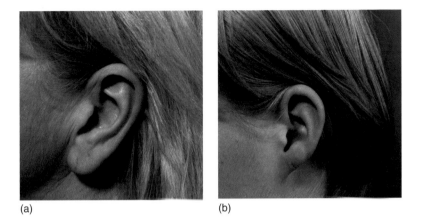

(a)   (b)

Figure 3.4   Ears are either (a) unattached with lobes, or (b) attached, without lobes.

The differences among parents and their children or among individuals in a population is called **variation**. One reason for this variation is the small *differences* between our genes. How can this be when all humans have the same set of genes? Although each individual has to contain the appropriate genes to be viable (i.e. to be able to survive), the set of genes does not have to be an *identical* copy of the set of genes of other individuals. Against the background of the same karyotypes and the same genes, we have some small differences in our genes. Thus, whilst we all share the same genes, **variants** of these genes can exist. These different forms of the same gene are commonly termed **alleles** by geneticists and, as we will see, they account for whether an ear is attached or unattached, and whether an individual's eye colour is blue or brown, for example. Each individual (apart from identical twins) has his or her own unique combination of alleles, i.e. their genetic make-up; the full set of genes is called the **genotype**.

However, as you will learn as you progress through the course, the phenotype of each individual is the result not only of the combined effect of their genes (their genotype) but is also influenced by their *environment*. In this context, environment means all the physical and social factors that interact with our genotype, such as the cytosol surrounding the nucleus of a cell, the *uterus* (womb) in which a fetus develops, the size of family and diet. Even identical twins have distinguishing characters, and you can imagine that a person raised under adverse conditions might develop and grow differently than they would have done if raised in a healthy environment. Some characters are influenced by the environment more than others. We can summarise the relationship between genotype and phenotype as follows:

genotype + environment = phenotype

17

In the next three chapters we explore the relationship between genotype and phenotype, by focusing on one or two particular characters, before we turn to examine the influence of the environment on the phenotype in Chapters 7 and 8. We begin Chapter 4 by describing the production of sperm cells and egg cells, which involves a different kind of nuclear division from mitosis.

Question 3.1

Explain whether or not each of the following is the same in every individual: (a) karyotype; (b) genotype; (c) phenotype.

Question 3.2

Which one of the following statements is incorrect?

(a) Pairs of homologous chromosomes have the same genes in a different order.

(b) The human karyotype contains 22 pairs of autosomes and two sex chromosomes.

(c) Variants of a gene contribute to an individual's uniqueness.

(d) An individual's phenotype is the result of the combined action of their genotype and their environment.

3.3   Summary of Chapter 3

The number of chromosomes is characteristic for a species; humans have 23 pairs of chromosomes composed of 22 pairs of homologous autosomes and two sex chromosomes. Females carry two X chromosomes and males carry an X and a Y chromosome.

Each chromosome has particular genes arranged in a specific order along its length, and each of the 24 different kinds of chromosome (i.e. the 22 autosomes, plus X and Y) carries different genes. Both partners in a homologous pair of chromosomes carry the same genes in the same order. These genes are present twice in the genome: one copy on one partner in a homologous pair of chromosomes, and the second copy on the other partner.

Although we all share the same genes arranged in the same order, variants of these genes, often called alleles, can exist.

The phenotype of each individual is the result of the combined action of their genes (their genotype) and their environment.

Chapter 4
Transmission of the genetic material

The process of reproduction can be separated into a number of stages: egg and sperm production and **fertilisation** (the combining of egg and sperm). We will examine these stages because they involve the transmission of a copy of each parent's genome to their offspring.

The focus of Chapters 4–6 is the relationship between genotype and phenotype. By examining the genome in egg cells, sperm cells and fertilised eggs, we can begin to explore answers to the question: why do members of a family such as mother, father, brothers and sisters, resemble each other but at the same time why do they each have a unique combination of characters? We will see that one reason for this is the large amount of *genetic variation* that is generated between egg or sperm cells, even in the same individual. Note that the term variation used in Section 3.2 for describing differences among individuals, can also be used to describe differences among egg cells and sperm cells. In this chapter our interest lies in the chromosomes, and in Chapters 5 and 6 we will home in on individual genes and characters.

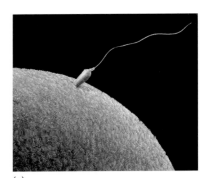

(a)

4.1 The formation of sperm and eggs

We all begin life as a single cell, which is formed from the combining of two **gametes**, the collective term for egg cells and sperm cells (Figure 4.1). We will examine the formation of sperm and eggs before exploring the content of their genomes.

A sexually mature male is continually producing sperm and releases about 500 million at each ejaculation. Sperm are produced in the testes, and production is most efficient at a temperature several degrees lower than the normal body temperature. For this reason, the testes are suspended outside the body cavity, and if they fail to descend from the position inside the body where they form, to this location, sperm production will not occur. Sperm formation is a complicated sequence of events taking about nine weeks, and many die at different stages along the way. Figure 2.2b shows that a sperm comprises a head, which contains the chromosomes tightly packed so that they can fit into the small space available, and a tail. Swimming is accomplished by means of the tail, which can beat rapidly, although it does not do so until after ejaculation.

There are substantial differences between sperm and eggs, and consequently their production pathways are very different. The egg is among the largest of human cells, almost visible by eye. Egg production takes place in the ovaries, which, unlike the testes, remain inside the body at body temperature. Normally only one egg is produced each month so that you might expect the whole of the development of an egg to take around one month to complete. You may therefore be surprised to learn that the process *can* take more than 50 years! This is because egg development begins *before* birth, so that at birth a girl will have partially formed eggs in her ovaries. Unlike sperm, which die a few days after their formation, the developing eggs remain alive, but enter a kind

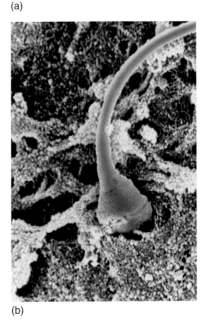

(b)

Figure 4.1 Gametes. (a) A sperm and part of an egg (non-human gametes). (b) A sperm has penetrated an egg (human gametes), and injected its nucleus. Both (a) and (b) are photographs taken with the aid of a scanning electron microscope.

19

of suspended animation. All of the eggs remain in this state until puberty, after which time some will be stimulated to carry on developing, culminating in the release of one mature egg each month. Although there are two million developing eggs at birth, only a few hundred will proceed to maturity and fewer still will be fertilised.

The genetic material contained in the **germline cells**, i.e. the gametes and the cells in the ovaries and testes that give rise to them, has a chance of immortality and could continue to survive through future generations. Some of your genetic material will be passed on to your children in your gametes, and their gametes will contain some of your genetic material, which will be passed on to your grandchildren, and so on from each generation to the next. By the same token, you inherited your genetic material from your parents' gametes, and they got it from their parents, and so on back in time. All the other cells in your body, called **somatic cells**, contain somatic genetic material that is not passed on to your descendants and will die with you.

4.1.1   Meiosis

This section describes the chromosome content of gametes. The process of gamete production involves a type of nuclear division that is different from mitosis (Chapter 2) and is called **meiosis**. Unlike mitosis, which occurs in somatic cells during growth and cell replacement, meiosis is confined to the egg-producing and sperm-producing cells in the ovaries and testes. The presence of pairs of homologous chromosomes (Section 3.1) is particularly important for reproduction and the passing on, or transmission, of genetic material between generations. Observing the behaviour of these pairs during the production of gametes provides us with a direct way of obtaining information about the inheritance of the genome and the genes it contains.

Meiosis is a much more complex process than mitosis and is remarkably similar in all animals and plants. The details of the process are not important here, but you should understand how differences between gametes can arise, because this variation has profound consequences for the characters of each individual.

The most striking way in which gametes differ from somatic cells in the body, and from the egg-producing or sperm-producing cells in the ovaries and testes from which they arise, is in the number of their chromosomes. The changes in chromosome number that take place in the human life cycle, including during meiosis and subsequent fertilisation of the egg by a sperm, are summarised in Figure 4.2. As a result of meiosis, each gamete contains half the number of chromosomes present in gamete-producing cells and somatic cells. Each gamete contains the *haploid* number of chromosomes, that is only 23 chromosomes: one from each of the 22 homologous pairs of autosomes, plus either an X or a Y chromosome. Put another way, the set of 23 chromosomes in each gamete is not a random selection from the 46 chromosomes of the parent, but consists of one of each pair of the 22 autosomes plus either an X or a Y chromosome.

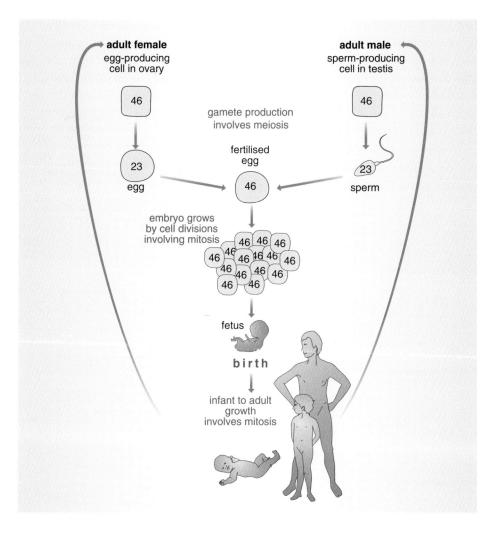

Figure 4.2   The changes in chromosome number in the human life cycle. Gamete cells contain 23 chromosomes, whereas all other cells of the body (with the odd exception) contain 46 chromosomes. We have omitted the nuclear membrane in each cell for simplicity, and we continue to do this in most subsequent figures.

■ How many chromosomes does a fertilised egg contain and from where did they come?

☐ It contains 46 chromosomes, which are in 23 pairs, including a pair of sex chromosomes: one member of each pair comes from the female gamete and the other member of each pair comes from the male gamete.

The full complement of 46 chromosomes in the human genome, the *diploid* number, is restored at fertilisation. As Figure 4.2 shows, all the somatic cells and the cells in the testes and ovaries arise from the same fertilised egg by the process of mitosis; the cells all contain copies of the same genetic material (with some exceptions).

■ From Figure 4.2, do the gamete-producing cells have the same chromosome number as the somatic cells?

☐ Yes; they have 46 chromosomes, the same number as somatic cells.

Each gamete-producing cell contains an identical copy of the genetic material in the somatic cells. Only the gametes contain half the chromosome number.

Now look at Figure 4.3, which illustrates the production of gametes in each parent and the possible combining of gametes at fertilisation with reference to the sex chromosomes only. We have omitted all the other chromosomes to make it easier to follow the sex chromosomes. First, we consider the production of gametes, and in the next section we examine fertilisation. Each one of the egg-producing cells in the ovaries of the female contains two X chromosomes, whereas the equivalent cells in the male each contain one X chromosome and one Y chromosome (top row of Figure 4.3). In the male, the X and Y chromosomes separate from each other during meiosis, the X chromosome to one sperm and the Y chromosome to another. Similarly, in the female, the two X chromosomes separate from one another, each one going into a different egg cell.

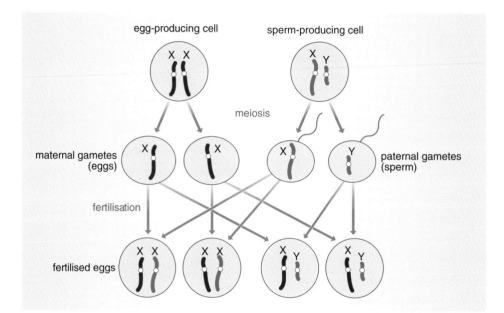

Figure 4.3   The distribution of human sex chromosomes during gamete formation and at fertilisation. Note that the chromosomes are drawn as single structures (unlike Figure 2.6a) in order to make it easier to follow the events.

■ On the basis of the middle row of Figure 4.3, what are the proportions of X-bearing and Y-bearing gametes produced by the male?

☐ Half of the gametes are X-bearing gametes and half are Y-bearing.

This answer can be expressed as a ratio in a number of ways; these are described in Box 4.1.

The behaviour of the sex chromosomes during meiosis is similar to that of all other pairs of chromosomes, that is the number is halved in each gamete. Thus the members of each of the 22 homologous pairs of autosomes in a gamete-producing cell also separate from each other during meiosis; one member of each chromosome pair enters each gamete. A consequence of the separation, or **segregation**, of members of homologous pairs of chromosomes (or the X and Y chromosomes) is that each gamete contains one member of each pair of autosomes and one sex chromosome (either X or Y).

Box 4.1 Ratios

Ratios are another way of expressing proportions. Ratios are usually written as two numbers separated by a colon (:). As the answer to the in-text question preceding this box shows, X- and Y-bearing gametes are produced by the male in equal numbers, so the ratio of X-bearing gametes to Y-bearing gametes is one to one, written as 1 : 1.

We are also interested in the proportion of the total number of gametes that are X-bearing gametes. The male produces two different types of gamete, of which one is X-bearing; so the ratio of X-bearing gametes to the total number of male gametes is 1 : 2.

Although not relevant in this case, it is important to note that ratios are usually simplified to the smallest whole numbers by dividing both sides by a common factor. For example, in a class of 4 boys and 8 girls, the ratio of boys to girls is 4 : 8, which is the same as 1 : 2, where both the numbers have been divided by 4.

You need to be careful about which ratio is being considered. Consider a practical example of a group of 20 people, 6 of whom have red hair and 14 of whom do not. The ratio of red-haired people to the *total* number of people is 6 : 20 (or 3 : 10). But now consider the ratio of red-haired people to non-red-haired people in the group: it is 6 : 14 (or 3 : 7).

Suppose that 2 out of 10 people in the UK have blue eyes. What is the ratio of people with blue eyes to those who don't have blue eyes?

The ratio is 2 : 8 (or 1 : 4).

Did you fall into the trap and answer 2 : 10 (or 1 : 5)? This is the ratio of people who have blue eyes to the *total* number of people. If we had asked what is the ratio of people who don't have blue eyes to those who do, the answer would have been 8 : 2 (or 4 : 1). So always read the question carefully and make sure when expressing ratios that it is clear what each number refers to.

Question 4.1

A class of children consists of 10 boys and 15 girls. What is the ratio of girls to boys?

We can now link the description of gamete production at the cellular level (Section 4.1) with the stages of meiosis. In males, meiosis begins at puberty and continues well into old age; each meiotic division takes just three hours. In contrast, in females the process of meiosis in an egg-producing cell *begins* before birth. But the halving of chromosomes during meiosis is halted within the egg-producing cell and is completed some time between puberty and menopause. Thus the process of meiosis and egg production in females is halted for many years before being completed. During a woman's reproductive life, one cell normally completes the meiotic division and gives rise to one egg during each menstrual cycle. The process of meiosis resulting in the production of an egg shortly after puberty has been halted for 10–15 years, and the process of meiosis resulting in the production of an egg just before the menopause will have been halted for about 50 years!

4.2 Fertilisation

Now that we have considered the production of gamete cells, including the process of meiosis, we can examine the next stage of reproduction, the process of fertilisation, which occurs inside the female's reproductive tract. As fertilisation occurs, the successful sperm stops swimming and a change takes place in the egg cell membrane, which prevents any other sperm from fusing with it. The nucleus of the sperm cell is injected into the cytosol of the egg cell (Figure 4.1b). The chromosomes of the fertilised egg thus consist of one set from the egg and one set from the sperm.

We have seen that fertilisation restores the number of chromosomes to 46 (Figure 4.2).

During in-vitro fertilisation (IVF), where eggs and sperm are brought together outside of the female's reproductive tract, the sequence of events of fertilisation and the subsequent restoration of chromosome number and early development is identical to the events outlined here. Generally, the fertilised eggs, now early embryos, are placed back into the recipient mother's uterus after 4–5 days of development and division.

■ Why is meiosis such an important feature of reproduction?

☐ If the chromosome number were not halved in the gametes prior to fertilisation, the fertilised egg would contain 92 chromosomes, twice the normal number in the parents' cells.

The fertilised egg grows and develops into an embryo by repeated mitotic divisions. The embryo in turn grows and develops into a fetus, baby, child and finally an adult. The life cycle shown in Figure 4.2 depicts all of the stages that a human must go through from conception through birth to reach adulthood. (This figure is similar to Figure 2.7 in that they both portray the human life cycle, but Figure 4.2 includes the important changes in chromosome number.)

One consequence of fertilisation can be examined by following the behaviour of the sex chromosomes. We can do this by returning to Figure 4.3, the top part of which we considered in Section 4.1. Figure 4.3 is a **mating diagram**, which shows the parents' gamete-producing cells, the gametes and the possible combinations of sex chromosomes at fertilisation. Recall from Section 3.1 that an individual with a Y chromosome will develop into a male.

■ From Figure 4.3, what is the expected ratio of female offspring to male offspring?

☐ Half of the sperm contain an X chromosome and every egg also contains one. Therefore, half of the fertilised eggs will be XX, and half will be XY, so the ratio of female to male offspring is 1 : 1.

The ratio of females to the total number of offspring is 1 : 2. Thus, for any fertilisation, the *chance* of producing a girl is 1 in 2, and the chance of producing a boy is the same, 1 in 2. The process of meiosis, which governs the separation, or segregation, of X and Y chromosomes during gamete formation, not only accounts for the occurrence of XX (female) and XY (male) individuals, but is also responsible for the production of the two sexes in the ratio of approximately 1 : 1 in any population.

Figure 4.4 represents a different way of showing the same information in Figure 4.3. Either way of presenting the details of a mating can be used, and when producing your own mating diagrams you can choose whichever is easier for you. In Figure 4.4, the fertilisations between the various combinations of gametes are shown in boxes. Along the top you can see the two types of gamete, X and Y, produced by a male; down the left-hand side you can see the two gametes produced by a female. Inside the other boxes are the products of fertilisation between the various gametes. Thus, for example, the top right-hand box records the outcome of the fertilisation of an egg with a Y-bearing sperm. An examination of the four boxes should convince you that the expected ratio of XX individuals to XY individuals is 2 : 2, which is the same as 1 : 1.

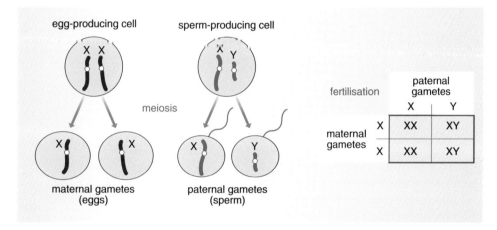

Figure 4.4   An alternative way of laying out the matings shown in Figure 4.3.

This ratio of 1 : 1 follows for two reasons. First, the two different gametes, X and Y, are produced in equal numbers in sperm. This is a consequence of segregation of the two sex chromosomes. Second, fertilisation is *random*; that is, an egg is equally likely to be fertilised by an X-bearing sperm as by a Y-bearing sperm. We will meet this 1 : 1 ratio in future chapters in relation to the inheritance of genes.

The 1 : 1 ratio of males to females is a consequence of:

segregation of chromosomes during meiosis into different gametes in equal numbers;

the combining of a female gamete and a male gamete at fertilisation occurring at random.

In Figures 4.3 and 4.4 we traced the behaviour of the sex chromosomes alone during the processes of gamete formation and fertilisation. However, the behaviour of autosomes during these two processes is the same as the behaviour of sex chromosomes, as shown in Figure 4.5. Note that in this figure the chromosomes coloured red in the fertilised egg originated from the mother (maternal chromosomes) and the blue-coloured chromosomes came from the father (paternal chromosomes). Thus the fertilised egg contains the diploid number of chromosomes: 23 homologous pairs, one member of each pair derived from the mother and the other from the father.

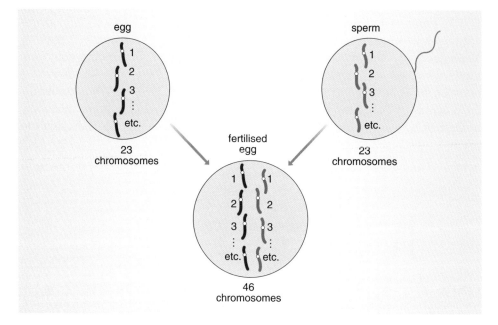

Figure 4.5   The chromosome content of both male and female gametes and the resulting fertilised egg (only four chromosomes are shown in each gamete, and four pairs in the fertilised egg). The fertilised egg contains half maternal chromosomes (red) and half paternal chromosomes (blue). In the fertilised egg, although each member of a pair of chromosomes contains the same set of genes, the two members of a pair differ due to the presence of different alleles.

4.3   Chromosome mixing during meiosis

We have accounted for the halving of chromosome number during meiosis, and the restoration of 46 chromosomes in the fertilised egg, as shown in Figure 4.5, but meiosis also results in gametes that are genetically different from each other. We return to meiosis to take a closer examination of the behaviour of chromosomes to see how variation arises between gametes and thus between individuals. The **recombination** of chromosomes during meiosis generates new combinations of genetic material, and is brought about either by *independent assortment* or *crossing over*. We examine these two processes in this section. The important principle to grasp is that these processes lead to genetic variation between the gametes of an individual.

The fertilised egg in Figure 4.5 will develop into an infant (who we will call individual A), who will grow into an adult who in turn will produce gametes (Figure 4.6). Recall that all the somatic cells and gamete-producing cells of an individual arise from the same fertilised egg by the process of mitosis; the cells all contain copies of the same genetic material. In the gamete-producing cells of individual A in Figure 4.6, only two of the 23 pairs of chromosomes are shown. During meiosis, when the chromosome number is halved, the members of each chromosome pair will separate and one of each pair will enter the resulting gametes. However, it is a matter of chance whether the red chromosome from a given pair enters a particular gamete, or whether the blue one enters it. (This is just like tossing a coin, it is a matter of chance whether you get a head or a tail.) Therefore, each gamete receives a *random assortment*, or an **independent assortment**, of the chromosomes, but always one of each chromosome pair.

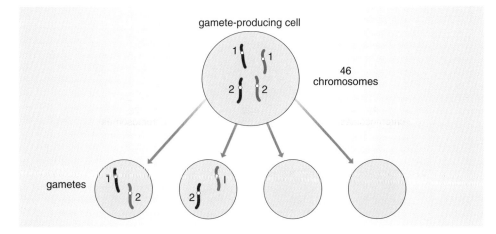

Figure 4.6 The different chromosome content of gametes produced by an individual (individual A, see text); two possible combinations are given. Only two pairs of chromosomes are shown in the gametes; the red chromosomes were inherited from individual A's mother, and the blue chromosomes from individual A's father.

Consider the two pairs of homologous chromosomes, labelled 1 and 2, in the gamete-producing cell of individual A in Figure 4.6. Four combinations of these chromosomes are possible in the gametes, but only two combinations are shown.

■ Suggest two other possible combinations of chromosomes in the gametes in Figure 4.6 that could be produced by independent assortment of chromosomes during meiosis. (Hint: you might find it helps to draw these in the spaces provided on the figure.)

☐ Red chromosome 1 and red chromosome 2; blue chromosome 1 and blue chromosome 2.

The more chromosome pairs there are in the gamete-producing cell, the greater the possible number of different combinations of red and blue chromosomes in the resulting gametes. As we have seen in Figure 4.6, two pairs of chromosomes could produce a total of four different combinations of red and blue chromosomes in the gametes. With the 23 pairs of chromosomes in human cells, a total of over 8 million different combinations exist!

However, the behaviour of chromosomes during meiosis is even more complex than described above! We have seen that the independent assortment of chromosomes during meiosis produces various combinations of red and blue chromosomes, but it does not break up the set of genes along each individual chromosome. However, a process known as crossing over does. This process occurs *before* partners of a homologous pair of chromosomes separate. **Crossing over** is the physical exchange of genetic material between the two chromosomes in a homologous pair, as a consequence of breakage and rejoining, as shown in Figure 4.7. Members of each pair come very close together during meiosis, and at this stage they may break, but always at identical points along their length, and rejoin with the homologous partner.

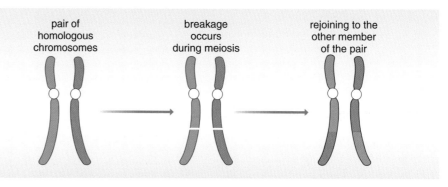

Figure 4.7   The process of crossing over between the two chromosomes in a homologous pair, which breaks up and rearranges the combination of gene variants on individual chromosomes. The chromosomes are drawn as single structures for simplicity.

This process brings about a considerable rearrangement of genetic material between each homologous pair of red and blue chromosomes. The genetic *difference* between the red and blue chromosomes lies not in the order of genes, which is identical between all people, but in the variants, or alleles, of each gene (Section 3.2). Thus, through the process of crossing over, new combinations of variants are produced, here represented by the rearrangement of segments of the red and blue chromosomes. The points at which this breakage and rejoining occurs are essentially random, but are always at the same distance from the ends of both partners of a homologous pair. Thus crossing over generates an infinite number of combinations of variation.

Crossing over typically occurs between one and three times along the length of each pair of homologous chromosomes, depending on their length. Thus the chromosomes of a gamete are not an exact copy of either member of a homologous pair.

In order to appreciate the effect of crossing over on the rearrangement of alleles between chromosomes over time, examine Figure 4.8. This traces the inheritance of one member of a pair of chromosomes over three generations, from child to mother, and to mother's parents.

■   From Figure 4.8, what is the composition of the chromosome in the person labelled 'child'?

☐   The chromosome in the 'child' is a patchwork, consisting of alternating portions of chromosome that originated in different grandparents.

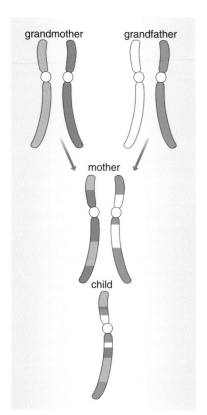

Figure 4.8   The effect of crossing over on the origin of various portions of a chromosome. The chromosome inherited by the child in the third generation is a patchwork of parts of all four grandparents' copies of that chromosome. The child's homologous partner chromosome, inherited from the father, is not shown. The chromosomes are drawn as single structures for simplicity.

Extending this notion back beyond three generations and to every chromosome, gives some indication of the effect of crossing over on the genome.

So we see that genetic variation between gametes produced by the same individual is the result of a number of processes: the segregation of members of homologous pairs of chromosomes (Figures 4.3 and 4.4); the random or independent assortment of homologous chromosomes (Figure 4.6); and crossing over between members of a homologous pair (Figure 4.7). These processes, combined with the process of fertilisation, contribute to the production of an individual with a unique combination of alleles.

> Variation between the gametes of an individual results from the processes of segregation, independent assortment and crossing over.

Question 4.2

Insert the missing terms in each of the following sentences.

(a) The process of _____ is involved in the production of gametes, which have the haploid number of chromosomes.

(b) The process of combining two gametes to produce a diploid cell is called

_____.

(c) Recombination generates new combinations of genetic material either by

_____ _____ or by _____ _____.

(d) The technical term for the separation of members of homologous chromosomes is _____.

Question 4.3

Why does a child not inherit a chromosome that is identical with that of either parent?

Question 4.4

Produce a flow diagram of the human life cycle (include arrows and labels but not drawings) to show the sequence of events during reproduction. Include the following terms in your labels: fertilisation, mitosis, meiosis, egg, sperm, fertilised egg, haploid, diploid.

It does not matter what sort of diagram you draw, provided that it helps you to understand and remember. Start by looking back through this chapter, making notes if necessary. Then draw a diagram to show the sequence in which the different events in reproduction occur.

Question 4.5

What are the main differences in the outcomes of cell division involving mitosis and cell division involving meiosis?

Question 4.6

In a few sentences, outline whether you would expect any differences in terms of the final chromosome make-up of an embryo that is formed during the process of *in-vitro fertilisation* (IVF) compared with an embryo conceived within the female reproductive tract.

4.4   To know or not to know the sex of an unborn baby

Once fertilisation has occurred and a pregnancy has been established, many parents are anxious to know whether a Y-bearing sperm or an X-bearing sperm won the race to fertilise the egg. The reasons why parents want to know the sex of their unborn baby are many and various.

If you were to conduct a straw poll among your acquaintances, particularly any who are expecting a baby, to establish whether they want to know the sex of their unborn child, you would probably find that many people do not mind what sex their baby is as long as it is healthy. However, some people have strong feelings about this, one way or the other, perhaps for cultural reasons or because they have a family history of a genetic disease that affects one sex, and therefore want a child of the other sex, or because they already have one or more children of a particular sex, and want some variety.

■ There are two ways of determining the sex of an unborn child. Can you suggest what these might be?

☐ The sex can be determined by examining either the chromosomes or the physical appearance of the fetus, which means waiting until the genitals are visible.

In order to look at the chromosomes of the unborn baby it is necessary to have some fetal cells, which can be obtained from the fluid in the womb by means of the technique of *amniocentesis* (described in Chapter 19). Distinguishing the sex of the fetus is usually possible by 17–18 weeks after fertilisation, at the time of a routine ultrasound scan. Unless there is good reason for telling the mother, some hospitals might withhold this information on the grounds that some people would procure an abortion if the baby were found to be the 'wrong' sex. We leave you to think about the ethics of this, but we will return to this sort of issue later in the course.

This chapter has considered the chromosomes of gamete-producing cells and gametes, and in the next chapter we focus on individual genes in these cells and their transmission from parent to offspring.

4.5   Summary of Chapter 4

Reproduction comprises two distinct processes: the production of gametes, which involves meiosis, and fertilisation. The two processes are accompanied by changes in the chromosome number, from diploid to haploid and from haploid to diploid, respectively.

Each gamete contains half the number of chromosomes, i.e. one member of each pair of homologous chromosomes and one sex chromosome (either an X or a Y chromosome). The fertilised egg is diploid and contains paired autosome chromosomes plus two sex chromosomes.

The chance of fertilisation producing a male is 1 in 2 and the chance of producing a female is also 1 in 2, thus the ratio of males to females is 1 : 1.

The 1 : 1 ratio is a consequence of the segregation of partners of homologous chromosomes during meiosis into different gametes in equal numbers, and because gametes combine at random at fertilisation.

Variation between the gametes of an individual results from segregation, and recombination, the latter consisting of independent assortment and crossing over. These processes, combined with the process of fertilisation, contribute to the production of an individual with a unique genotype, i.e. a unique combination of alleles.

The sex of a fetus can be determined by examining either its chromosomes or its physical appearance.

Chapter 5
The inheritance of genes

The behaviour of chromosomes during meiosis and fertilisation can explain the way that genes, which are integral parts of chromosomes, are transmitted in particular patterns from generation to generation. Unlike the previous chapter, which considered whole chromosomes, this and the following chapter focus on **genes** — the *units of inheritance*. We will trace the inheritance of genes but we will also follow the particular characters influenced by these genes, and examine the relationship between characters and genes. We will jump between these two perspectives, and in so doing we shall be jumping from the fundamental work of late 19th century biologists, who could only trace characters from generation to generation, to that of late 20th century geneticists, who worked at the level of the gene.

Thus in this chapter we continue our exploration of the relationship between genotype and phenotype, which we began in the previous chapter, but here at the level of individual genes and individual characters rather than at the level of whole chromosomes. By tracing the inheritance of genes we continue to examine the reasons why members of a family resemble each other but at the same time why each person has a unique combination of characters.

5.1   A family history

Why does an individual have a particular set of characters? To answer this question, we need to look at the family history. Relatives are more likely to share variants of genes, or alleles (Section 3.2), with each other than are unrelated people because they have an ancestor in common. The more closely related two people are to each other the more alleles they have in common.

Let's consider the tendency to develop tuberculosis.

■   If every individual in a family of two parents and four children has a condition, such as tuberculosis, should you conclude that the condition was bound to be genetic in origin (as a result of family members sharing similar genes)?

☐   No. One may suspect a genetic origin, but there could be something about the environment that they all share that leads them all to succumb to the same disease.

Following a family history for a particular character, or condition, over a number of generations to trace whether it is *familial*, i.e. whether it runs in families, can show whether the character is genetically influenced. This can also clarify the pattern of inheritance from generation to generation; as you will see, there is more than one pattern.

In this chapter we will look at specific characters, such as blood groups, in order to explore patterns of inheritance in family members and examine how these patterns contribute to the production of variation between individuals.

A word of warning is appropriate here about the terminology sometimes used to describe the relationship between genes and characters. Biologists often use a shorthand such as the 'gene for brown hair' or the 'brown hair gene', and we shall do this. This shorthand suggests a direct causal relationship between a particular gene and the production of brown hair. This is an oversimplification because the gene involved in making hair brown is primarily involved in pigment formation throughout the body, not just in hair colour. Thus, while convenient to use, the shorthand can give a very misleading impression of the relationship between genes and characters such as hair colour, and you should bear this in mind.

5.2   Patterns of single-gene inheritance: dominant and recessive alleles

Here we focus on the behaviour of single genes during gamete production and fertilisation. We can consider a gene as a small section of DNA in a chromosome, which issues instructions for the production of a character. A single human chromosome carries many genes (Section 3.1), each with its own function and each with its own specific location on that chromosome, such as gene *A* in Figure 5.1. As this figure shows, a diploid cell contains two copies of a gene for a particular character situated at corresponding locations on the two homologous chromosomes. The technical term for the location of a gene on a chromosome is **locus** (plural loci).

The character that we will examine is a blood group called the Rhesus system, which, unlike the attached ears shown in Figure 3.4, produces no visible features. Individuals are either Rhesus positive or Rhesus negative. You may have heard of this character in relation to Rhesus blood incompatibility between mother and fetus. If the mother is Rhesus negative and the fetus is Rhesus positive, the red blood cells in the fetus can be destroyed as a consequence of incompatibility. Therefore, before a blood transfusion is given, this particular blood group is checked for in women of child-bearing age.

Phenotype, as well as meaning the sum total of all characters (as defined in Chapter 3), has another more restricted meaning; it is used as a shorthand way of referring to the appearance of just one character, for example the Rhesus system phenotype. In the case of the Rhesus system gene there are two variants of the gene, two alleles, one associated with Rhesus positive phenotype and one associated with Rhesus negative phenotype. Within a whole population, the presence of alleles of a single gene for any given character (such as Rhesus positive or Rhesus negative, and attached or unattached ears) gives rise to what is seen as normal variation.

Why should individuals within a family have different phenotypes for the Rhesus system? In order to answer this question we will examine a mating between an individual who is Rhesus positive and one who is Rhesus negative.

It is conventional in genetics to represent each allele by a letter, or letters (either capital or lower case), printed in italics; different alleles of the same gene are given the same letter symbol. In this example, we will use the letter *R* for the allele associated with Rhesus positive phenotype, and *r* for the allele associated with Rhesus negative phenotype.

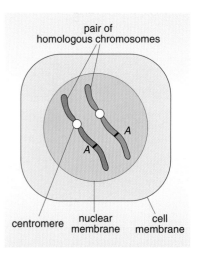

Figure 5.1   A gene, labelled *A*, is a small section of a chromosome at a particular locus. For simplicity, only one pair of homologous chromosomes is shown in the hypothetical cell. The length of the gene relative to the length of the chromosome is very much smaller than shown here.

The terms 'allele' and 'gene' can be confusing because the terms are used interchangeably in some situations. For example, the 'allele for Rhesus positive' and the 'gene for Rhesus positive' both refer to the same thing in an interchangeable way. This stems from the fact that the alleles are of course genes themselves.

Genotype, as well as meaning the full set of an individual's genes (Section 3.2), is also used to refer to a specific gene, for example, the Rhesus system genotype.

■ Recall that an individual has two copies of every gene in their somatic cells. What are the possible genotypes involving the two alleles, *R* and *r*, that any individual could be?

☐ Any one individual could be *R R*, *r r*, or *R r*.

An individual with two copies of the *R* allele is said to have the *R R* genotype; such individuals will be Rhesus positive. A person with two copies of the *r* allele has the *r r* genotype and will be Rhesus negative. We can follow what happens to the *R* and *r* alleles, first during meiosis when gametes are produced, and second at fertilisation when gametes combine, as shown in the mating diagram in Figure 5.2. Of course, the gametes contain a copy of each of the other human genes too, but here we are considering only the gene for the Rhesus system.

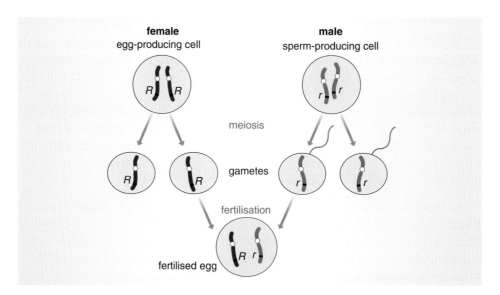

Figure 5.2   A mating diagram between a female with the genotype *R R* and a male with the genotype *r r*, illustrating the behaviour of these alleles during gamete formation and fertilisation. For simplicity only one fertilisation is shown.

The two copies of the Rhesus system gene are located on a pair of homologous chromosomes, one copy on each member of the pair, as shown in the egg-producing and sperm-producing cells at the top of Figure 5.2. It is important to note that because members of a homologous pair of chromosomes separate during gamete formation (Section 4.1.1), the alleles that they contain also separate.

■ How many copies of the Rhesus system gene are present in each gamete?

☐ Only one copy is present in each gamete. (Remember that homologous chromosomes segregate, or separate, at meiosis, one going to one gamete and the other to a different gamete, as shown in Figure 5.2.)

■ What are the genotypes of the gametes produced by each of the parents in Figure 5.2?

☐ In this example, the female's gametes will be *R*, whereas the male's gametes will be *r*.

■ What are the possible genotypes of the children of this couple with respect to the Rhesus system gene?

☐ Each child must receive one allele from each parent and therefore they must all be *R r* or *r R*, and these are the same genotype.

The convention is to write the allele with the capital letter first, so the children's genotype would be written as *R r*. Notice not only that all of the children have the same genotype, *R r*, but also that it is different from those of both parents. We need some way to distinguish between situations in which the two copies of a particular gene are the same and ones in which the two copies are different. Where the two copies of a gene are the same, as in the case of each parent in Figure 5.2, they are said to be **homozygous** and the individual is a **homozygote**. Where the two copies of the gene are different, they are said to be **heterozygous** and the individual is referred to as a **heterozygote**.

■ Are the parents and offspring in Figure 5.2, homozygotes or heterozygotes?

☐ The parents are both homozygotes, and the offspring is a heterozygote.

But what is the phenotype of offspring with the heterozygous genotype *R r?* One of their alleles (*R*) is associated with the Rhesus positive phenotype, but the other (*r*) is associated with the Rhesus negative phenotype. In fact, *R r* offspring are Rhesus positive. The character that is manifest (or appears) in a heterozygote is said to be the **dominant** phenotype. The character that is not manifest in a heterozygote is said to be the **recessive** phenotype. In this case, Rhesus negative is recessive to (or masked by) the dominant character, which is Rhesus positive. Strictly speaking, it is the phenotype — rather than the allele — that is dominant or recessive; however, alleles are usually referred to as being dominant (represented by a capital letter) or recessive (represented by a lower case letter) on the basis of their associated phenotype.

Two important features of this mating of two different homozygotes should be noted. First, one of the characters (Rhesus negative) has vanished in the children. Second, it doesn't matter whether the father or mother has the dominant phenotype and which one has the recessive, the result is the same: all the children are heterozygotes with the dominant phenotype.

Understanding the patterns of inheritance for recessive and dominant alleles helps us to learn more about normal variation between individuals and why particular characters tend to run in families. These patterns are even more important in the inheritance of genetic diseases, which is considered in the next chapter.

5.3   X-linked characters: colour blindness

The small Y chromosome (Figure 3.3) carries very few genes, most of which are involved in directing the embryo to develop testes and other male characters. However, the larger X chromosome carries a number of so-called **X-linked genes** that are not involved in sex determination. Consequently, females carry two copies of each X-linked gene, one on each X chromosome, but males carry only one copy of each X-linked gene on the single X chromosome, there being no counterpart on the Y chromosome. Because males do not have a homologous pair of X chromosomes, the genes on the X chromosome have a pattern of inheritance that is different from that of the genes on the autosomes. Such a pattern is described as **X-linked inheritance**.

This can be illustrated by examining the gene associated with red colour vision. It is carried on the X chromosome, and an allele exists that causes red colour-blindness. In a female, an allele for normal colour vision is dominant over an allele for red blindness. Red blindness is therefore a recessive character. If we represent the normal vision allele as *C*, and the recessive red blindness allele by *c*, we can use a mating diagram to examine what happens in a mating between a heterozygous female (*C c*) who has normal colour vision, and a male with normal colour vision, as shown in Figure 5.3.

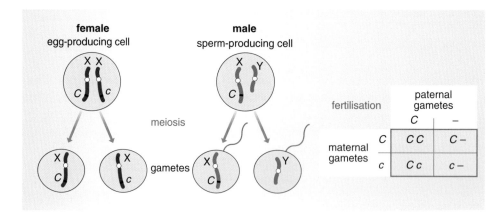

Figure 5.3   Mating diagram illustrating the behaviour of alleles on the X chromosome associated with normal colour vision (*C*) and with red blindness (*c*) during gamete formation and fertilisation. These alleles are missing from the Y chromosome.

■   What are the genotypes of the gametes produced by the female parent in Figure 5.3?

☐   The gametes are either *C* or *c* because the female is *C c*. Two types of gamete will be produced, half with the normal allele, *C*, and half with the red colour-blindness allele, *c*, as shown in Figure 5.3.

■ In what ratio would these two gametes be produced, and why?

☐ The ratio would be 1 : 1, because the pairs of X chromosomes on which they are located separate into different gametes in equal proportions.

The male in Figure 5.3 will also produce two types of gamete, one bearing the X chromosome with the *C* allele and the other bearing the Y chromosome. You can see that the allele *C* of the female might combine with either the X chromosome with *C* or the Y chromosome of the male at fertilisation. Over a large number of fertilisations a *C*-bearing egg would combine with a *C*-bearing sperm in half of the fertilisations and combine with a Y-bearing sperm in the other half. Similarly, the *c*-bearing egg might combine with either the *C*-bearing sperm or the Y-bearing sperm.

The genotypic ratio of a mating, such as the one shown in Figure 5.3, is a consequence of two factors (as explained in Chapter 4 for pairs of homologous chromosomes).

The two copies of a gene separate into different gametes in equal numbers (because pairs of homologous chromosomes behave this way).

Which type of sperm fertilises which type of egg is entirely random.

■ What are the possible genotypes of the children of the couple in Figure 5.3, for both sex and red blindness?

☐ There are four possible genotypes: *C C* (female), *C c* (female), *C* – (male), and *c* – (male).

■ What would be the relative numbers of these genotypes?

☐ Because fertilisation is random, over a large number of fertilisations the four genotypes will be produced in equal numbers; that is, in the overall ratio 1 : 1 : 1 : 1.

Half of the children would be female (two X chromosomes) and half would be male (one X and one Y chromosome). All the daughters would have normal colour vision with *C C* and *C c* genotypes in a 1 : 1 ratio. Half of the males would have normal colour vision (*C* –; they would only have one copy of the gene) but the other half would be red blind (*c* –).

■ Why would half of these males have red blindness, even though this phenotype is described as recessive?

☐ They would have red blindness because their genotype is *c* –; there is no dominant *C* allele (normal colour vision) present to mask the single recessive *c* allele. Males only have one copy of this gene, on the X chromosome.

■ The frequency of phenotypes for recessive X-linked characters in a family or population is much higher in males than in females. Why should this be so?

☐ Males have to inherit only *one* copy of the recessive allele for the phenotype to show, whereas daughters have to inherit *two* copies of the recessive allele (one from each parent) in order for the recessive phenotype to be manifest.

Question 5.1

Why are X-linked phenotypes never passed from father to son?

5.4   Multiple alleles: the ABO system

So far, characters with just two alternative phenotypes have been described. However, some genes have more than two possible alleles. One well-known example is that of the ABO blood group system, of which there are four different phenotypes, or blood groups, A, B, AB and O. The genetic basis of the ABO system is well known and is based on at least three alleles at a single locus, denoted by the symbols A, B, and O. (Note that, for historical reasons, the naming of these alleles is different from the standard convention.)

A person's blood group depends on which of these alleles they inherit. Identifying the ABO blood group is vital for blood transfusion. Blood must not be transfused unless the blood groups of both the recipient and the donor are first checked. It is safe to transfuse blood from an individual of one group into another individual of the same group. However, when blood is transfused between individuals with different blood groups, strict rules must be followed because some of the blood groups are incompatible with each other, resulting in the clumping together of red blood cells. (This contrasts with Rhesus blood groups where incompatibility is usually confined to mother and fetus; see Section 5.2.)

■ Three alleles of the ABO system exist, but how many of them are present in any one individual?

☐ Only two, one on each member of a pair of homologous chromosomes.

An individual may be homozygous for any one of the three possible alleles (that is, $A\,A$ or $B\,B$ or $O\,O$) or heterozygous for any possible combination ($A\,B$ or $A\,O$ or $B\,O$). To determine the phenotype (that is, the blood group) arising from these genotypes, you need to know that both the alleles A and B are dominant to O (or put another way, O is recessive to both A and B).

■ What is the blood group of individuals with the following genotypes: $A\,O$, $B\,O$, and $O\,O$?

☐ Blood group A, B and O, respectively.

When A and B are present together in an individual we see the simultaneous expression of both alleles, as neither is dominant to the other, and the individual has the blood group AB. In such cases the alleles are said to be *codominant*. In a sense, codominance is no dominance at all, since the presence of one allele does not mask the presence of the other allele but rather the effects of both alleles are manifest! The ABO system also shows that alleles of a gene can show different dominance relationships with one another, for the A and B phenotypes are both dominant to the O phenotype but not to each other.

This example reveals an important feature of inheritance: the phenotype of a particular character is a result of the relationship between two alleles of a gene, and this relationship varies between different combinations of alleles. Recall that, although we talk of dominant alleles, it is the phenotype that is dominant not the alleles (Section 5.2).

The existence of **multiple alleles** of the same gene is quite common; a great variety of characteristics is known to be associated with multiple alleles and others are sure to be found in the future. Although the pattern of inheritance seems more complicated for multiple alleles than for genes with just two alleles, the same rules are obeyed: only two copies of a gene (either the same or different forms) are present in each individual, these are separated and reduced to one during gamete production, and two are restored at fertilisation.

Multiple variants of a gene represent an important source of variation within the human population. As humans have many thousands of genes, many with multiple alleles, you can begin to get a measure of the extent of variation that exists within humans.

Alternative alleles (dominant and recessive), X-linked alleles, codominant alleles and multiple alleles all contribute to phenotypic variation.

Understanding the patterns of inheritance for recessive, dominant, X-linked, codominant and multiple alleles helps us to learn more about normal variation between individuals and why particular characters tend to run in families. These patterns are even more important when the inheritance of genetic diseases is considered, a subject that we turn to in the next chapter.

Question 5.2

Match each of the following descriptions (a)–(f) with one of the terms (i)–(vi).

Descriptions:

(a) An individual in which both copies of the gene are the same.
(b) The alternative forms of a gene.
(c) A phenotype that masks the presence of the allele for a contrasting character.
(d) A genotype with two different alleles of a gene.
(e) A phenotype not expressed in the heterozygote.
(f) The phenotype that manifests both copies of a gene that are different from each other.

Terms:

(i) alleles; (ii) codominant; (iii) heterozygous; (iv) homozygote; (v) dominant; (vi) recessive.

Question 5.3

(a) Determine the possible genotypes of the children produced by two individuals, one of blood group AB and the other of blood group O. (Hint: draw a mating diagram.)
(b) How do the phenotypes of these children compare with those of the parents?

5.5   Summary of Chapter 5

Genetics is based on the concept of the gene as the unit of inheritance.

A particular phenotypic character is determined by the two copies of a gene that an individual possesses.

When two individuals who are homozygotes, one for the dominant character and the other for the recessive character, mate, the dominant character appears in the heterozygous children and the recessive character is masked.

The genotypic ratios of a mating result from the separation of the two copies of a gene to different gametes in equal numbers, and because gametes combine at random at fertilisation.

The absence of genes on the Y chromosome, other than those involved in sex determination, results in X-linked genes (those on the X chromosome) having a pattern of inheritance that is different from that of the genes on the autosomes.

The phenotype of a particular character is a result of the relationship between the two copies of a gene that are present in an individual, and this relationship varies between different alleles (e.g. dominance, codominance). A gene can have more than two alleles in the population but there are only two copies of a gene in any single individual and only one copy of X-linked genes in males.

Chapter 6
The inheritance of genetic disorders

Once the pattern of inheritance is known for a character, it is possible to make predictions about that character in future generations. Although this might not be important for characters such as attached ears, it is crucially important to parents, doctors and genetic counsellors when a debilitating or potentially fatal disease is involved. (Genetic counselling is discussed in Chapter 19.)

The previous chapter was primarily concerned with the inheritance of normal variation and how particular patterns are seen according to whether the phenotype is dominant, recessive, X-linked or codominant. Here we move on to look at disease phenotypes that are considered to be outside the normal range of variation.

Human diseases can be classified in a number of ways, from those caused by nutritional factors (such as rickets), to those caused by infectious agents (such as polio or tuberculosis), to those which are influenced by the genes a person has inherited. It is important here to recall that human genes contain many different variants, most of which have few consequences. Many of these variants do, however, contribute to the normal range of variation we see in the human population and some have more serious health consequences and result in what are called **genetic disorders** or *genetic diseases*. There are many thousands of genetic disorders, most of them rare, but it is important to realise that the alleles that result in disease are found in genes that we all contain in our genomes. In the case of genetic disorders, individuals inherit a version of the gene that is defective in some way; most of us contain non-disease or *normal* alleles of these genes. Disease alleles follow exactly the same patterns of inheritance as non-disease alleles, so the rules already described in Chapter 5 also apply to their inheritance.

Some genetic disorders occur when the individual inherits only one copy of a single defective gene (*dominant disorder*); others require both copies of the gene to be defective (*recessive disorder*); and some genetic diseases are X-linked. (Note the abbreviation of 'dominant genetic disorder' to 'dominant disorder'.) About 1 in 30 children born in the UK has a genetic disorder and these account for about one-third of all hospital admissions of young children.

We have seen that the inheritance of characters determined by a single gene, such as the Rhesus blood group system, follows a distinctive pattern from generation to generation. Some genetic disorders are also determined by a single gene, and hence their pattern of inheritance can be predicted. Other genetic disorders, however, such as coronary heart disease, involve many genes.

In later chapters we will discuss disorders that involve many genes, but first, in this chapter, we will consider two cases of single-gene disorders. The first is Huntington's disease, a dominant disorder that leads to the onset of degeneration of the nervous system in adult life. The second is a recessive disorder, cystic fibrosis, the commonest genetic disease of childhood in the UK.

6.1 Pedigree charts

With any single-gene disorder it is useful to know whether it is related to a dominant or recessive allele, and whether it is X-linked or not, because the number of children likely to be affected varies in these different situations. The matings that we showed diagrammatically in Chapter 5, i.e. the mating diagrams in Figures 5.2–5.4, can be used in those cases where we know the genotypes of some, or most, of the individuals in a family. However, controlled matings cannot be carried out with humans in the same way that they can with mice or maize. So human geneticists draw up **pedigree charts**, or *family trees*, over many generations, in order to trace the inheritance patterns of a character. Thus the basic method of genetic analysis in humans is to make observations on people or to track events that have already taken place, rather than designing and carrying out an experiment or a mating between known genotypes, as in the case of mice, for example.

Pedigree charts trace *phenotypes*, and describe the occurrence of a particular phenotype within the family over several generations. The degree to which the character recurs in different members of the same generation and between generations provides the first clue as to the mode of its genetic transmission, i.e. whether it is dominant or recessive. Pedigree analysis is useful not only for medical research but also in the day-to-day counselling of prospective parents who are concerned about genetic disease in their children.

The pedigree chart in Figure 6.1 traces a family for four generations: I, II, III, and IV; individuals are numbered from top to bottom so that each can be identified. Within a family, individuals are also usually placed with the oldest on the left, and those who manifest the character, in this case Huntington's disease, are shaded so that lines of inheritance can be easily tracked. A short horizontal line, linking two individuals, such as individuals 1 and 2, is a mating line. The children are connected to each other by a horizontal line and to the parents by a vertical line. By studying the pedigree chart in Figure 6.1, you can see that female 1 and male 2, of generation I, had three children, numbered 3, 5 and 6, the first of whom was affected. These three children are generation II. Person 4 'entered' the family as the husband of female 3.

In order to check that you understand a pedigree chart, or family tree, try answering the following questions about Figure 6.1.

■ How many children did the couple 3 and 4 have, and of what sex?

☐ Two male children, 8 and 9, and one female, 10.

■ How many of these children were affected with the disorder?

☐ Two, 8 and 9.

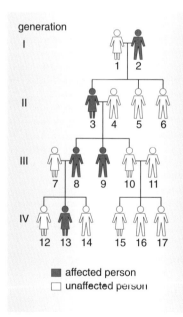

Figure 6.1 A typical Huntington's disease pedigree chart spanning four generations. Shaded individuals are affected with the disorder.

6.2 Huntington's disease: a dominant disorder

Figure 6.1 gives a pedigree chart for a family with Huntington's disease (HD), a degenerative neurological disease. It is a progressive disorder causing motor (movement), cognitive (thought) and psychiatric disturbances. The disease starts in adult life, usually between the ages of 35 and 45, and patients survive with progressive degeneration for between 10 and 15 years. HD affects 1 in 20 000 Caucasians, but is far less common in other world populations, being found in only 1 in 300 000 Asians and fewer than 1 in 1 million Africans. There is no known cure, only treatment for the various symptoms.

Let's consider the pattern of inheritance of the disease shown in the pedigree chart in Figure 6.1 and try to deduce whether the disorder is the result of a recessive or a dominant disease allele. For this exercise we will assume that all of the individuals in the chart who have the HD genotype are already manifesting the progressive degeneration.

■ What is the most obvious feature of this pedigree chart with reference to affected individuals?

☐ The most striking feature is that every affected person has an affected parent, who also had an affected parent, and so on. Therefore, there is at least one affected family member in each generation.

■ This is a typical pattern seen for a **dominant disorder**. Can you suggest why?

☐ A person needs to inherit only one copy of a disease gene from their affected parent to develop the disease.

Let's explore this in more detail. By knowing the patterns of inheritance of genes, described in Chapter 5, it is possible to make some predictions about the phenotypes and genotypes of each generation in a pedigree chart. First consider whether it is possible to determine the genotype of individuals in Figure 6.1 for HD, from observing their phenotype. To understand this, complete Figure 6.2 (derived from Figure 6.1), by writing the genotypes of individuals 1, 2, 3, 5 and 6 in the spaces provided, as you progress through the following questions. Assign *HD* for the Huntington's disease allele because it is dominant, and *hd* for the normal allele because it is recessive. (Note that we are assigning *two* letters to the gene here.)

■ What must be the genotype for individual 1 with respect to Huntington's disease?

☐ Since the individual is unaffected she must be homozygous for the normal allele, so her genotype is *hd hd*. (Write this in the appropriate space in Figure 6.2.)

We know that any individual who is unaffected must have two copies of the normal gene, *hd hd,* since the possession of only one *HD* allele would result in the disease phenotype. You can now also determine the gametes that person 1 would produce, and note these in Figure 6.2.

■ What must be the genotype for individual 2 with respect to Huntington's disease?

☐ Since the individual is affected he may be either homozygous (*HD HD*) or heterozygous (*HD hd*) for the disease allele.

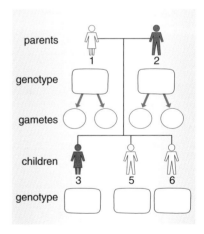

Figure 6.2   The genotypes for Huntington's disease for individuals 1 and 2, their gametes, and their children 3, 5 and 6. (The individuals are derived from the pedigree chart in Figure 6.1.) The blank spaces are for you to fill in as you work through the text.

We cannot distinguish between the two possibilities; it is possible to say that one copy of the gene must be *HD* but it is not possible to identify the second copy without further information, so we write his genotype as *HD ?*. Note this in Figure 6.2, and then note the gametes that he would produce, *HD* and *?*.

■ What must be the genotype for individual 3 with respect to Huntington's disease? (Hint: use the genotypes of the gametes that you have noted down.)

☐ According to Figure 6.1 the individual is affected, so she must have inherited the disease allele from her father, and we know that she must have inherited a normal allele from her mother, so she must be heterozygous, *HD hd*, for the Huntington's disease gene. (Note this down in Figure 6.2.)

■ Now determine the genotypes of individuals 5 and 6.

☐ They must both be *hd hd*, because they are unaffected.

Consequently, we can infer that individuals 5 and 6 must have received a normal allele from their mother and a normal allele from their father. You can use this information to go back and determine the genotype of the second gene copy of the father, person 2. The father must be a heterozygote, *HD hd*, since he transmitted an *HD* allele to child 3 and an *hd* allele to both children 5 and 6. You can now complete the genotypes of all the individuals in Figure 6.2.

6.2.1   Genetic ratios and probability

A mating diagram between a homozygous recessive individual (*hd hd*) and a heterozygous individual (*HD hd*), i.e. persons 1 and 2 in Figure 6.2, is shown in Figure 6.3. The fertilisations in Figure 6.3 show the *expected* genotypic ratio of affected to unaffected children.

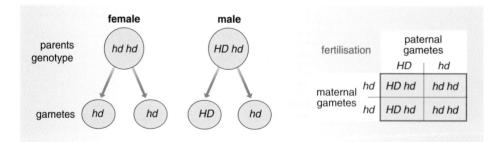

Figure 6.3   A mating diagram between a homozygous recessive individual and a heterozygous individual for Huntington's disease and the expected genotypic ratio of affected to unaffected children. Note that we have omitted the chromosomes; this is the usual way of drawing a mating diagram.

■ From Figure 6.3, what are the expected genotypic and phenotypic ratios of the children?

☐ The genotypic ratio is 1 : 1 (two heterozygous *HD hd* to two homozygous recessive *hd hd*). The phenotypic ratio is also 1 : 1 (two affected to two unaffected).

The phenotypic ratio of 1 : 1 (one of the dominant phenotype to one of the recessive phenotype) is of fundamental importance in genetics.

One of the important things that can be learnt from the study of pedigree charts is that many of the outcomes of inheritance are statistical ones; that is, they are to do with probability, as explained in Box 6.1.

Box 6.1   Chance and probability in genetics

When tossing a coin there is an even chance that heads or tails will turn up, i.e. each is equally likely. The probability of throwing heads is described mathematically as 1 out of 2, or $\frac{1}{2}$. **Probability** is a quantitative value for the chance or likelihood that a given outcome will occur. Probabilities have values between zero and one, and a probability of one is a certainty.

In general, the probability of a particular outcome, such as heads, is defined mathematically as:

$$\text{probability of outcome} = \frac{\text{number of ways to get that particular outcome}}{\text{total number of possible outcomes}}$$

In the case of throwing a six-sided die and getting a 4, there is only one way of getting that outcome, but there are six possible outcomes, so the probability is $\frac{1}{6}$.

■ What would be the probability of throwing an even number with the die?

□ $\frac{3}{6}$ or $\frac{1}{2}$, because three of the six possible different outcomes are even numbers.

■ What is the probability that a gamete produced by individual 3 in Figure 6.1, who is heterozygous *HD hd*, will contain the Huntington's disease allele?

□ The probability is $\frac{1}{2}$, since there are two possible outcomes and each one is equally likely. Only one of these corresponds to the Huntington's disease allele.

■ Can you recall from Section 4.2 why each of these two possibilities is equally likely?

□ It is because the two copies of a chromosome separate from each other into different gametes in equal numbers at meiosis.

We assumed that all of the individuals in Figure 6.1 who carry the *HD* allele are already manifesting the disease phenotype. In reality, individuals in such a family have to live for decades with the possibility that they might succumb to the disease in later life. The gene that underlies Huntington's disease has now been identified and a test is available to identify the *HD* allele so it is possible to check whether an individual has inherited a disease allele before the symptoms are manifested. Having inherited a disease allele for a dominant single-gene disorder, an individual is certain to develop the degenerative disease. We will discuss the impact of a diagnosis of HD within a family and the personal dilemmas that this brings, in Chapter 19.

Question 6.1

A female homozygous for the dominant phenotype 'white forelock', on a head of otherwise coloured hair, and a heterozygous male, are expecting a child. Assign *WF* and *wf* to the two alleles, and draw a mating diagram, with a layout as Figure 6.3. Then predict the genotypic and phenotypic ratios of their children.

6.3   Cystic fibrosis: a recessive disorder

Recessive disorders are those in which two defective copies of a gene must be inherited before the disease phenotype is expressed. Put another way, in a recessive disorder, the presence of one normal allele masks the effect of one disease allele and thus the person is unaffected. The most common single-gene recessive disorder in populations of north European descent is cystic fibrosis (CF), with as many as 1 in 2500 children in the UK and USA being affected. It is rarer in other populations, being found in 1 in 12 000 Africans and 1 in 25 000 Asians. Individuals with CF release excess salt from the sweat glands in the skin, and produce thick, sticky mucus that clogs the lungs, leading to infection, and in some individuals also blocks the pancreas (which produces digestive enzymes that are released into the gut), leading to problems in the gut. Most affected individuals, particularly males, are infertile because their reproductive ducts are blocked. Affected children develop symptoms in early childhood and even with intensive physiotherapy the life-expectancy is often only 30 to 35 years.

A pedigree chart illustrating the inheritance of CF is shown in Figure 6.4.

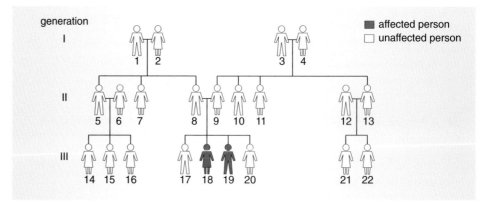

Figure 6.4   A typical pedigree chart for a recessive disorder, in this case cystic fibrosis.

■   What is the most striking difference between the pedigree chart shown in Figure 6.4 and the one shown earlier in Figure 6.1 for a dominant disorder?

□   Far fewer individuals are affected by the recessive disorder than by the dominant disorder.

■ Why is this?

□ As CF is a recessive disease, affected individuals must inherit two copies of the defective allele, one from each parent.

The parents will therefore carry only one disease allele, that is, they are heterozygous; they would manifest the disease themselves if they were homozygous.

Individuals who are heterozygous for a recessive disease are called **carriers**. When two carriers, such as individuals 8 and 9, mate, some of their children can be affected whereas others can be unaffected.

■ Can you determine from the pedigree chart who transmitted the disease allele to individual 8?

□ No, it is not possible to determine which of his two parents, 1 or 2, transmitted the disease allele in their gamete.

The mating diagram for the two heterozygotes, 8 and 9, is given in Figure 6.5. A mating between two carriers is of genetic importance, so we will analyse the ratios of the genotypes and phenotypes in some detail.

■ From Figure 6.5, what is the expected genotypic ratio of the children?

□ The expected genotypic ratio is 1 *CF CF* : 2 *CF cf* : 1 *cf cf* (one homozygous dominant to two heterozygous to one homozygous recessive).

The phenotype of each of these genotypes can be determined since we know that the allele *CF* is dominant to *cf*.

■ In what ratio would individuals with the normal phenotype and individuals with the cystic fibrosis phenotype be expected to occur in the children in Figure 6.5?

□ The expected ratio is three normal (the dominant phenotype) to one cystic fibrosis (the recessive phenotype), since three of the four possible fertilisations have at least one dominant *CF* allele.

The phenotypic ratio of 3 : 1 (three of the dominant phenotype to one of the recessive phenotype) is of fundamental importance in genetics.

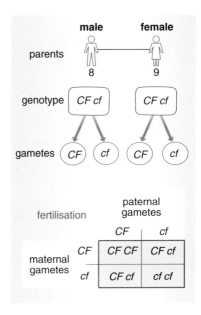

Figure 6.5   A mating diagram between the two individuals 8 and 9 in Figure 6.4 who are heterozygous for the cystic fibrosis gene. (*CF* represents the normal allele, and *cf* the disease allele.)

6.3.1   What is the risk of another affected child?

A common problem in genetic counselling is that of assessing the risk that a second child might be affected by a recessive disease following the birth of an affected child. Again the outcome of each birth is a statistical one; that is, it is to do with probability, as explained in Box 6.2.

Box 6.2 Probability for two or more separate events

Let's begin by determining the probability that two carriers will have an affected child.

■ What is the probability that an offspring of a mating between two persons who are heterozygous for cystic fibrosis (*CF cf*) will have the cystic fibrosis genotype? (Hint: you might find it helpful to look at the mating diagram in Figure 6.5.)

□ The probability is $\frac{1}{4}$, because there are four possible outcomes (*CF CF*, *CF cf*, *cf CF* and *cf cf*), and only one of these (*cf cf*) corresponds to the cystic fibrosis genotype. Another way of stating this is as a ratio of 1 : 3 (one affected to three unaffected).

■ What is the probability that two carriers with an affected child will have a second child that is affected?

□ The probability of the second child being affected is the same as the probability of the first child being affected, that is $\frac{1}{4}$.

■ Can you think why the probability does not change following the birth of one affected child?

□ This is because the outcome of any mating is completely *independent* of any other mating.

The probability of a second child being affected is still $\frac{1}{4}$ because it is based on the same two events as the probability of the first child being affected, namely:

• on an equal number of *CF* and *cf* gametes being produced by each heterozygous individual *CF cf*; and

• on male and female gametes combining at random at fertilisation.

• Similarly, the probability of the third child being affected, and so on, is also $\frac{1}{4}$.

Question 6.2

A phenotypically normal man in his early twenties learns that his father has Huntington's disease. He is informed that his father is heterozygous for the disease; his mother is unaffected and a test reveals that she does not have a disease allele.

(a) What is the probability that he will develop symptoms of the disease?

(b) What is the probability that his younger sister will develop the symptoms in later life?

6.3.2 Why do ratios deviate from those expected?

We predicted that the ratio of unaffected to affected children born to two cystic fibrosis carriers would be 3 : 1. Before we leave the pedigree in Figure 6.4, we will look at how closely an *observed* ratio fits the *expected* phenotypic ratio of 3 : 1.

Look at the ratio of unaffected children to affected children born to the carriers, 8 and 9, in Figure 6.4. There are four children, individuals 17, 18, 19 and 20, and the observed ratio is 2 : 2 or 1 : 1, yet we expected a ratio of 3 : 1. Why is there a deviation in the ratio of unaffected to affected individuals, i.e. why is the observed ratio not the same as the expected ratio of 3 : 1? The short answer is 'chance'. The *predicted* or *expected* ratio does not tell us the *actual* ratio of unaffected to affected individuals in a particular family, but rather the most probable ratio, as explained in Box 6.3.

Box 6.3 More about chance and probability in genetics

In genetics, the observed deviations from predicted ratios such as 3 : 1 are similar, in principle, to what you observe when you toss a coin. The *expected* ratio of heads to tails is 1 : 1 because each is equally likely; that is, each has a probability of $\frac{1}{2}$. If you were to toss a coin a million times, the result would be a ratio very close to 1 : 1. If you tossed it only ten times, however, the result *might* be quite a marked deviation from a 1 : 1 ratio (e.g. six heads and four tails — a ratio of 3 : 2 — instead of five heads and five tails).

In the case of couple 8 and 9 (Figure 6.5), suppose that exactly half of the eggs (of individual 9) contained the allele *CF* and the other half contained the allele *cf*. Imagine also that of the millions of sperm ejaculated by individual 8, exactly half contained *CF* and the other half contained *cf*. Which of the millions of sperm wins the race to fertilise any one egg is totally independent of whether the sperm contains *CF* or *cf*. Purely by chance, the proportion of *CF*-bearing sperm that succeed in this way may differ between one couple and another couple. One family would develop rather more unaffected children than the expected ratio of three unaffected to one affected children. In another couple the opposite might occur, with rather fewer unaffected children than consistent with the expected ratio of three unaffected to one affected children. Similarly, in any one family the proportion of *cf*-bearing eggs fertilised may differ from that of another family.

If a sufficiently large number of births are investigated, giving a very large total number of fertilisations counted, then the ratio will be very close to 3 : 1, but for any one family, such as the one in Figure 6.4, it may deviate quite markedly from 3 : 1.

The appearance of the disease for the first time in a family, as in the example in Figure 6.4, is the usual way in which CF cases clinically come to light; over 85% of cases have no apparent family history of the disease. This is a consequence of the disease being recessive. The proportion of new cases with no family history is dependent on the frequency of carriers within the population. The higher the frequency of carriers in the population, the greater the chance of two heterozygotes mating. In the case of CF, about 1 in 20 people in the UK is a carrier. The chance of two carriers meeting and having children in this case is quite high and explains why CF occurs so frequently in the UK population.

generation

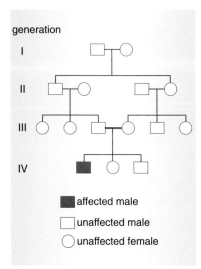

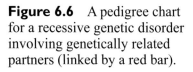

Figure 6.6 A pedigree chart for a recessive genetic disorder involving genetically related partners (linked by a red bar).

The chance of a mating occurring between two carriers is increased if their parents are genetically related in some way. Look at the family in the pedigree chart in Figure 6.6. This pedigree, unlike previous ones in the course, is drawn as geneticists and doctors draw them: females are shown as circles and males as squares; all other symbols are unchanged, e.g. affected individuals are shaded. From now on we will draw all pedigree charts like this one.

■ How are the parents of the affected child in Figure 6.6 genetically related to each other?

☐ The two parents of the affected child are related by their grandparents, which means they are first cousins.

The tendency of recessive disorders to appear with a high frequency in the offspring of inter-cousin marriages was recognised long before the genetic principle was understood, and it led to the prohibition of such marriages in many societies. Recessive disorders have a higher frequency today in societies where marriages between cousins remain common.

Before leaving the study of pedigree charts, read Box 6.4.

Box 6.4 An important note about pedigree charts

It is clear from Figure 6.4 that cystic fibrosis is not a dominant phenotype, since the parents (individuals 8 and 9) of the affected children do not manifest the disease yet they both must have transmitted a disease allele to the affected children. Likewise the grandparents (individuals 1–4) do not manifest the disease yet individual 1 or 2 must have transmitted a disease allele to individual 8 and similarly individual 3 or 4 must have transmitted a disease allele to individual 9.

However, it is not always so straightforward to determine whether a phenotype is dominant or recessive from a pedigree chart, because the phenotype can apparently work out to be either dominant or recessive. However, when using pedigree charts to determine whether a disease phenotype is dominant or recessive, it is important to bear in mind that we are dealing with rare diseases in the general population. You can work through Figure 6.1 assigning genotypes to each individual assuming, wrongly, that HD is recessive. You would soon discover that most individuals in this pedigree must have at least one disease allele for the disease to be manifest with such high frequency. For example, individuals 1, 4 and 7, who were introduced into this family through marriage, would all have to be heterozygous for HD because they have a normal phenotype but pass on the disease allele to at least one of their children. Given that we are dealing with a rare disease, it is highly unlikely that all three unrelated individuals would be carriers.

In Chapters 4–6 we have examined the relationship between genotype and phenotype, exploring how differences between genotypes contribute to the huge amount of variation that exists between individuals. We have seen that an understanding of the way that the two copies of a gene segregate at meiosis, of the relationship between dominant and recessive alleles and of probability enables us to predict the outcome of many matings. In the next few chapters we explore environmental factors and how these interact with the genotype to affect the phenotype.

But before that, test your understanding by trying the questions that follow. To help you, we have provided some hints in Box 6.5.

Box 6.5 General hints for tackling problems in genetics

Here we will offer some guidelines on how to set about solving genetics problems. You need to bear in mind that such problems cannot be solved by rote learning; each one has to be tackled afresh using your understanding of genetic principles, common sense, and sometimes trial and error. Here is a list of guidelines, which should help you to tackle a wide range of genetics problems; you may need to adjust the *order* in which you work through the steps according to the information given.

1   Read the question and make sure that you understand all of the terms that are used (e.g. heterozygous, etc.).

2   Draw out a pedigree chart or mating diagram. If you need to determine whether a phenotype is dominant or recessive then a pedigree chart may suffice. If you need to determine genotypes of individuals and gametes then you will probably find a mating diagram more useful (two types were introduced in Figures 4.3 and 4.4 and either is acceptable). Occasionally you might need to draw both.

3   Use information about the dominant allele or character to determine the phenotypes of each generation. Alternatively, some problems start with phenotypes and you have to determine genotypes.

4   Assign letters to the alleles of the genes that are involved, if they are not specified in the question.

5   Use the genotypes of each generation to deduce the genotypes of the gametes, and use the genotypes of the gametes to determine the genotypes of the offspring. (With some problems you may be working from the genotypes of offspring back to the genotypes of the parents.)

6   Calculate the ratios of the genotypes and of the phenotypes from the mating diagram.

7   Ask yourself whether the results are consistent with what you have learned about genetics and probability.

Question 6.3

Two individuals with hair that is frizzy and breaks easily, have a child who also has the same phenotype; their second child is unaffected.

(a) Is frizzy hair a dominant or recessive phenotype?

(b) Are each of the parents a heterozygote or a homozygote?

Question 6.4

Figure 6.7 shows two human pedigree charts: (a) Tay–Sachs disease, a degenerative disease of the nervous system, and (b) familial hypercholesterolaemia, which increases the predisposition to coronary heart disease. For each pedigree:

(i) State whether the condition is dominant or recessive, giving reasons for your answer.

(ii) Assign letters to alleles and determine the genotypes of as many individuals as possible.

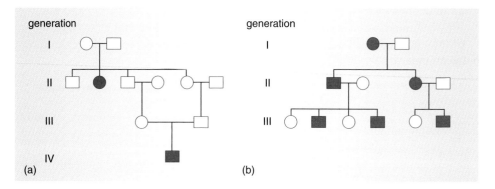

Figure 6.7   Two human pedigree charts: (a) Tay–Sachs disease and (b) familial hypercholesterolaemia; for use with Question 6.4.

6.4   Summary of Chapter 6

The alleles of genes involved in genetic disorders follow identical patterns of inheritance to alleles of non-disease genes.

Pedigree charts trace phenotypes, dominant or recessive, and describe the occurrence of a particular phenotype (such as a genetic disorder) within families over several generations.

Matings between a heterozygous individual and a homozygous recessive individual are expected to produce children with 1 : 1 phenotypic and genotypic ratios (one heterozygous to one homozygous recessive).

Matings between two carriers (heterozygotes) give rise to children with an expected phenotypic ratio of 3 : 1 (three with the dominant phenotype to one with the recessive phenotype).

Probability is a quantitative value for the chance or likelihood that a given outcome will occur. The probable outcome of any mating is completely independent of that of any other mating. The expected phenotypic ratio of offspring does not tell us the actual ratio of phenotypes of individuals, but rather the most probable ratio.

Chapter 7
The influence of the environment on the phenotype

Genes play an important role in the development of our characters, but so does the environment. Recall, from Section 3.2, that an individual's phenotype is the sum of the combined action of their genes and the environment in which they grow and develop:

genotype + environment = phenotype

This chapter explains how the environment plays a crucial role in the development of the phenotype, and hence is another source of variation between individuals. This is because the environment is never the same for any two individuals.

All of the characters that we have considered so far are influenced by single genes. However, some characters, called **multifactorial characters**, involve two or more genes. All genes can interact with the environment, but for multifactorial characters there is a *strong* interaction between genotype and the environment. *Multifactorial inheritance* is an important concept in human genetics because a significant proportion of characters and disorders are multifactorial. Physical characters such as height, weight, and skin colour are multifactorial, but so are aspects of behaviour, health and the ability to score highly in IQ tests. So in examining the role of the environment, we will focus in the main on the multifactorial character of height. In the next chapter we will consider multifactorial inheritance of genetic disorders, such as coronary heart disease.

The relative influence of genetic factors and environmental factors on multifactorial characters is intriguing. We consider this concept and explore the use of identical twins for estimating such *relative influence* on variations between individuals (section 7.3.1).

7.1   Environmental factors

In order to appreciate the effect of the environment on the phenotype, let's take a striking example: temperature and coat colour in Siamese cats. In these cats (Figure 7.1), the pattern of brown extremities — feet, face, ears and tail — and cream-coloured body is transmitted to their descendants. The kittens are all cream-coloured at birth; some days later, pigment appears in their new fur, first along the margin of the ears and gradually over their extremities. If the kittens grow and develop in a warm environment, the amount of brown fur is less than if they develop in cold temperatures. Although it appears that the brown and cream pattern is itself inherited, in fact what is really inherited is the capacity of the fur to form brown pigment, depending on the particular temperature at the time of growth. So a single genotype may produce different phenotypes, depending on the environment in which the organism develops.

Figure 7.1 Siamese cats of the same litter showing the variation in the distribution of brown colour on the body. The cat on the left grew and developed in a colder environment than the cat on the right and hence has more brown fur.

Temperature is just one example of an environmental factor that affects phenotype. When we are considering the development of the phenotype, **environment** has the very broadest meaning, ranging from the cytosol surrounding the nucleus within a cell, to a specific environment such as the uterus, or more general environmental factors such as human culture and the Earth's climate. It includes any factor, whether social or physical, *other than the genes*, that can interact with the genotype. The phenotype changes during the lifetime of an individual, and is continuously affected by many aspects of an individual's changing environment.

■ Given this very broad definition, can you give some examples of environmental factors that affect physical or mental growth and development of humans?

□ You may have thought of some of the following (there are many others): diet, education, lifestyle, number of children in the family, level of income, amount of pollution.

Some of these factors may influence the phenotype only at one particular stage of development; for example, biological environments such as the uterus are particularly important during fetal development. On the other hand, diet affects the phenotype throughout an individual's lifetime.

7.2 A multifactorial character: height

A good example of a multifactorial character is height in humans. All of the characters that we have considered in previous chapters have one of a number of contrasting phenotypes that can be classified into a number of discrete classes, such as attached or unattached ear, and Rhesus positive or Rhesus negative, as shown in Figure 7.2. Such characters that vary in this way show *discontinuous variation* within a population.

■ From Figure 7.2, what percentage of people in the UK are Rhesus negative?

☐ About 15%.

However, other characters, such as height, do not fall into a few distinct classes; they show *continuous* variation in the distribution of phenotypes in the population, as shown in Figure 7.3. The easiest way to appreciate the continuous nature of a multifactorial character is by plotting the values or measurements of the character in a large number of individuals, on a graph. The original measurements, presented in the form of a graph known as a histogram in Figure 7.3, have been interpreted as a smooth curve on the same figure.

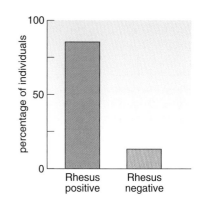

Figure 7.2 A character that has discontinuous phenotypes: the bars show the percentages of people in the UK that are Rhesus positive and Rhesus negative.

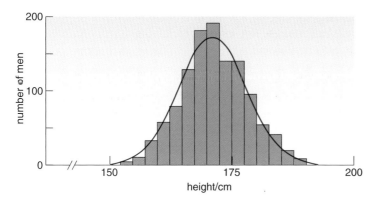

Figure 7.3 The distribution of phenotypes for a multifactorial character: the height of 1164 adult British men in 1946. The original measurements are presented as a histogram with 2.5 cm height intervals and interpreted as a smooth curve (shown in red). The gap on the horizontal axis indicates that the axis has been shortened. (The mean height of adult British men nowadays is considerably greater than it was in the 1940s.)

To check that you can read the graph in Figure 7.3, answer the following question before proceeding.

Question 7.1

(a) What quantity is plotted on the vertical axis of the graph in Figure 7.3?

(b) What quantity is plotted on the horizontal axis, and in what unit is it measured?

(c) In 1946, did more men have a height greater than 175 cm or less than 175 cm?

The distribution of height in Figure 7.3 shows that the majority of individuals had a height that is close to the *mean* value (about 172 cm) for the population, with numbers decreasing on either side of this mean value. Very few individuals who are very tall or very short, are found at the two extremes. Such a symmetrical distribution, giving a bell-shaped curve, is described as a *normal distribution.*

The fact that the phenotype varies continuously does not mean that the variation is the result of some new genetic mechanism. A multifactorial phenotypic character, such as height, is due to the joint action of *many* genes, each of which has a small individual impact on the phenotype. So height, for example, is the cumulative effect of multiple genes, each at a different locus, scattered throughout the chromosomes. Consequently, unlike the single-gene characters discussed earlier, it is difficult to predict the patterns of inheritance for multifactorial characters. Added to this, environmental factors also play a large part in the development of the phenotype of multifactorial characters.

■ Can you suggest some environmental factors that might affect human height?

☐ You might have thought of diet and severe periodic bouts of illness during childhood.

Studying Figure 7.3 should convince you that the critical difference between characters that vary continuously and those that fall into discrete classes (Figure 7.2) is the range of the phenotypic differences. For multifactorial characters (such as height) there is a potentially infinite number of slightly different phenotypes.

7.3   Distinguishing between genotype and environment

If phenotype is the result of the dynamic interaction of the genes with the environment, we might ask: how much are characters determined by the genes and how much are they influenced by the environment? This question is difficult (if not impossible) to answer, because a person's phenotype is a product of growth and development brought about by a certain genotype in a *succession* of environments. The phenotype at a given moment is determined not only by the environment that prevails at that moment, but also by the succession of preceding environments experienced during the individual's lifetime. Every person is the product of their genotype and their environments or, put another way, we are more than the 'sum of our genes'.

Over the last 40 years or so, there has been heated debate among biologists as to the relative contribution of the genotype (sometimes referred to as nature) and the environment (nurture) to the development of characters. From this so-called *nature–nurture debate* there has emerged a reasonable consensus for the view that the two are generally inseparable. This interactionist view is epitomised by the words of the eminent biologist and expert in animal behaviour, D. O. Hebb who, writing in 1953 about attempts to differentiate between instinct (nature) and learning (nurture) in the development of behaviour, suggested that such attempts are

> 'exactly like asking how much of the area of a field is due to its length, and how much to its width' (Hebb, 1953).

Nevertheless, some attempts have been made to partition the causes of variation for some characters. The difficulty of this task is illustrated by the example of human birth weight which, although it might be considered a character of the baby, is also affected by a number of genetic and environmental factors outside the baby.

■ Can you suggest some genetic and environmental factors that might affect human birth weight?

☐ You might have thought of some of the following: fetal genotype, maternal genotype, maternal diet, and the environment within the uterus during the time when the fetus was developing there.

This example illustrates the complexity of the interactions between the genotype and the environment.

7.3.1   Twin studies and multifactorial characters

Studying identical twins is one way of estimating the relative influence of environmental and genetic factors on variations between individuals for characters such as height. Identical twins raised together are compared with those in which members of each twin-pair are separated at birth and raised in different households. The two individuals in each twin-pair are genetically identical because both are formed from a single fertilised egg, which splits early in development to form two distinct embryos with identical genes, as shown in Figure 7.4a. Thus, identical twins separated at birth can be studied to examine the effect of different environments on the same genes. They represent a sort of 'natural' experiment to test whether two individuals who are genetically identical may develop differently.

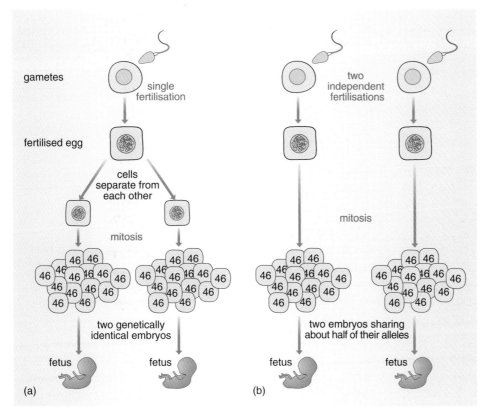

Figure 7.4   The early stages in the production of twins: (a) identical twins formed from the splitting of a single fertilised egg, and (b) non-identical twins produced from two different eggs, each fertilised by a different sperm.

■ Will identical twins always be the same sex?

□ Yes; since they have identical genotypes, they must be the same sex.

Non-identical twins, on the other hand, are genetically different, because they develop from two different eggs, each fertilised by a different sperm (Figure 7.4b). Hence non-identical twins might be the same sex or different sexes.

■ What could studies on non-identical twins raised together be used to measure?

□ They could measure the effect of different genotypes in a similar environment.

Table 7.1 compares the phenotypes of four multifactorial characters in identical twins when raised in the same household and when raised apart, and in non-identical twins (same-sex pairs) when raised in the same household. There are differences in all four characters between the two individuals in each pair of twins (within-pair differences). First, consider identical twins raised together.

Table 7.1 Average difference between individuals in pairs of twins for four multifactorial characters.

Multifactorial character	Average difference between individuals of a pair		
	Identical twins raised together (no. of pairs = 50)	Identical twins raised apart (no. of pairs = 19)	Non-identical twins raised together (no. of pairs = 52)
height/cm	1.7	1.8	4.4
weight/kg	1.9	5.4	4.5
head length/mm	2.9	2.2	6.2
head width/mm	2.8	2.9	4.2

■ What is the average difference between the heights of the two individuals in each pair of identical twins raised together?

□ The difference is 1.7 cm.

This difference is an effect of the environment during pregnancy and after birth, which gives rise to small phenotypic differences in spite of the twins having *identical* genotypes and being raised together. For example, the twins may receive different nutrition during pregnancy because the blood supply from the mother to one twin is greater than that to the other twin.

By themselves, the results from identical twins raised together are not very informative; they become significant, however, when comparisons are made between them and the corresponding findings for the other two groups of twins.

■ What does a comparison between identical twins raised together and non-identical twins raised together reveal?

□ This shows that the average differences between the individuals in each pair are larger for all four characters in *non-identical* twins raised together than in *identical* twins raised together.

The middle column of figures in Table 7.1 contains the important average within-pair differences for identical twins raised apart. It is important to note that in this study the home environments for the two members of a pair raised apart were not strikingly different.

Consider the genetic influence on each particular character in Table 7.1 by comparing identical twins raised together with identical twins raised apart.

■ What do the results suggest about the genetic influence on weight compared with that on height, head width and head length?

☐ The results indicate that a greater genetic influence exists for height and head dimensions than for weight; the latter is more subject to environmental influences. (If you are unsure about this, notice that height and head dimensions are similar for identical twins, regardless of whether they were raised together or apart, but their weight differences are much greater in twins raised apart, suggesting that this character is strongly affected by their environment.)

So even within the group of multifactorial characters, the amount of influence exerted by the environment or by the genes varies according to the particular character. Although the twin method has contributed to the analysis of many multifactorial characters that have otherwise been difficult to interpret genetically, it is not without drawbacks. The chief limitation is that it gives no insight into the genes concerned or their pattern of inheritance.

The data shown in Table 7.1 illustrate that no character is inherited ready made; the phenotype arises during the growth and development of the individual in particular environments. This takes us to the extremely important point that what is biologically inherited is not a character itself: you do not actually inherit a fixed character such as a specific height or the shape of your father's nose. What is inherited is the *information*, in the genes, to produce that character. (We examine this information later in the course.)

7.4 Height around the world

More can be learnt about genetic and environmental influences on multifactorial characters by broadening the view to compare populations that live in different parts of the world. There are enormous differences in both the rate of growth and the ultimate height of children belonging to different countries. Here we consider the latter character, ultimate height. Studies have shown that people with good nourishment in Asia, such as the Japanese, end up about 6 cm shorter than Western Europeans.

■ Assuming that environmental conditions were ideal in both populations, what do these data suggest about genetic influences on ultimate height?

☐ They suggest that there are genetic differences between different populations for this character.

So even among children who are well nourished there are clear indications that genes influence height differently in different populations.

However, there are a number of environmental factors that lead to differences in ultimate height within and between populations.

■   What environmental factors might contribute to these differences?

☐   Many are due to differences between rich and poor, urban and rural dwellers, well nourished and under nourished.

As living conditions improve, adult height increases, although in some countries ultimate height has almost stabilised, at least in the offspring of the financially better-off.

The example of height shows that the interaction between genotype and environment is important for the development of the phenotype. It is possible to explain this interaction in the following way. However good the diet that promotes the growth of a particular individual, there is a maximum height above which he or she cannot grow that is determined by their genotype. On the other hand, the potential height may never be reached because of an inadequate diet and/or the extent of childhood diseases that the individual has suffered.

The genotype sets the boundaries within which the phenotype develops in different environments.

In the next chapter, we continue to examine the effects of the genotype and the environment on other multifactorial characters, that is those that are associated with genetic disease.

Question 7.2

This question examines the differences in height between pairs of identical twins and non-identical twins. This distribution of differences in height (reflected in the profiles of the graphs) is given in Figure 7.5.

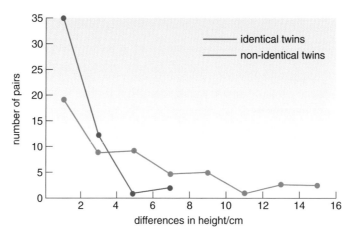

Figure 7.5   Distribution of height differences of 50 pairs of identical twins raised together (blue line) and 52 pairs of non-identical twins raised together (orange line).

(a)   How many identical twin pairs had a height difference of 1 cm?

(b)   Describe in words the distribution of differences in height for identical twins.

(c)   Overall, is the height difference for non-identical twins greater than for identical twins?

Question 7.3

What is the difference between multiple alleles of a gene (Section 5.4) and multifactorial inheritance?

7.5 Summary of Chapter 7

The phenotype, which changes during the lifetime of an individual, is continuously affected by many aspects of an individual's changing environment.

Characters that show continuous variation are influenced by several genes, each with a small effect, as well as by environmental factors, hence they are called multifactorial characters.

The symmetrical distribution of a multifactorial character, such as height, in a population gives a bell-shaped curve, which is described as a normal distribution.

It is difficult to measure the relative contributions of genetic and environmental factors to the variation of multifactorial characters. Studying identical and non-identical twins is one way of estimating the relative influence of environmental and genetic factors on variation between individuals for characters such as height.

There are differences in the ultimate height of children belonging to different countries of the world, which are due to both genetic variation and environmental factors.

The genotype sets the boundaries within which the phenotype develops in different environments.

Chapter 8
Genetic disorders with multifactorial inheritance

We have seen that the inheritance of characters caused by a single gene (such as the Rhesus blood group system or the ABO blood group system) follows a distinctive pattern from generation to generation. But for multifactorial characters, such as height discussed in the previous chapter, there is no distinctive pattern of inheritance. Multifactorial inheritance is an important concept in medical genetics because many common disorders are multifactorial, and they occur much more frequently in most populations than do than single-gene disorders. Multifactorial disorders include a host of debilitating diseases of old age, such as diabetes, coronary heart disease, high blood pressure, rheumatoid arthritis and Alzheimer's disease. They also include developmental abnormalities in the fetus, such as cleft lip with or without cleft palate (a condition in which the two halves of the roof of the mouth do not fuse) and spina bifida (a condition in which the bones of the spinal column fail to fuse).

Many of the principles that we learnt about height also apply to **multifactorial disorders**. Significantly, a number of genes and environmental factors are involved in each multifactorial disorder. Multifactorial disorders recur within families, but they do not show any particular pattern of inheritance in an individual family. This absence of a pattern of inheritance makes it difficult to predict the likelihood of genetic relatives inheriting or manifesting such disorders. Research involves unmasking not only the identity of genes that render people *susceptible* to these disorders, but also the environmental factors that affect them, some of which are difficult to define.

We will look at the phenotypes of multifactorial disorders from two perspectives. First, we focus on one particular environment, within the uterus, and second, we consider one particular disorder, coronary heart disease.

8.1   The environment within the uterus

There is no doubt that certain chemicals or infectious agents entering the uterus can have serious adverse effects on the developing fetus. Some agents are not harmful to the mother yet can damage the fetus. The majority of agents that produce malformations (such as the drug thalidomide, prescribed to pregnant women in the 1960s to combat morning sickness) are especially damaging in the early stages of pregnancy, when limbs and major organs are taking shape. Another example is the *virus* that causes rubella (also commonly called German measles). If infection occurs in the first three months of pregnancy it may result in serious eye, ear and cardiovascular (heart and blood vessel) malformations in the fetus, while the mother experiences only the mild symptoms of rubella.

In contrast, the harmful effects of excessive alcohol consumption by the mother are not restricted to a sensitive period during pregnancy, but extend through the entire nine months. The consumption of over 80 grams per day of alcohol, i.e. a full bottle of wine or about five pints of beer, during pregnancy is believed to be the major cause of mental retardation in new-born babies in the UK.

The nutritional environment inside the uterus has been implicated in possible long-term effects on the individual's susceptibility to a range of disorders in their adult life, including coronary heart disease, stroke, bronchitis and diabetes, as well as features such as obesity. Such dietary effects are difficult to prove because of the long timescale involved, but evidence has accumulated over recent years to suggest that the time in the uterus is an important one for the development of the *adult* phenotype (see Section 8.2.2). This illustrates an important point raised in Section 7.3.

> An individual's phenotype at a given moment is determined not only by the prevailing environment but also by the succession of preceding environments experienced by the person.

The examples considered in this section reveal that the phenotype arises during the growth and development of the individual in particular environments and that early environments may have a prolonged effect on the phenotype.

Question 8.1

A correlation has been found between a deficiency of folic acid (found in green vegetables and cereals) in the diet of pregnant women and the development of spina bifida in the fetus. However, not all women with this deficiency give birth to a baby with spina bifida. Comment on these observations using the principles that you have learnt in this chapter so far.

8.2   Coronary heart disease

Some progress has been made in defining the genetic components of multifactorial disorders but many genes that affect them have yet to be identified. We will take as an example of a multifactorial disease, coronary heart disease (CHD) — the number one killer in many high-income countries. Genetic studies of CHD are directed towards finding genetic differences that predispose an individual to disease, identifying environmental factors (called **risk factors** in relation to disease), and detecting individuals at risk of succumbing to the disease. We deal here with the first two of these three areas, the third one we consider later in the course.

It is the principles that are important here, rather than the specific details. However, we give some details in order to show

- the complex roles of genes that predispose individuals, or make them susceptible, to develop the disease
- the significant environmental contributions to the progression of the disease.

8.2.1   Genetic susceptibility to CHD

Two biological features contribute crucially to CHD: high blood pressure (hypertension) and deposition of fatty plaque on the walls of the arteries (atherosclerosis). We discuss these two features in turn.

Studies of twins suggest that a large proportion of differences in individuals' blood pressure could have a genetic basis. In addition, it has long been known that high blood pressure runs in families, suggesting a genetic influence. At least 10 genes are now known to be involved in controlling blood pressure. They work by controlling the amounts of water and salt that are transferred between the kidneys and the blood. The levels of both of these constituents of blood control blood pressure. Some genetic defects have been found to have a significant effect on blood pressure. For example, a mutation in a gene involved in the uptake of salt from the kidney into the blood brings about an increase in the amount of salt reabsorbed from the kidney. Hence, more salt is retained within the blood instead of being excreted in the urine.

Deposition of plaque on the walls of arteries results from an imbalance between the amount of fat eaten and its use and breakdown in the body, especially the fat *cholesterol*. (You can identify this type of fat on food labels of some margarines and oils.) Cholesterol plays a vital role in the body, but an excess amount may accumulate as plaque in arteries, as shown in Figure 8.1.

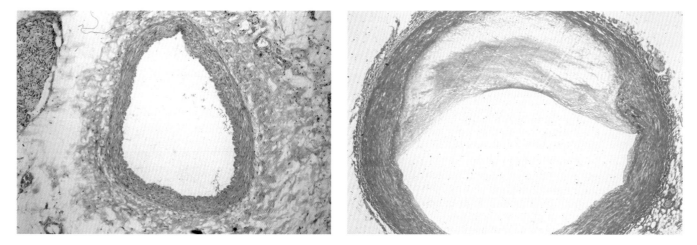

Figure 8.1   Arteries that supply the heart, cut across to show the inside: (left) a normal artery; (right) an artery partially blocked by plaque at the top of the inside.

Many genes control the amount of cholesterol in the body, by affecting the way the body absorbs, produces, transports, converts or breaks down the fat. For example, some genes are involved in the uptake of cholesterol from the blood into cells in the liver, but in individuals with certain gene variants, the fat stays in the blood and can build up in the walls of the arteries as plaque. This means that some individuals have a genetic predisposition to maintaining high levels of cholesterol in the blood.

A large number of genes are involved in the development of a multifactorial disease, such as CHD, in the same way as we saw for a multifactorial character such as height (Section 7.2). In the case of height, the genes, taken one by one, have a small effect on the phenotype, and in the case of a multifactorial disorder it is the disease alleles of genes, taken one by one, that contribute to the phenotype. It is the presence of disease alleles in the genotype that makes an individual *susceptible* to the disease in question.

8.2.2   Environmental risk factors

We have seen that genes are only one set of contributory factors to the intricate process of the life experience, including the health of the individual; environmental risk factors are also significant. Diet is an important risk factor for CHD, since obesity plays a part. Reducing the amount of fat in the diet may reduce body weight. In addition, it can reduce the amount of cholesterol in the blood in some individuals, but this depends on their genotype. Similarly, obesity or a high salt diet can lead to high blood pressure (hypertension) in some individuals. These observations reveal the important interplay between genes and environment; different genes interact with different risk factors.

In addition to diet, other environmental factors are implicated in CHD, such as smoking, drinking excessive amounts of alcohol and lack of exercise. Intriguingly, a more important risk factor for CHD depends on the status of a person's job; the less control a person has over their work, the higher the likelihood of a heart attack. In fact, this risk factor is a more accurate determinant of an individual suffering a heart attack than high blood cholesterol, drinking excessive amounts of alcohol, smoking or lack of exercise.

The reason is as follows. The body produces *hormones* to help you cope with stress. A hormone is a chemical messenger produced in a gland and transported in the blood to tissues where it exerts its effect. Hormones released in response to stress increase in level, not according to the amount of work you do, but to the amount of freedom you have in carrying out the work. These particular hormones increase the heart rate, increase the rate of breathing and raise blood pressure. This relationship between work status and CHD shows how much our health can be at the mercy of our environment.

We now turn to another environmental risk factor. In the 1980s, researchers proposed that certain adult diseases, such as CHD, are caused or made more likely by impaired development of the fetus in the uterus. The theory that adults may develop life-threatening conditions as a result of events that occurred when they were developing in their mother's womb is called *fetal programming*. We now know that inadequate nutrition and stress of the mother during pregnancy affect fetal development. We examine the first of these two factors here: the effect of poor maternal nutrition on hypertension in adult life.

In order to demonstrate the relationship between maternal nutrition and hypertension in later life, researchers had to find out the birth weight of those individuals who suffered from hypertension as adults. Low birth weight is an indicator that babies had been developing poorly in pregnancy, which in turn is linked to poor maternal nutrition. Hence, researchers found old maternity and infant welfare records with relevant records of birth weight of individuals who were now in their 40s or older. The individuals were asked about their medical history, smoking habits and family history of CHD. Their weight and blood pressure were then measured.

It turns out that weight of the baby is a better predictor of hypertension than lifestyle measures of the adult, such as cigarette smoking or obesity. Furthermore, this predictor was independent of current adult body weight. Lifestyle certainly influences health, but so do conditions experienced by the developing fetus in the uterus, such as maternal nutrition. How the two important risk factors, status of a person's job and maternal nutrition when developing in the womb, interact with each other to affect CHD is not yet understood.

8.3   The continuum of human disease

Before leaving our description of the relationship between genes and environment, we will end this chapter by bringing together several threads from this and previous chapters. As we have discussed, normal human variation can arise from differences in one single gene or in multiple genes, as can diseases. In most cases, the environment that we are exposed to throughout our life and our own behaviours act upon these genes. As a result, human diseases can be represented as a continuum ranging from those almost entirely due to a genetic component, as is the case for many genetic diseases, to those that have only a minor genetic contribution, as shown in Figure 8.2.

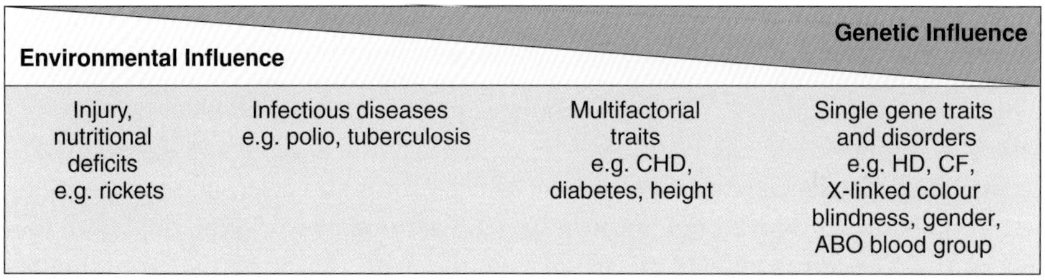

Environmental Influence			Genetic Influence
Injury, nutritional deficits e.g. rickets	Infectious diseases e.g. polio, tuberculosis	Multifactorial traits e.g. CHD, diabetes, height	Single gene traits and disorders e.g. HD, CF, X-linked colour blindness, gender, ABO blood group

Figure 8.2   The interplay between genetic and environmental contribution to human health is a continuum. For some diseases, such as Huntington's disease, the major component is genetic. In contrast, many diseases arise due to injury or nutritional deficits, which are less influenced by genes.

The health of an individual involves their genotype, the conditions and experiences over the whole of their lifetime from conception onwards and the interactions between all these factors. Responsibility for health is not just in the hands of the individual, but also lies with society in ensuring adequate nutrition and other resources for its members.

Activity 8.1   Environmental factors

In this activity you will study an article that examines the influence of environments on the development of certain medical conditions.

In Chapters 7 and 8 we have considered the effect of environmental factors on phenotypes, and in Chapters 5 and 6 we examined the influence of genes on the phenotype. A person's phenotype is a result of the interplay between these factors. However, to understand how genes influence characters we need to explore the chemical substances involved, and this is what we turn to next.

Question 8.2

Match the following situation with one of the explanations (a)–(e) given in the list below. Give reasons for your choice of response.

A study was conducted on twins in which at least one member of each pair had club-foot at birth. The results are shown in Table 8.1.

Table 8.1 Percentage of twin-pairs in which at least one member was born with a club-foot.

Twin type (number of pairs)	Both members of a pair affected/%	One member of a pair affected/%
identical twins (40)	32	68
non-identical twins (134)	3	97

(a) Assortment of chromosomes at meiosis accounts for this situation.

(b) The club-foot phenotype is recessive.

(c) The club-foot phenotype is dominant.

(d) The environment within the uterus accounts for these observations.

(e) The club-foot phenotype is a multifactorial character influenced by both genetic and environmental factors.

8.4   Summary of Chapter 8

Some environmental factors influence the phenotype only at sensitive periods of development, whereas others affect the phenotype over a longer timescale.

Many disorders that cause a host of common debilitating diseases of old age, such as CHD, and developmental abnormalities in the fetus are multifactorial.

The environment inside the uterus may have a prolonged effect on the phenotype.

A number of genes and risk factors (diet, excessive alcohol consumption, smoking, lack of exercise, status of a person's job, nutritional environment inside the uterus) may be involved in the progression of a multifactorial disease, such as CHD.

Fetal programming is the name given to the theory that an individual's health in later years is predetermined by events that occurred during the time they were developing and growing in their mother's womb.

Human disease can be seen as a continuum across a spectrum that represents the interaction between one or multiple genes and the environment.

Chapter 9
Introducing the substances of life

So far we have focused on characters of individual people, and we have considered genes as units of inheritance arranged along a chromosome. However, in order to understand how the genome functions, we need to look at DNA, the chemical that makes up the genome, and examine the substances that make up the cells. This chapter builds on an understanding of the structure and function of cells described in Chapter 2, and you may need to refer back to that. Cells are composed of a number of different substances but the most important one for understanding the functioning of the genome is a substance called *protein*. The reason is that genes, composed of DNA, specify proteins.

In this chapter we examine the structure and function of proteins. An individual protein can be referred to as a protein molecule. These molecules illustrate very clearly the precise relationship between structure and function. Proteins have a tremendous amount of structural diversity, and this enables them to carry out a vast range of functions in the body. We explore how this structural diversity comes about.

We then turn to look at the molecular structure and function of DNA in the next chapter, but we describe both proteins and DNA without the use of chemical formulae, chemical structures or chemical notation.

9.1   The components of cells

The chemical composition of a typical cell is given in Table 9.1. By far the greatest amount of matter in the cell is water, and clearly water plays a crucial role in the cell (Section 2.1).

Table 9.1 Chemical composition of a typical cell.

Type of molecule	Amount of matter/% of total
water	70
proteins	18
fatty substances	5
carbohydrates (including sugars)	2
DNA and other nucleic acids	1
Others	4

■ Apart from water, what type of molecule is present in cells in the largest proportion?

☐ Proteins.

■ How much of the cell content is proteins?

☐ 18%. (Don't forget to specify %, since if you just say 18, nobody will know if you mean molecules or portions!)

Notice that fatty substances and carbohydrates (including sugars) also make up a significant proportion of the content of a cell.

A comparison between Table 9.1 and a table of nutritional information on, say, a box of breakfast cereal or a packet of meat, reveals remarkable similarities. These food products also contain proteins, fats and carbohydrates. The food we eat — cereals, such as maize, wheat or oats, fruit, vegetables and meat — was once living material, emphasising the similarity between the chemical compositions of all living organisms.

■ From Table 9.1, what is striking about the relative proportions of DNA and proteins?

☐ The amount of DNA is relatively small; there is about 18 times as much protein as DNA.

You may wonder why we need proteins in our diet. Children need them for growth, i.e. for making more cells, but adults need them too, for maintenance, that is, for replacing worn-out and damaged cells. Proteins contribute to the structures in the cell (such as mitochondria; Figure 2.1), and also many of the chemicals in the cytosol are proteins. Both carbohydrates and fatty substances also contribute to the structure of cells, for example, one particular type of fatty substance forms the basic building blocks of cell membranes, and they are both also important sources of energy. However, it is the knowledge of the structure and function of proteins that is important for understanding the structural and functional differences between cells, as well as for understanding the function of DNA, so we will look at proteins in some detail.

9.2   Proteins

Although nutritional information on food packets lists 'protein' as if it were a single substance, it is in fact a class of substances, and there are tens of thousands of *different* types of **protein** molecules in every human. All life is based on proteins.

To understand why proteins are important, we need to recall some of the points introduced in Section 2.1, about the structural differences between different types of cell. Although all cell types have many features in common, for example, they all contain endoplasmic reticulum and mitochondria (Figure 2.1) there are also characteristic structural differences between the different types (Figure 2.2).

These similarities and differences between cell types stem from differences in the nature of the proteins they contain. Each type of specialised cell contains some proteins that are common to all cell types, for example those in the mitochondria, but they each contain some proteins that are specific to that cell type. Such proteins determine the specialised functions of that cell and hence whether it is part of the blood system or muscle or liver tissue, for instance. To take a specific example, haemoglobin is a protein found only in red blood cells, and it gives these cells the capacity to carry out their role of carrying and distributing oxygen around the body.

Each different protein has its own specialist job to do and each type of protein has its own unique chemical structure. Our aim here is not to be comprehensive but to give a few examples, sufficient for you to appreciate the diversity of functions of proteins. The examples we have chosen are listed in Table 9.2, with a summary of their location and function; we will return to these examples in later chapters.

Table 9.2 Examples of proteins, their location and function.

Type of protein	Location	Function
haemoglobin	red blood cells	carries oxygen
myoglobin	muscle cells	carries oxygen
enzymes (many different kinds)	throughout the cell including the nucleus	speed up chemical reactions
transport proteins (many different kinds)	part of the cell membrane	control movement of substances in and out of cell

Proteins are very large molecules, made by linking together hundreds, or in some cases thousands, of building blocks called **amino acids** to form a long chain, as shown in Figure 9.1.

Figure 9.1   The structure of a protein is made by linking together a large number of building blocks called amino acids, of which there are about 20 different types. Each different pattern represents a different amino acid. The links between amino acids are shown in black.

Most proteins are not extended chains but have a compact globular shape. This is achieved by regions of the linear chain of amino acids coiling up, and the coiled regions folding back on themselves to form *supercoils*, as shown in Figure 9.2 for myoglobin. The part of the myoglobin molecule that can combine with oxygen is picked out as a red disc in Figure 9.2, and this is held within a crevice by the folds of the chain. Hence the *shape* of myoglobin is important for the protein to carry out its function. This is true for all proteins.

Figure 9.2   The structure of the protein myoglobin. The black dots represent amino acids. The blue 'folded sausage' shows the three-dimensional structure and the red disc shows the location of the (non-protein) oxygen-carrying region.

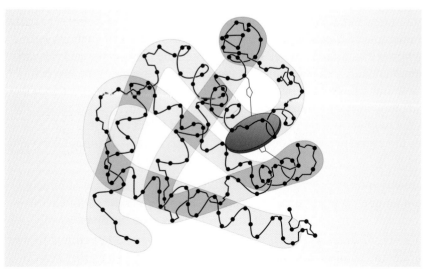

Myoglobin is rather unusual in that it has a small non-protein region that interacts with another substance, in this case oxygen. Other proteins rely on specialised 'pockets' in the protein surface for their interaction. These *binding sites* are precisely shaped so that each provides an exact fit with another substance of a specific type. The binding of a protein to a specific substance serves a myriad of different functions in cells. This is illustrated particularly clearly by enzyme proteins.

Enzymes are proteins that speed up chemical reactions and are crucial for survival, for, without enzymes, these reactions would proceed too slowly to sustain life. Each enzyme speeds up a different reaction. The majority of enzymes are present within cells but some of them are released from the cell, into the inside of the gut, for example, where they break down food into smaller units, which can then be absorbed by the body.

To understand the role of enzymes in the cell we will consider just one example, the enzyme *lactase*, which regulates the breakdown of *lactose* (the principal sugar found in milk) into smaller components. No enzyme other than lactase can do this work; this specificity is determined by the three-dimensional shape of its binding site (Figure 9.3a). Lactose has a highly specific three-dimensional shape, which exactly fits the binding site in the enzyme lactase. They fit together so precisely, like a key in a lock, that no other enzyme can bind to lactose and break it down (Figure 9.3b).

We have looked at one single chemical reaction, that of the enzyme lactase. But thousands of different interlinked reactions are taking place in every cell all the time, and each one is brought about by a different enzyme. Because of this specificity, the presence (or absence) of a particular enzyme determines whether a particular reaction actually occurs in the cell.

It is important to realise that cells are complex 'factories', with many different processes going on at once. So at a given moment, a fully functional cell may be replicating its genetic material (DNA) between cell divisions, building large molecules such as proteins, taking in small molecules from outside the cell membrane, and breaking down complex molecules. Such activities require enzymes, each one specific to the particular reaction.

Transport proteins form part of the cell membrane, as shown in Figure 9.4. There is a large variety of different types of transport protein, each of which is specific for the movement of a particular substance through the cell membrane. Thus the one that allows the movement of glucose, a small sugar molecule, is different from the one that allows the movement of a particular amino acid.

We learnt above that each cell type has its own characteristic set of proteins. Thus the nature of proteins, including enzymes, holds the key to the unique character of a particular cell, in terms of both that cell's specialised structure and its functions.

9.3　The structure of proteins

Having introduced some proteins with different structures and therefore different functions, we now explore how these structures are built up. To do this we will consider myoglobin, the protein shown in Figure 9.2.

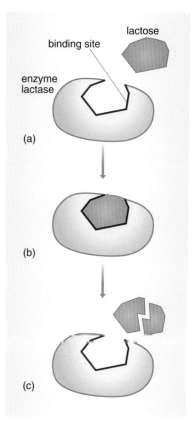

Figure 9.3　(a) The specific binding site on the enzyme protein lactase matches the shape of the substance lactose. (b) Lactose exactly fits the binding site in lactase. (c) Lactose is broken down into smaller components, which then leave the binding site.

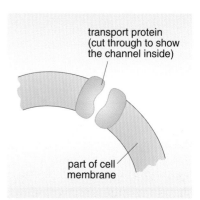

Figure 9.4　A transport protein within the cell membrane.

Muscles need a plentiful supply of oxygen while they are working to produce movement. Myoglobin, an oxygen-carrying protein in muscles, is largely responsible for the red colour of meat. In Figure 9.2, the myoglobin protein is represented as a long, contorted blue tube. The string of black dots within the blue tube represents the chain of amino acids.

Even though there are only around 20 different naturally occurring amino acids there are many thousands of different proteins, each with a particular biological function. Thus it is clear that there must be an enormous variety of protein structures. How can this be, given that they are made from only 20 different amino acids? The answer is that when several hundred of the 20 different types link up to form a protein chain, there is a huge number of possible *sequences*. Some amino acids may not be used at all in a protein whereas others may occur many times. For example, there are 153 amino acids in myoglobin and since there are only 20 different sorts, some occur a number of times. Every protein is different because it has its own unique sequence of amino acid building blocks along its length. The sequence of amino acids in a protein is termed its *primary structure*.

Figure 9.5 shows part of the primary structure of a protein. Compare this with the sequence of the amino acids of the protein in Figure 9.1.

Figure 9.5 Part of the primary structure of a protein, for comparison with Figure 9.1. Each different pattern represents a different amino acid.

■ Are the two proteins in Figures 9.1 and 9.5 the same or different proteins, and why?

☐ The two proteins are different because they each have a different sequence of amino acids.

■ Would you expect the sequence of amino acids in the protein myoglobin to be the same as the sequence of amino acids in the enzyme lactase, and why?

☐ No, they would be different because the two proteins have different functions.

The primary structure of a protein such as myoglobin appears to give no clues about the overall shape of the protein. Yet, amazingly, a particular sequence of amino acids always folds spontaneously into a particular three-dimensional shape. This is because different amino acids in the chain interact with one another to establish 'ties' between them, but only if they are compatible. So all protein molecules with the same amino acid sequence fold in the same way, provided the conditions in the cell are the same. Because the 'ties' will be in exactly the same positions, every copy of myoglobin finishes up with the same convoluted three-dimensional shape outlined in blue in Figure 9.2. Thus the primary structure of a protein determines its three-dimensional structure. If one critical amino acid is lost or missing from the sequence, it ceases to function properly as myoglobin.

The function of all proteins depends ultimately on the amino acid sequence of the protein chain.

■   Is the three-dimensional shape of lactase different from that of myoglobin, and why?

☐   Yes, the two proteins have different primary structures and hence have different three-dimensional shapes.

The surface of a protein is pitted with crevices and depressions and covered with protuberances, all of an exact shape and size. Every pit or protuberance occurs in just the same position on every molecule of that particular protein. As we discussed in Section 9.2, the precise three-dimensional shape determines the specificity of biological activity, or function, of the protein.

The primary structure of a protein determines its three-dimensional shape, which determines its biological function.

Proteins are very large molecules, and in the next chapter we look at the structure of another very large biological molecule, DNA.

Question 9.1

Which of the following statements is incorrect?

(a) All proteins yield amino acids when they are broken down into their constituent building blocks.

(b) A molecule of any protein contains all 20 amino acids.

(c) The shape of the binding site of a protein determines the substance(s) with which it can interact.

(d) Two protein molecules with an identical sequence of amino acids have the same three-dimensional structure and, therefore, the same function.

(e) All enzymes are proteins, but not all proteins are enzymes.

9.4   Summary of Chapter 9

Cells are specialised to perform different functions according to the particular proteins that they contain. Some proteins are common to all cells, but others are specific to one cell type.

Each different protein molecule has its own particular sequence of amino acids.

The primary structure of a protein — the amino acids and the sequence in which they are linked — determines its three-dimensional shape, which in turn determines its biological function.

Chapter 10
What is your genome made of?

This chapter explores the chemical nature of the genome. Genomes are composed of DNA, and a knowledge of the structure of DNA is essential to understand how it can function as hereditary material. DNA is remarkable, breathtakingly simple in its structure yet capable of directing all the living processes in a cell, the production of new cells and the development of a fertilised egg to an individual adult.

DNA illustrates beautifully the precise relationship between molecular structure and biological function that we saw also exists for proteins (Chapter 9). DNA has three key properties: it is relatively stable; its structure suggests an obvious way in which the molecule can be duplicated, or replicated; and it carries a store of vital information that is used in the cell to produce proteins. In this chapter, we will examine the chemical nature of DNA, which accounts for both its stability and the way it can be replicated — the first two of these three key properties. The third property, how DNA functions as the genetic material, i.e. how the information in DNA specifies proteins, is the subject of the next chapter.

Note that, in the same way that we use the word 'protein' to describe many different molecules of similar structure, so we use 'DNA' as a general term to describe many different substances of similar structure.

10.1   The chemical structure of DNA

It was in 1953 that James Watson and Francis Crick (Figure 10.1) working in the UK, deduced and published the three-dimensional structure of DNA. It was the year that might be described as the dawn of molecular biology, for their publication was to have far-reaching consequences in terms of our understanding

Figure 10.1   James Watson and Francis Crick in 1953 with the double helix model of DNA, which they built to help them to determine its structure; the model was assembled from metal clamps used to hold test-tubes and other bits of laboratory apparatus.

of the nature of life, i.e. how cells function at the molecular level. So monumental was this work that they were awarded, together with Maurice Wilkins, the Nobel Prize for Medicine with Physiology in 1962. In this section we shall examine in some detail the structure of the DNA molecule.

Watson and Crick showed that **DNA** or **deoxyribonucleic acid** has a *double helix* structure: two helical strands like spiral staircases, coiled round one another. It is this structure that accounts for the stability of DNA, one of its key features. Its simplest representation is shown in Figure 10.2. We will first consider the composition of each separate strand by taking it apart to reveal the building blocks of this molecule. Then we will show how the two strands interact to form the characteristic double helix structure of DNA.

Much as a protein is a string of amino acids, so each strand of the double helix is a string of building blocks, called **nucleotides**. Each nucleotide consists of three components: phosphate, a sugar molecule and a **base** (Figure 10.3). (The type of sugar is deoxyribose, hence the molecule is known as <u>deoxyribo</u>nucleic acid.) The phosphate and the sugar are the same in each nucleotide but the base can differ. There are four different bases in DNA: *adenine, guanine, cytosine* and *thymine*. When illustrating a length of DNA we can simplify the name of each base to a single capital letter, so that **A** = adenine, **G** = guanine, **C** = cytosine and **T** = thymine, as shown in Figure 10.4.

In each strand, the phosphate of one nucleotide is joined to the sugar of another nucleotide, and so on down the strand, as shown on the left (in white) of the single strand shown in Figure 10.4. The strand of alternating phosphates and sugars is known as the *sugar–phosphate backbone*, and the bases protrude away from this towards the other strand of the helix.

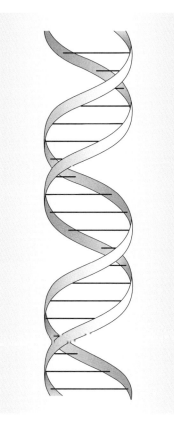

Figure 10.2   A simplified model showing the double helix structure of DNA.

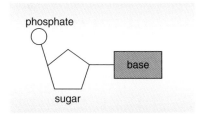

Figure 10.3   A nucleotide composed of phosphate, a sugar molecule and a base.

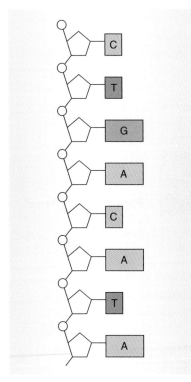

Figure 10.4   A short segment of a single, straightened strand of DNA, in which the bases, adenine, guanine, cytosine and thymine, are denoted simply as A, G, C, and T, respectively. The sugar–phosphate backbone is shown in white. (This figure represents one strand of the double helix.)

■ How many nucleotides are shown in the DNA segment in Figure 10.4?

☐ The simplest way of answering this question is to count the number of rectangles that represent the bases; there are eight.

There is a simplified way of describing the structure of DNA in text, and that is to write out the sequence of bases in a single strand, representing each base by its initial letter A, G, C or T (as we did in Chapter 1). We will use this shorthand extensively from now on.

■ What is the base sequence in the portion of the DNA molecule shown in Figure 10.4, starting from the top?

☐ CTGACATA.

These sequences are usually written or printed in lines like the letters or characters on this page. This is a convention, like reading left to right and top to bottom of this page. There may be many hundreds of thousands of bases within a single strand of a DNA molecule, in a long linear sequence. Such a sequence might appear as follows (reading from left to right):

….AAACGCGCGTATATAAATCGCTAGCTTCAACGACTGCTGACGTAGTTCCC….

You may be surprised to learn that DNA molecules are by far the largest known molecules on Earth. Recall from Chapter 3 that one DNA molecule runs the full length of the chromosome. If the DNA molecules of all the chromosomes in the nucleus of a single human cell were uncoiled, stretched out straight and laid end to end, they would measure about two metres. If all the DNA in all your cells were stretched out end-to-end, it would reach to the Moon and back about 10 000 times!

If you look at the comparatively short sequence of 50 bases printed above, and think about how many ways a simple coding language of just four letters could be rearranged in such a sequence, you will gain some appreciation of the huge variety of sequences that is possible. Take, for example, a short chain of just eight nucleotides. Since there are four different bases, there are four options for each position, and therefore $4 \times 4 \times 4 \times 4 \times 4 \times 4 \times 4 \times 4 = 65\,536$ possible different sequences for a DNA molecule of just eight nucleotides! A DNA molecule consisting of thousands of nucleotides therefore represents a vast store of potential information, the full consequences of which should become apparent as you study subsequent chapters.

So far we have considered a single strand of DNA, but Figure 10.2 showed that DNA has a *double* helix structure. Here each of the two 'ribbons' spiralled around each other represents the sugar–phosphate backbone of Figure 10.4, whilst the horizontal bars represent the bases of the two strands.

The key to understanding the structure of DNA and how it functions in the cell lies in the interaction between the bases in each strand at the core of the molecule. Along the length of a strand within the double helix, each base makes a specific pairing with a corresponding base in the other strand. These interactions are known as **base-pairing**, for which there are very precise rules.

T pairs only with A, and C pairs only with G. These pairs are called *complementary base pairs*.

These pairs of complementary bases sit 'flat' within the double helix, rather like the steps of a spiral staircase, as shown in Figure 10.2. The relative proportions of each base in DNA is related to the base-pairing rules just outlined.

■ If you were to extract some DNA from cells, and isolate and purify the four bases, how many A bases would you expect to find relative to T bases? Similarly, how many C bases would you find relative to G?

☐ A consequence of the base-pairing rules is that the amount of A in a DNA molecule is always equal to the amount of T; the same applies to the amount of C relative to that of G.

The alignment of base pairs within a DNA molecule is shown in Figure 10.5. Here the helix is shown unwound, with the two sugar–phosphate backbones now parallel but still on the outside; the complementary base pairs form the core of the molecule. Since the sequence of bases on one strand is complementary to the sequence of bases on the other strand, the two strands of the double helix are described as *complementary*.

The structure of DNA can be summarised as follows. The complementary base pairs sit at the core of the molecule, and are arranged flat like the steps of a spiral staircase. The two sugar–phosphate backbones lie to the outside of the helix, each spiralled around the other.

Watson and Crick, in their famous 1953 paper published in the journal *Nature*, wrote:

> We wish to suggest a structure for …. deoxyribose nucleic acid (DNA). This structure has novel features which are of considerable biological interest …. It has not escaped our notice that the specific pairing we have postulated immediately suggests a possible copying mechanism for the genetic material.

In the following section we consider how new DNA molecules are produced (the scientific term for this is *synthesised*), and show how true Watson and Crick's prediction was. But first try Question 10.1.

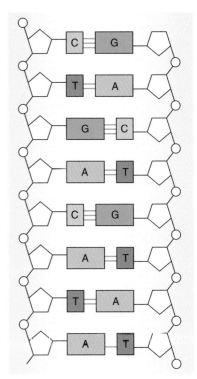

Figure 10.5 A portion of a DNA molecule with the helix unwound, showing the complementary base pairs between the two strands held together by base-pairing interactions (shown as orange lines).

Question 10.1

In a fragment of double-stranded DNA, there is a total of 100 bases, of which 30 are C. Calculate the total number of each of the following items in the DNA fragment: (a) complementary base pairs; (b) G bases; (c) T bases; (d) A bases.

10.2 DNA replication

You know from Section 2.2.1 that cell division involving the nuclear division of mitosis produces two progeny cells, which contain identical genetic material, which is also identical with that of the original parent cell. This is how a fertilised egg grows into an adult many-celled organism (Figures 2.7 and 4.2). For one cell to become two new ones with identical genetic material, the DNA in each chromosome must undergo a process in which an identical copy is made.

We begin by examining how DNA is replicated, and then look at the chromosome to explore the relationship between DNA molecules and chromosome structure.

10.2.1   How DNA is replicated

As noted above, Watson and Crick postulated that DNA base-pairing provides a mechanism by which the DNA might be copied. This DNA copying mechanism, usually referred to as **DNA replication**, is the process we consider here.

The separation of the two strands of DNA is an early event in the process of DNA replication. Once the strands have been separated, new DNA strands are synthesised; the enzyme that brings about this process is called *DNA polymerase*, which adds nucleotides to each separated strand according to the base-pairing rules.

Figure 10.6 shows the principal stages of DNA replication. The two strands of the double helix shown in Figure 10.6a unwind, starting at one end, to expose the bases on each strand. The two complementary single strands are shown separated in Figure 10.6b. Each of these strands now acts as a *template*, a mould, for DNA replication. The base-pairing rules are the basis of this process; that is, the nucleotides are added in a manner that places complementary bases opposite each other — C always opposite G and vice versa, A always opposite T and vice versa. At the same time, the two new sugar–phosphate backbones are formed.

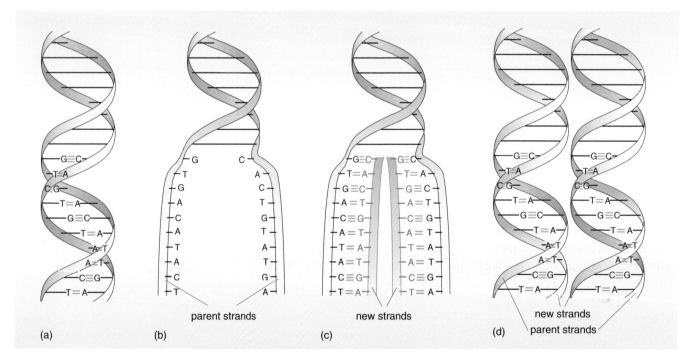

Figure 10.6   The process of DNA replication. (a) A portion of a DNA double helix showing 10 labelled complementary base pairs. (b) Part of the double helix has unwound and come apart at one end, revealing two single strands. (c) Part of each strand has been replicated, but the two double-stranded DNA molecules have not yet wound into two daughter double helices. The new DNA strands are shown in green. The process continues until all of the parent DNA molecule has been replicated. (d) The two double-stranded DNA molecules wind into two daughter double helices. Each double helix is composed of an original, parent strand and a newly synthesised strand.

The result is the production of two identical double-stranded DNA molecules (Figure 10.6c). Initially each double-stranded DNA molecule is unwound, as shown in Figure 10.6c; later, the paired strands wind around each other to form the characteristic double helix structure, as shown in Figure 10.6d.

This process has been termed *semi-conservative replication*, meaning 'half-conserved replication'. This is because in each new DNA double helix, one of the two original strands is conserved, i.e. is unchanged, from the original parent molecule; these are labelled as the parent strands in Figure 10.6b. The second strand in each daughter DNA double helix has been newly synthesised in its entirety; these are labelled as the new strands in Figure 10.6c. Or, to put it crudely, each daughter double helix is only 'half new'; each has one parent strand and one new strand, as shown in Figure 10.6d.

Figure 10.6 shows just a small portion of DNA being replicated. The process continues until the whole of the DNA molecule has been replicated, and the two daughter DNA molecules form the characteristic double-helix structures shown in Figure 10.6d, as opposed to the unwound products of replication shown in Figure 10.6c. Before the cell can divide to produce identical progeny cells, all of the DNA molecules in the cell have to replicate to produce two identical copies.

This, in outline, is how DNA is copied during most cycles of cell division. If you compare Figures 10.6a and 10.6d you will see that both DNA molecules in (d) are a faithful copy of the sequences of bases of the parent molecule in (a).

An important consequence of DNA structure is that the genetic information it contains is copied into more DNA.

10.2.2 Chromosome structure and DNA replication

DNA replication is closely linked to chromosome replication, which in turn is linked to cell division, which includes the nuclear division of mitosis (Section 2.2.1). This raises an intriguing question: how many DNA molecules are present in a chromosome?

Chromosomes are composed of DNA intimately associated with proteins. When the chromosomes become visible at the beginning of mitosis (Figure 2.5), the DNA has already been replicated, and the chromosomes are double structures; that is, each chromosome consists of two chromatids. During mitosis, the two chromatids of each pair separate to opposite ends of the cell so that at the end of mitosis each chromosome is a single unit (Figure 2.6d). Evidence suggests that such a single (unreplicated) chromosome contains one continuous DNA double-stranded molecule running along its length, as shown in Figure 10.7a. That makes a very long molecule! This suggests that, because genes are linked together along the length of a chromosome (Section 3.1), each gene must be a short section of a DNA double helix molecule.

Before the next round of cell division begins, each chromosome forms paired chromatids when the DNA is replicated. Each chromatid contains one DNA double helix along its length, as shown in Figure 10.7b. If you look at the chromosomes that are undergoing mitosis in Figure 1.1 and Figure 2.6a, you will see that each one is double along its length, like the one in Figure 10.7b.

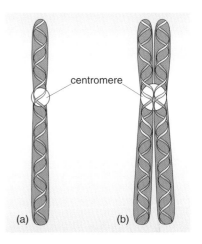

Figure 10.7 The number of DNA molecules in a chromosome: (a) a chromosome prior to replication contains a single DNA molecule; (b) a chromosome that has been replicated and consists of two chromatids, each comprising a single DNA double helix molecule. In reality, in each chromatid each DNA double helix is associated with protein, which condenses into a coil and then into a supercoil.

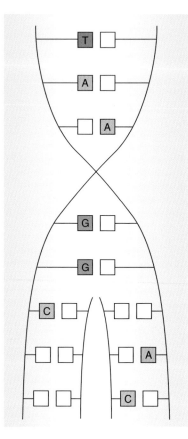

Figure 10.8   Part of a double-stranded DNA molecule during replication.

Question 10.2

Some concepts are difficult to grasp on first reading. One technique that you may find helpful is to rephrase the concept or idea in your own words. Try rephrasing the concept of semi-conservative replication in your words.

Question 10.3

Figure 10.8 shows part of a double-stranded DNA molecule during the process of replication. Each square represents a base.

(a) Identify the missing bases in the figure and write the correct letter (A, G, C or T) in each of the blank squares.

(b) At what stage of the cell cycle would the DNA in Figure 10.8 be undergoing replication?

In this chapter, we have examined the molecular structure of DNA, which accounts for both its stability and the way it can be replicated. In the next chapter we look at how the information in a sequence of DNA bases can be 'translated' into a sequence of amino acids in a protein.

10.3   Summary of Chapter 10

DNA (deoxyribonucleic acid) is composed of two strands spiralled around each other to form a double helix molecule. Each strand consists of a string of nucleotides; each nucleotide is composed of phosphate, a sugar and a base.

Four bases, adenine (A), guanine (G), cytosine (C) and thymine (T), make up the core of the DNA double helix. These form complementary base pairs, so that an A of one strand always pairs with a T of the other strand, and C and G always pair with each other. The outer part of the double helix consists of the two sugar–phosphate backbones.

The information carried by DNA is in a simple coding language of just the four bases, A, G, C and T. Using only these four letters, a DNA molecule represents a vast store of information.

The process of DNA replication is semi-conservative. During replication, the DNA double helix unwinds, and each of the two parent strands forms a template on which a new strand is produced. DNA polymerase adds nucleotides to each separated strand according to the base-pairing rules. Two identical double helices are thereby produced, each consisting of a parent strand and a newly synthesised strand.

An unduplicated chromosome consists of a long DNA double helix molecule, and the two chromatids of a duplicated chromosome each consist of a DNA double helix molecule. Each gene is a short section of a DNA double helix molecule.

Chapter 11
Using information stored in DNA

One important property of DNA is that it carries genetic information in the simple coding language of just four bases. These bases, which can be arranged in a huge variety of sequences, represent a vast potential store of information (Section 10.1). In this chapter, we consider how this information is used by the cell. The key structural feature of complementary base pairs, which plays an important role in both stability and replication, is also the basis for how DNA functions as genetic material.

How does the simple coding language of DNA relate to the nature of the gene; that is, how do genes function? Genes, composed of DNA, specify proteins. *How* genes do this is the topic of this chapter. The essence is that the structure of DNA can be related directly to the structure of proteins. As you saw in Chapter 9, proteins come in a huge range of sizes and shapes, and this diversity arises from different combinations of just 20 amino acids. We will examine how the simple coding language of just four letters (bases) in DNA contains information for thousands of different proteins, each with its own unique sequence of amino acids. How the proteins in cells relate to the phenotype of characters will be explored in Chapters 12 and 13.

The production of proteins is far more complex than the relatively straightforward process of DNA replication, partly because many other molecules are involved. We review the overall scheme in barest outline and then go on to examine each step in turn.

11.1   One gene–one protein

We have seen that a gene is a short section of a long DNA double helix molecule, which comprises a linear sequence of base pairs (Section 10.2.2).

■ What is the basic (primary) structure of a protein?

☐ A protein is a linear sequence of amino acids.

There is a direct and specific relationship between the linear sequence of base pairs that makes up a gene, and the linear sequence of amino acids in a protein molecule. This relationship, presented in a very simplistic manner in Figure 11.1,

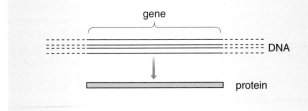

Figure 11.1   The relationship between a gene and the protein for which it codes. DNA is shown here as a double strand with the helix unwound.

is known as the one gene–one protein hypothesis. Each gene codes for a different protein. Thus the gene for haemoglobin specifies the protein haemoglobin, and the gene for myoglobin specifies the protein myoglobin (Section 9.2). How the DNA sequence of a gene gives rise to the protein, i.e. how the protein is synthesised, is the subject of the rest of this chapter.

11.2   The flow of information from DNA to RNA to protein

The information flow from DNA to protein is more complex than shown in Figure 11.1. The genetic information encoded within the DNA of a gene is carried via an intermediary molecule, **ribonucleic acid** (**RNA**). Information within a cell can therefore be seen as passing from DNA, via RNA, to a protein. This flow of information can be expressed in another way.

DNA makes RNA makes protein.

This statement implies that there are two separate steps in this information flow: from DNA to RNA and from RNA to protein; these are called, respectively, transcription and translation. **Transcription** of DNA produces RNA (Section 11.3) and the subsequent **translation** of this RNA produces proteins (Section 11.4). These steps are summarised in Figure 11.2.

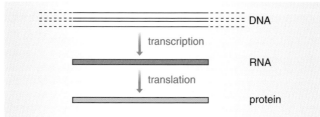
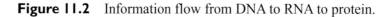

Figure 11.2   Information flow from DNA to RNA to protein.

11.3   From DNA to RNA: transcription

In the process of transcription, the information in a gene, i.e. the DNA base sequence, is copied, or transcribed, to form an RNA molecule. RNA is therefore an intermediary in the flow of information from DNA to protein. Before we consider the details of transcription, we will first look at the structure of RNA.

The name ribonucleic acid suggests that chemically it is related to DNA. Like DNA, RNA is a chain of nucleotides.

■   What are the three component parts of a nucleotide?

☐   Each nucleotide consists of three parts: phosphate, a sugar and a base (Section 10.1).

There are some important differences between DNA and RNA. One way in which RNA and DNA differ is in the sugar component; RNA has *ribose* (not deoxyribose as in DNA) hence <u>ribo</u>nucleic acid. A second difference is in the nucleotide bases.

■   What are the four bases in DNA?

☐   The DNA bases are adenine (A), guanine (G), cytosine (C), and thymine (T)

In contrast, the RNA bases are adenine (A), guanine (G), cytosine (C) and *uracil* (**U**). Why one of the four bases in RNA is different from the equivalent base in DNA is not understood.

There is a third important structural difference between DNA and RNA. Recall that the basic structure of DNA is a double helix of two spiralled strands, i.e. it is double-stranded. In contrast, RNA is usually a single strand, as shown diagrammatically in Figure 11.2.

The similarities in structure between DNA and RNA suggest that RNA is synthesised in a manner similar to DNA replication, i.e. using the DNA as a template. This is indeed what happens. The process of transcription is illustrated diagrammatically in Figure 11.3. As in DNA replication, the starting point is a double helix molecule of DNA (Figure 11.3a). The length of DNA sequence corresponding to a gene unwinds and the two strands separate (Figure 11.3b). Here the process of transcription diverges from the familiar one of DNA replication, because synthesis of RNA molecules occurs on only one of the two strands: only one DNA strand is the template for RNA synthesis, and this is termed the *template strand*. The other DNA strand, which is not used as a template in RNA synthesis, is termed the *non-template strand* (Figure 11.3b).

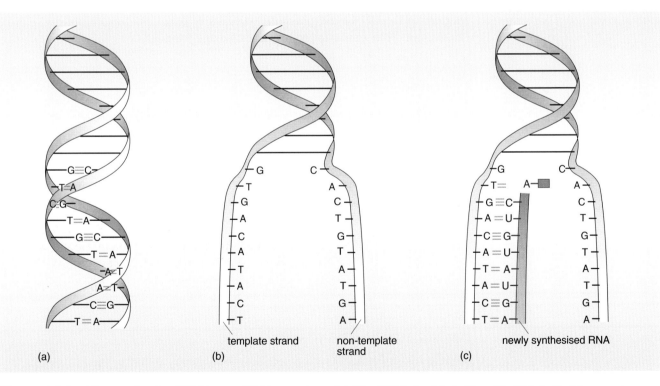

Figure 11.3   The synthesis of RNA on a DNA template. (a) The DNA double helix with 10 labelled base pairs. (b) The two strands of the helix unwind; note that only one of the strands is used as the template for RNA synthesis. (c) A short length of RNA (shown in red) is being synthesised: a nucleotide with base A is about to be added to the RNA strand. In reality, the RNA molecule would be much longer than the chain of nine nucleotides shown here.

The basic mechanism of RNA synthesis is the same as that for DNA, in that pairing of complementary bases is the key to the process. The enzyme that brings about the synthesis of RNA is *RNA polymerase*, and is a different enzyme from the DNA polymerase that brings about DNA synthesis.

■   Which bases are paired together in DNA?

☐   C pairs with G, and A pairs with T.

■   Considering these base-pairing rules in DNA, together with the information in Figure 11.3, what base-pairing rules would you expect to apply to transcription?

☐   The T of DNA is replaced with U in RNA, so A–U is a 'new' base pair. The C–G base pair remains the same. T–A is still a possible base pair, but clearly the T has to be in the DNA template and not in the newly synthesised RNA.

Table 11.1 Base-pairing rules in transcription.

DNA base	RNA base
A	U
G	C
C	G
T	A

The base-pairing rules in transcription are summarised in Table 11.1.

Thus, the template strand of DNA forms the template on which an RNA molecule is synthesised, according to the base-pairing rules shown in Table 11.1. The enzyme RNA polymerase brings about the growth of the RNA strand by the successive addition of nucleotides containing bases complementary to those in the template strand, as shown in Figure 11.3c.

Most importantly, unlike DNA replication, in transcription only relatively short regions of the DNA molecule, corresponding to genes, are transcribed into RNA molecules. Thus transcription produces genetic messages.

An aside

Inevitably in a short course we cannot cover all concepts, and many questions might occur to you as you study. One question that puzzles many students is: what distinguishes the template from the non-template strand? How does the cell 'know' which is the template strand? RNA polymerase first binds to the template strand of DNA at a particular sequence of bases in the DNA, which marks the beginning of the gene. You can think of this particular sequence as an *extension* of the DNA sequence that codes for a protein because it is immediately adjacent to the gene.

Question 11.1

Which of the descriptions (a)–(e) apply to: (i) both DNA and RNA; (ii) DNA but not RNA; (iii) RNA but not DNA?

(a) Consists of strand(s) of nucleotides; (b) typically found as single strand; (c) typically found as double helix; (d) contains U but not T; (e) synthesised on a DNA template.

11.4 From RNA to protein: translation

The second process in the production of proteins is translation. Here the base sequence of an RNA molecule is converted into the amino acid sequence of a protein chain. This is a more complex process than transcription. As you have seen, the DNA base sequence of a gene is transcribed into an RNA base sequence; the language of both consists of a mere four characters. Translation is the conversion from the four-character language of RNA into the corresponding 20-character language of a protein. In any language, not all of the characters are used in every word, and in the same way not all 20 amino acids are used in every protein (Section 9.3).

11.4.1 Messenger RNA

The RNA that we have been discussing and which has preserved within it the sequence of DNA bases, although now in an RNA code, is called, more fully, **messenger RNA (mRNA)**. Thus any given mRNA molecule carries the code for a specific protein. The code in mRNA consists of consecutive three-base sequences, or triplets (e.g. AUG, CCU). Each triplet is termed a **codon**, and there are many different ones. Each codon contains the information for a particular amino acid. Thus the *genetic code* consists of a linear series of nucleotides read three at a time, and each triplet specifies an amino acid.

Let's explore this with a particular example. Suppose that a sequence of bases in a tiny section of an mRNA molecule is:

…AUGCCUGCUGUUGGAAAG…

This message forms a series of three-letter 'words', or codons: in this example they would be:

–AUG–CCU–GCU–GUU–GGA–AAG–

Each of these six codons codes for a different amino acid. For example, the RNA codon AUG codes for the amino acid methionine (abbreviated to Met), and CCU codes for the amino acid proline (Pro). The sequence of codons within a molecule of RNA enables the sequence of amino acids in the protein for which it codes to be determined, since there is a direct and precise relationship between the two sequences, as shown in Figure 11.4. The details of the genetic code will be examined in Section 11.6. In the context of translation, all you need to appreciate is that an mRNA molecule consists of a very specific sequence of consecutive codons. (You are not expected to remember individual codons or names of amino acids.)

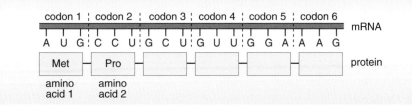

Figure 11.4 The relationship between the codons in mRNA and the amino acids in a protein. Met is the abbreviation for the amino acid methionine and Pro is the abbreviation for the amino acid proline.

A significant feature of the genetic code in mRNA is that it is a copy of the code present in one strand of the DNA of a gene, the non-template strand (except that U has replaced T). This follows because the sequence of bases in an mRNA molecule is determined by the base sequence of the DNA template on which the mRNA was synthesised during transcription. The consequence of the genetic code being carried on an mRNA molecule is that a given protein is coded for by a particular mRNA molecule consisting of a specific sequence of codons.

■ Since there are thousands of different proteins, how many different mRNA molecules must there be?

☐ There must be thousands of different mRNA molecules, each transcribed from a different gene.

11.4.2   Transfer RNA

So mRNA carries the code for a protein, but how is the correct sequence of amino acids in a protein, such as the one in Figure 11.4, brought about? In other words, how does each amino acid 'recognise' a particular codon in the mRNA? Although we have described the flow of information as 'RNA makes protein' (Section 11.2) the process of translation is far more complex, in that it requires the interaction of several components. An amino acid cannot 'recognise' a particular codon in the mRNA. This is achieved by another type of RNA molecule, called **transfer RNA (tRNA)**. tRNA brings an individual amino acid to the mRNA where it will be incorporated into a growing protein molecule. A stylised structure of a tRNA molecule is shown in Figure 11.5.

Figure 11.5   A stylised structure of a tRNA molecule showing its functional regions.

Figure 11.5 shows two significant features of tRNA, which demonstrate the relationship between the structure and function of the molecule. First, there is a site that is available to bind an amino acid. Second, there is a region at the other end of the molecule called an **anticodon**. The anticodon is composed of three bases, as shown in Figure 11.6. For each amino acid there is a different tRNA molecule. Enzymes are involved in recognising each amino acid and binding it to its specific tRNA.

The process of translation depends on the interaction between mRNA and tRNA, as shown in Figure 11.6. The three bases of the anticodon pair with the three bases of the corresponding mRNA codon. Thus the amino acid is placed at the correct codon of the mRNA because the tRNA molecule recognises that codon; the tRNA molecules are the link between the mRNA codon and the amino acid. Thus tRNA allows the mRNA code to be translated into a sequence of amino acids. You can think of the sequence of events in translation as:

mRNA → [tRNA + amino acid] → protein

■ What base-pairing rules must apply to the interaction between the codon and the anticodon?

☐ Here one RNA molecule is forming base pairs with another RNA molecule, so the base-pairing rules would be C–G (and vice versa) and A–U (and vice versa).

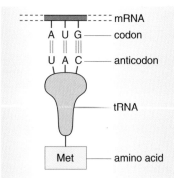

Figure 11.6   The interaction between one tRNA molecule attached to the amino acid methionine (Met) and a short mRNA sequence of one codon.

Thus, the interaction between mRNA and tRNA forms the basis of translation, as shown in Figure 11.7. The first tRNA to bind at the mRNA does so at a very particular **start codon** (labelled codon 1 in this figure), which always has the base sequence AUG and codes for the amino acid methionine. Once this first tRNA has bound, a second follows suit (Figure 11.7a) and the two amino acids become linked together (Figure 11.7b). The first tRNA is then released and the third tRNA binds (Figure 11.7c).

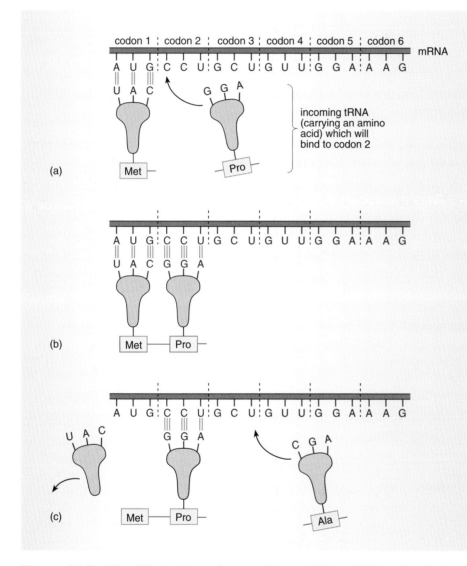

Figure 11.7   Simplified scheme for translation. (a) One tRNA molecule is already bound to mRNA and a second is about to bind. (b) Two tRNA molecules are now bound to mRNA, and the two amino acids are linked together. (c) The first tRNA molecule is released and a third is about to bind.

The binding and subsequent release of tRNA molecules is repeated along the length of the mRNA chain, with amino acids being added sequentially, one at a time, to the growing protein chain, as shown in Figure 11.7.

The final event in protein synthesis is termination of translation. This is brought about by a specific **stop codon** in the mRNA, which 'tells' the translation machinery that its job is complete. Recall that each protein has a precise number and particular sequence of amino acids in its primary structure (Section 9.3). When the stop codon is reached, synthesis stops, no further tRNA molecules bind to the mRNA, and so the completed protein is released from the mRNA. As it is being synthesised, the protein folds up into its own characteristic shape (Section 9.3).

11.5   Where do transcription and translation occur in the cell?

So far we have described the processes of transcription and translation without considering where each occurs within the cell.

■   Given that transcription — the production of mRNA — requires a DNA template, where do you think this process occurs in the cell?

☐   It must occur in the nucleus where the DNA in the cell is located.

However, once mRNA is produced, it leaves the nucleus and protein synthesis — translation — occurs in the cytosol. Thus transcription and translation are separated both in space within the cell and in time, in that one occurs after the other, as shown schematically in Figure 11.8. Thus the role of mRNA is to carry a coded message from the nucleus where the information is stored, to the cytosol where the coded message is translated into a specific protein; hence its name — *messenger* RNA.

Figure 11.8   The sites of transcription and translation within the cell. (a) mRNA is produced in the nucleus. (b) mRNA passes through the nuclear membrane into the cytosol. (c) Protein synthesis occurs in the cytosol on ribosomes (not shown here).

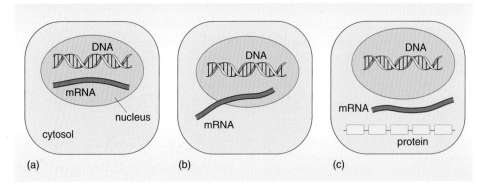

Translation occurs at particular sites within the cytosol; it occurs on ribosomes. Ribosomes are large aggregates of proteins and **ribosomal RNA (rRNA)**. Hence three types of RNA are involved in the process of translation but only one of them, mRNA, codes for proteins.

Question 11.2

Fill in the blanks in each of the following sentences about RNA and protein synthesis. (In some cases more than one word is required to fill a blank.)

(a)   The enzyme _____ copies a stretch of DNA into RNA in a process known as _____ .

(b) Only the _____ strand of DNA is 'read' in the process of RNA synthesis.

(c) There are three different types of RNA molecule: _____ , _____ and _____ .

(d) The transfer of information from the mRNA base sequence to the amino acid sequence of a protein is known as _____ .

(e) The mRNA sequence has a triplet code, and each triplet is known as a _____ .

(f) _____ binds to both an amino acid and mRNA; it attaches to the latter via its three-base _____ .

11.6   The genetic code

The description of the mechanism of translation in Section 11.4 has revealed that there is a code carried within the base sequence of mRNA and the corresponding DNA. For each mRNA codon that is read, one specific amino acid is attached to the growing protein chain. The set of correspondences between base triplets in DNA or mRNA and amino acids in proteins is known as the **genetic code**, which we introduced in Section 11.4, but which is examined here in greater detail.

The DNA and corresponding mRNA codons form the basis of the genetic code, whereby each triplet of three bases specifies a particular amino acid.

■ Look back at Figure 11.7 and write out the sequence of bases in the mRNA that codes for the amino acid methionine (Met), i.e. the codon for Met, and the codon for the amino acid proline (Pro).

☐ AUG codes for Met, and CCU for Pro.

Figure 11.7 shows the codons for six amino acids, but as you know there are 20 commonly occurring amino acids in proteins. There are also four different bases in RNA, but only three are included in any one codon. These four bases can be arranged in 64 different combinations of a three-letter codon, i.e. $4 \times 4 \times 4 = 64$, since there are four possibilities for the first base of a triplet, four possibilities for the second, and four for the third.

■ What can you conclude from the fact that there are 64 possible mRNA codons but only 20 amino acids?

☐ One possible conclusion is that there are several codons for each amino acid. An alternative possibility is that many codons do not code for amino acids.

Both answers are in fact correct to a certain extent. Actually, 61 codons code for particular amino acids, and the other three are stop codons.

■ What is the role of a stop codon?

☐ It signals termination of translation.

A considerable amount of work from the mid-1950s till the mid-1960s was required before the full genetic code was deciphered. It is shown here in Table 11.2. This shows the 64 different codons arranged in terms of the order of the three bases. Let's consider one example: the codon UUU, in the top left-hand corner of the table. This is the sequence coding for the amino acid phenylalanine, here abbreviated to Phe. (The abbreviations for all the amino acids are given below the table; you are not expected to remember the details of this table!) The table shows that for most of the 20 amino acids found in proteins there are several codons. The fact that most amino acids have several codons has led to the description of the code as being a *degenerate* genetic code.

Table 11.2 mRNA codons and the amino acids for which they code. (Note that AUG, the codon for Met, is also the start codon.)

first base		second base				third base
		U	C	A	G	
U	UUU UUC } Phe	UCU UCC } Ser	UAU UAC } Tyr	UGU UGC } Cys	U C
		UUA UUG } Leu	UCA UCG	UAA stop UAG stop	UGA stop UGG Trp	A G
C	CUU CUC } Leu	CCU CCC } Pro	CAU CAC } His	CGU CGC } Arg	U C
		CUA CUG	CCA CCG	CAA CAG } Gln	CGA CGG	A G
A	AUU AUC } Ile	ACU ACC } Thr	AAU AAC } Asn	AGU AGC } Ser	U C
		AUA AUG Met	ACA ACG	AAA AAG } Lys	AGA AGG } Arg	A G
G	GUU GUC } Val	GCU GCC } Ala	GAU GAC } Asp	GGU GGC } Gly	U C
		GUA GUG	GCA GCG	GAA GAG } Glu	GGA GGG	A G

The abbreviated names of the 20 amino acids are as follows: Ala = alanine, Arg = arginine, Asn = asparagine, Asp = aspartate, Cys = cysteine, Gln = glutamine, Glu = glutamate, Gly = glycine, His = histidine, Ile = isoleucine, Leu = leucine, Lys = lysine, Met = methionine, Phe = phenylalanine, Pro = proline, Ser = serine, Thr = threonine, Trp = tryptophan, Tyr = tyrosine, Val = valine. You do not need to remember these abbreviations, nor which codons correspond to which amino acids.

■ The fourth codon in the mRNA sequence in Figure 11.7 is GUU. From Table 11.2, for which amino acid does this triplet code for?

☐ GUU codes for valine (Val).

Table 11.2 shows that the codon AUG codes for the amino acid methionine. As described in Section 11.4.2, the codon AUG is also the start codon for initiating the translation of all proteins. Methionine can therefore appear both at the beginning of and within a protein.

The final aspect of the genetic code we should mention is its *universal* nature. What this means is that the mRNA codons shown in Table 11.2 apply in all of the organisms where the code has been examined. In fact, the processes of information storage in DNA, replication, transcription and translation, are fundamentally similar in all organisms on Earth. Thus all organisms, from simple single-celled organisms such as bacteria to many-celled organisms such as trees and humans, have a genome that contains information in its DNA needed to construct and maintain that particular type of organism.

Question 11.3

Below is the start of the base sequence in the template strand of a section of a DNA molecule.

TAC–CTC–GGT–CAT–CCC–T...

(a) If the above sequence is transcribed, what will be the corresponding mRNA base sequence?

(b) If the mRNA sequence is translated, what will be the amino acid sequence of the product?

(c) Write out the corresponding DNA sequence of the non-template strand.

11.7   Genes, proteins and cells

Almost all of the cells in the body of an individual contain exactly the same genes (Sections 2.2.1 and 4.1.1). Yet there is a huge variety of different kinds of cell in the body of an individual, some of which are shown in Figure 2.2. How are these differences between cells brought about?

We learnt in Section 9.2 that variation between cells of different types stems from differences in the nature of the proteins they contain. Genes code for proteins, and each gene carries the specification for just one protein. All of the cells of the body (with a few exceptions) contain a gene for haemoglobin and a gene for myoglobin, and so forth — thousands of genes in all, each one unique. But they are not all *active* in any one cell type; there are mechanisms for 'switching' genes on and off. A 'switched-on' gene is actively engaged in the production of the protein it codes for, and synthesis of the protein ceases when the gene is 'switched off'. However, the genes specifying proteins that are common to all types of cell (Section 9.2) are active in all cells. The protein is often described as the *gene product*, i.e. the product of the active gene.

■ How can the protein myoglobin be produced only in muscle cells and no other cells in the body?

☐ The gene for myoglobin is active ('switched on') in muscle cells but the gene is not active ('switched off') in other cell types.

Although most cells in an individual carry the same set of genes, not all of the genes are active in all of the cells.

If analogies help, you can think of the genome as a recipe book that contains the recipe (gene) for every dish (protein) in the body; in each cell type a different set of recipes (genes) is used and thus a different menu of dishes (proteins) is produced.

In this chapter we have seen that genes contain the information for the production of a specific sequence of amino acids, which folds into a three-dimensional structure that makes a functional protein. Earlier, a gene was defined as a unit of inheritance, which influences a particular phenotype. There is a direct relationship between a person's genotype and the proteins synthesised in their cells, as we will see in Chapter 12. But what is the relationship between the proteins synthesised within a person's cells and the phenotype of a character? We will go on to explore this relationship in Chapter 13.

Activity 11.1   DNA: the medium and the message

You should now study this video sequence, which illustrates the key points of Chapters 10 and 11.

11.8   Summary of Chapter 11

There is a direct and specific relationship between the linear sequence of base pairs in a gene and the linear sequence of amino acids in a protein. The flow of information is: DNA makes RNA makes protein.

Transcription is the process of RNA synthesis, in which information coded in one of the strands of DNA becomes coded in mRNA. RNA polymerase adds RNA nucleotides one at a time, and the base-pairing rules apply: G of DNA binds to C of RNA, and vice versa; T of DNA binds to A of RNA, but A of DNA binds to U of RNA.

In the process of translation, the four-character language of mRNA is translated into the 20-character language of proteins. A codon of mRNA binds to a triplet anticodon of a tRNA molecule, to which is attached a specific amino acid.

The process of transcription occurs in the nucleus of the cell, and the process of translation occurs in the cytosol of the cell.

The genetic code consists of 64 triplet codons, each of which codes for a specific amino acid or is a stop codon. The genetic code is degenerate in that some amino acids are specified by more than one codon, and it is a universal code, which applies to all organisms.

The majority of cell types in an individual carry the same set of genes, but not all genes are active in all cell types.

Chapter 12
Mutation

As we have seen in Chapters 5 and 6, tracing the patterns of inheritance of genes must start with parental differences, such as Rhesus positive versus Rhesus negative blood group. Where do these underlying genetic differences come from? The answer is that the genetic material has a natural tendency to undergo change in a spontaneous process called *mutation* — a term that means genetic change.

Geneticists recognise two different levels at which mutation takes place. In **gene mutation**, small changes in the sequence of a gene occur and this gives rise to gene variants and alleles. A different kind of mutation involves parts of, or whole, chromosomes and is called **chromosome mutation**. We review these two types of mutation and the mechanisms by which each type arises.

12.1 Gene mutation

The idea of mutation may conjure up an image of a monstrous fly or a humanoid with a single eye in the middle of its forehead, but these images are born of science fiction! Nevertheless, the idea that a mutation is a *difference* is a correct one, since the process of mutation accounts for genetic variations between individuals.

Gene mutation is *the* fundamental source of *heritable* variation.

■ Can you recall what the term 'allele' means?

☐ An allele is a different form of a gene (Section 3.2).

Gene mutation may bring about a change of one allele to another, such as a change in an allele for Rhesus positive to one for Rhesus negative, or vice versa. All the variation that is due to genetic differences rather than environmental factors, such as different blood groups, must have arisen by mutation. These differences have then been copied and transmitted from parent to offspring. Some may have *no* effect on the phenotype; some are useful in that they confer an advantage on that individual, such as an increased resistance to disease; and some can have harmful consequences, such as cystic fibrosis or Huntington's disease (Chapter 6).

It is important to realise that mutation can occur in the genetic material in any cell in the body, but only those that occur in the egg-producing and sperm-producing cells of the germline (Section 4.1) are transmitted to the next generation via gametes; mutations that arise in other cells are not. Some gene changes transmitted in gametes are new, and arose as the egg and the sperm were formed. In fact, it is highly probable that each of us has received at least one new mutation in our genes from one of our parents.

Other gene changes transmitted in gametes, however, are descended from mutations that happened many generations ago. One famous example is a mutation in a single gene that causes haemophilia in the generations of interrelated royal families in Europe. Their pedigree chart is shown in

Figure 12.1. Haemophilia is a recessive disease in humans in which blood clotting is impaired owing to the absence of a blood-clotting factor normally present in blood. The original haemophilia allele arose as a mutation in the reproductive cells of either Queen Victoria or one of her parents and spread into other aristocratic families by intermarriage.

■   What is the striking feature of the pedigree in Figure 12.1?

☐   The affected individuals are all male.

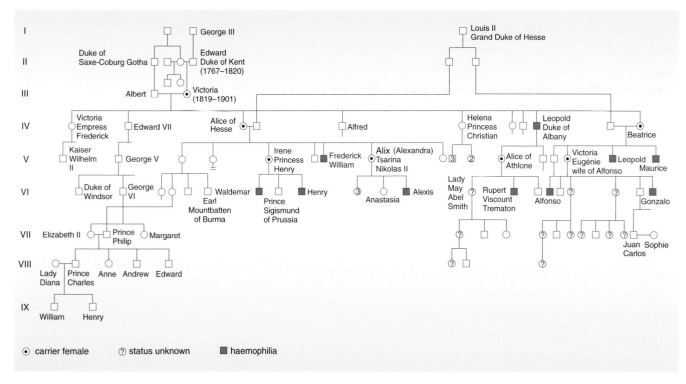

Figure 12.1   A pedigree chart of the royal families of Europe. A recessive allele causing haemophilia arose in the reproductive cells of Queen Victoria or one of her parents, through mutation. Carriers (heterozygotes) are also shown. There is uncertainty about the carrier status of some female individuals, shown by a question-mark (?). A number inside a circle or a square indicates the number of females or males, respectively; it is a device to save space.

■   What does this suggest about the location of the gene for haemophilia?

☐   It suggests it is on the X chromosome (i.e. X-linked, see Section 5.3). Recall that an X-linked recessive gene is always manifest in males because males have only a single X chromosome; there is no equivalent gene on the other sex chromosome, i.e. the Y chromosome.

The defective allele, carried by Queen Victoria on one of her X chromosomes, was transmitted to one of her sons, Leopold, Duke of Albany, who suffered from the disease, and to some of her daughters, who were carriers (heterozygotes). Many of her grandsons and great grandsons also suffered from the disease. For example, the son of the last czar of Russia, Alexis, inherited the allele from his mother, Alexandra, granddaughter of Queen Victoria. Haemophilia is rare in females because they would have to inherit two copies of the recessive allele in order for the recessive phenotype to be manifest.

So much variation in the human genome exists, that no two people (apart from identical twins) alive today, or who have ever lived, have identical DNA sequences in their genome. This is a reflection of the enormous size of the human genome — three billion base pairs. So although we all have the same set of genes, the human genome sequence is not one sequence but many variations on a common theme. Without the process of mutation there would be no genetic variation, in which case all humans would have identical genotypes and the only differences that would exist between us would result from environmental differences!

12.2   From gene mutation to protein structure

How does mutation occur? To answer this question we need to return to the structure and replication of DNA. As we saw in Chapter 10, the double helix structure of DNA and base-pairing account for its stability. The process of DNA replication is generally remarkably efficient and accurate, so that a parent DNA molecule is faithfully reproduced as two new, identical helices (Figure 10.6). However, this process is not always perfect and errors sometimes occur. For example, the enzyme DNA polymerase may occasionally add the wrong nucleotide.

Two examples of the types of error that might occur during the process of DNA replication are shown in the left-hand side of Figure 12.2. For example, the 'wrong'

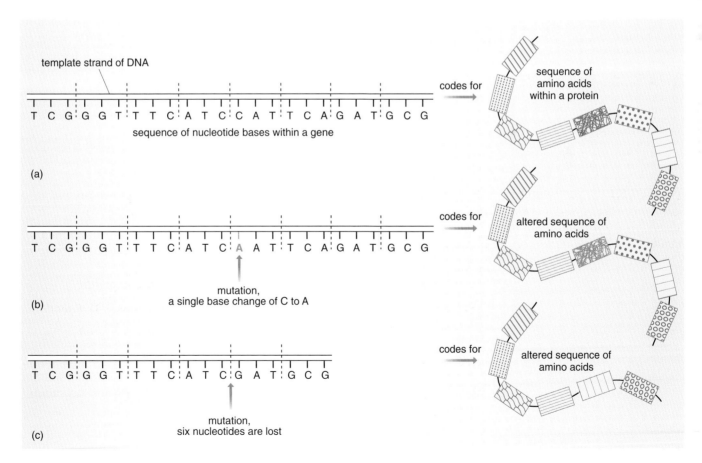

Figure 12.2   Gene mutation. (a) The normal nucleotide sequence on the template strand of DNA codes for a protein. (b) Mutation of a single base change in DNA gives rise to a protein with an altered sequence of amino acids. (c) Mutation resulting in the loss of six nucleotides (including their bases) gives rise to a protein with an altered sequence of amino acids. The intermediate, mRNA, has been omitted in each of (a)–(c).

base may be added to the growing DNA chain, such as an A where a C should have been (Figure 12.2b), or one or a few nucleotides may be lost (Figure 12.2c). Alternatively, a few additional nucleotides might be inserted. These types of gene mutation can occur in any portion of DNA, and are essentially random events. Each of the three gene copies in Figure 12.2a–c, respectively, would be variants of the same gene.

■   What is the difference between a nucleotide and a base?

☐   A nucleotide consists of phosphate, a sugar and a base (Figure 10.3), so a base is one component of a nucleotide.

A change in the sequence of bases within a gene results in a change of information that the gene carries. Recall (Chapter 11) that the genetic code forms the key to understanding the information flow from DNA to RNA to protein. Sequences of three bases in DNA relate directly to mRNA codons, which in turn provide the template on which a precise sequence of amino acids is joined together to form a protein. It requires only a very small change in a DNA sequence to produce a change at the level of the functioning protein.

■   If an error is made during DNA replication so that a base is 'misread' and the 'wrong' base inserted, consider what will happen at transcription. How will the mRNA be affected?

☐   The error in the template strand of DNA is transferred to the mRNA, so that a different message (codon) will be produced.

■   What effect will this different message have on the amino acid sequence of the protein produced at translation?

☐   An incorrect codon could result in a different amino acid being inserted into the growing protein chain.

As you can see from Figure 12.2, modifications to a DNA sequence can lead ultimately to changes in the amino acid sequence of a protein. The 'wrong' sequence would be copied as faithfully in future cell divisions as would the 'correct' sequence, so the new DNA variant that arose by mutation would be perpetuated.

Let's consider the examples in Figure 12.2 in more detail. The DNA molecule in Figure 12.2a contains eight triplets, which correspond to eight mRNA codons. The fifth triplet is CAT, for which the corresponding mRNA would be GUA. From Table 11.2, GUA codes for the amino acid valine (Val). In Figure 12.2b, mutation has resulted in this DNA triplet being changed from CAT to AAT.

■   What would be the corresponding mRNA codon, and for which amino acid does it code?

☐   The mRNA codon would be UUA and Table 11.2 shows that this codes for the amino acid leucine (Leu).

So the mutation of a single base change in Figure 12.2b has resulted in a protein with a small change in the sequence of amino acids. In the mutational event in Figure 12.2c, six nucleotides — two triplets — are deleted.

■ What would be the effect of this deletion on the protein for which this gene codes?

☐ It would result in the absence of two amino acids in the protein.

Had only one nucleotide been deleted, then all subsequent triplets in the sequence would be changed. For example, if the mutation in Figure 12.2b had resulted in the loss of the single orange nucleotide A, the subsequent triplets in the sequence would have shifted to the right by one nucleotide to read: ATT, CAG, ATG, and so on to the end of the gene.

Recall from Chapter 9 that the function of a protein depends on its three-dimensional shape, which is determined by its primary sequence of amino acids. Both examples of mutation in Figure 12.2 lead to a change in the sequence of amino acids in the protein. The effect of these changes on the function of the protein will depend on the position of the changed amino acid(s) in the protein.

■ Thinking back to the structure and function of a protein, such as an enzyme (Section 9.2), which part of the enzyme is most likely to be affected by a change of amino acid sequence?

☐ The part of the protein that contributes to a binding site. (Recall that the binding site provides an exact fit with another substance of a specific type, Figure 9.3. A change in the binding site might affect this fit.)

Why some mutations are harmful and others are not depends on how much they disrupt the normal function of the protein. We look at some examples in the next chapter.

12.3   The rate of DNA mutation

However, not all of the errors that arise during DNA replication result in mutation. There are 'surveillance' processes in cells that can detect most of the errors that arise during DNA replication. For example, there are enzymes that can identify a wrongly placed base in the growing DNA chain, remove it, and replace it with the 'correct' base. These DNA repair enzymes can be viewed as being analogous to quality control systems in an industrial production line, such that 'faulty' products are removed before they leave the 'factory'. Hence the error is usually short-lived, because the incorrect base(s) are removed and replaced by the correct one(s). However, if errors pass undetected by the repair enzymes — an event that must happen relatively rarely, considering the total number of DNA bases replicated — the result is a mutation. In fact, all of the variants in the human genome are DNA changes that escaped detection by repair enzymes!

In addition to mutation brought about by mistakes made during DNA replication, environmental agents, termed *mutagens*, can produce DNA changes by mutation. Many environmental agents are chemicals that occur naturally in the environment, for example, the toxin called aflatoxin produced by moulds on badly stored food such as peanuts.

Other mutagens are physical agents, such as various forms of radiation, including ultraviolet light from the Sun and X-rays. If you have ever had an X-ray, you are probably aware that considerable precautions are taken to protect your reproductive organs, and those of the radiographer, from the mutagenic effects of X-rays. This is primarily to prevent mutation occurring in the DNA of the testes or ovaries.

12.4   Chromosome mutations

In addition to small changes at the DNA level, mutation can also occur at a chromosome level; the change might be the loss or gain of a portion of a chromosome or the loss or gain of a complete chromosome. In either case of chromosome mutation many genes are involved. Since such a large portion of DNA is involved the change is visible in the karyotype.

■ Can you recall what the karyotype is? (You may need to refer back to Section 3.1.)

☐ The karyotype is the number, size and shape of the chromosomes in the cell.

The commonest example of a chromosome mutation leads to Down's syndrome (Figure 12.3), a typical karyotype of which is shown in Figure 12.4.

Figure 12.3   A three-year-old girl with Down's syndrome, playing with bubbles.

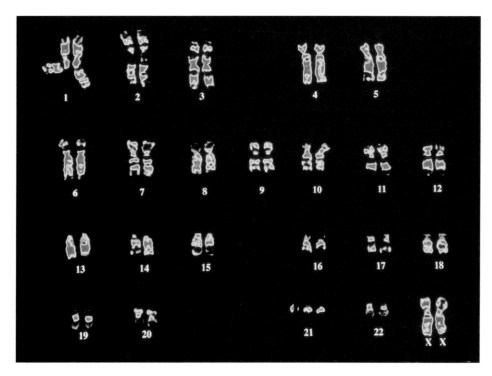

Figure 12.4   False-colour photograph of the chromosomes of a female with Down's syndrome, arranged as a karyotype.

■ Compare the karyotype of a female with Down's syndrome (Figure 12.4) with a typical female karyotype (Figure 3.1). How do these karyotypes differ?

☐ The Down's syndrome karyotype has 47 chromosomes instead of 46; there are three copies of chromosome 21, instead of the usual two copies.

The presence of the extra chromosome 21 has a profound effect on the phenotype; Down's syndrome children usually have a particularly loving nature, short stature, poor muscle tone, and a small round head, as well as showing varying degrees of learning disability. Why the presence of an extra chromosome 21 has these effects on the phenotype is an area of current intensive research.

The reason for the occurrence of an extra chromosome is that occasionally a pair of homologous chromosomes fails to separate during meiosis in the gamete-producing cells. (Normal separation for one pair of homologous chromosomes is shown in Figure 5.2.) Consequently, both chromosomes move to the same gamete and this results in a gamete with *two* copies of the same chromosome instead of the usual one copy. When this gamete combines with a normal gamete at fertilisation, the result is a fertilised egg with *three* copies of this chromosome. The cells derived from this egg during development have the same karyotype of 47 chromosomes.

Intriguingly, the presence of an extra chromosome in a gamete is more frequent in women than in men and is more frequent in older than in younger women. Why should this be so? Recall that meiosis takes about three hours in men, but in contrast it begins in a developing female embryo whilst still inside the uterus. The process is halted at an early stage before the female baby is born and is completed at some time between puberty and the menopause (Section 4.1.1). During a woman's reproductive life, one cell completes the meiotic division and gives rise to one egg during each menstrual cycle. The process of meiosis may be halted for between about 10 (puberty) and 50 years (prior to menopause). As the duration of meiosis increases, the risk of chromosome mutation, such as the failure of homologous chromosomes to separate, also increases.

Hence the older a woman is, the greater the likelihood that she will produce an egg with a chromosome mutation such as an extra chromosome 21. This is clearly demonstrated by comparing the number of Down's syndrome babies born to mothers of different ages, as shown in Figure 12.5.

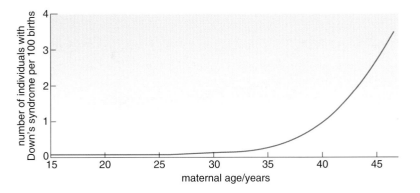

Figure 12.5   A graph showing the increase in frequency of Down's syndrome with maternal age.

■ From the graph in Figure 12.5, what is the frequency (as number per 100 births) of individuals born with Down's syndrome for mothers aged 20 years and those aged 45 years?

☐ The frequency of individuals born with Down's syndrome is very low (about 0.1 per 100 births, i.e. about 1 in 1000) in mothers aged 20 years but rises steeply to about three per 100 births in those aged 45 years.

It is estimated that about three-quarters of the fertilised eggs that would develop into a Down's syndrome child spontaneously abort (as miscarriages), and many live-born Down's syndrome children die soon after birth. Those who survive are usually infertile.

The vast majority of human embryos with other types of major chromosome abnormality spontaneously abort, and chromosome mutation is believed to account for about half of all spontaneous abortions.

Gene mutation, the ultimate source of new variations that exist between individuals, contributes to the overall range of phenotypes within the entire human population and explains why each individual is genotypically unique.

Now that you understand something about gene mutation and how it can affect protein structure, in the next chapter we move on to examine the link between the protein product of a gene and the overall phenotype of the individual. We will do this by examining how alterations in proteins (Section 12.2) result in a changed phenotype.

Question 12.1

Match *one* of the following events with each of the definitions (a) to (d): gene mutation, chromosome mutation, mutagen.

(a) An individual has a karyotype of 45 chromosomes including one X chromosome; one sex chromosome is missing.

(b) The change of one base within a gene to a different base.

(c) A chemical that induces mutations in cells in the laboratory.

(d) The deletion of a nucleotide within a gene.

12.5   Summary of Chapter 12

A gene mutation can bring about the change of one allele of a gene to a different allele or variant. A mutation may involve a change of base(s), the loss of nucleotide(s), or the insertion of nucleotide(s).

A mutation in the DNA of a gene can lead ultimately to a change in the amino acid sequence of a protein, which may disrupt the function of the protein.

In addition to errors made during DNA replication, environmental agents can produce mutations.

Chromosome mutations sometimes arise because homologous chromosomes fail to separate at meiosis. Down's syndrome is an example of a chromosome mutation.

Chapter 13
From protein to phenotype

The primary aim for medical science in trying to understand any genetic disease is to determine the link between the cause — a mutation in the DNA sequence — and its symptoms. An important concept in medical genetics is that genetic diseases are an extreme manifestation of genetic change. Such changes are superimposed upon a background of normal variation, and are all generated through the random process of mutation.

In Chapter 12 we saw that mutation of DNA can lead to changes in the amino acid sequence of a protein. Proteins are the intermediates between genes and the characters of an individual; it is the functioning of proteins that brings about the particular character. Here we will explore the mechanism by which an abnormal protein produced as a result of DNA mutation gives rise to a *clinical phenotype*, i.e. the signs and symptoms of the person who has a disease. Studying alleles that cause disease and their gene products can also help us to learn about the function of the normal protein.

So the central question in this chapter is, what is the relationship between the phenotype of an individual and the protein molecules that are part of his or her cells? We describe two specific examples to illustrate the link between protein product and clinical phenotype: cystic fibrosis and Huntington's disease.

13.1   Cystic fibrosis

The disorder cystic fibrosis (CF) was described in Section 6.3. The lungs and gut, particularly the pancreas, are the major organs affected, becoming blocked by a thick sticky mucus. CF individuals also have an elevated salt content in their sweat, and their reproductive ducts are usually blocked, causing infertility.

A lot is known about the gene involved in CF and the protein for which it codes. In about 70% of cases of CF, the disease results from a mutation in which three consecutive nucleotides are lost from the gene for CF, leading to the loss of one amino acid in the protein. Consequently, we will consider two alleles of this gene: the normal allele, which includes these three nucleotides, and the mutant *cf* allele, which lacks them. Although the change in the DNA in the *cf* allele is relatively minor, it has a profound effect on the functional protein.

■   Is the origin of alleles causing genetic disease such as CF different from that producing alternative alleles, such as the *A* and *B* alleles of the ABO blood group system?

☐   No, the process of mutation underlies the formation of both types of allele (see Chapter 12).

The exact position of the gene for CF on chromosome 7 was identified in 1989. (Chromosomes are shown in Figures 3.1 and 3.2.) Once a gene sequence has been identified, using sophisticated techniques it is possible to extract, and then visualise, pieces of DNA that contain a specific gene such as the gene for CF, as described in Box 13.1.

Box 13.1 Visualising pieces of DNA that contain a specific gene

In this procedure DNA is extracted from many thousands of cells (usually white blood cells, or from a small scraping of skin or from the mouth, both of which would contain thousands of cells). A section of the DNA of the gene of interest is then amplified using a technique called PCR (which is an abbreviation for the polymerase chain reaction). It is not the details of this procedure that are important, but rather the underlying basic principle of finding differences in the DNA sequences of normal and mutant genes.

PCR allows any short section of DNA to be copied many billions of times over (Figure 13.1a), so that it is possible to see the DNA using special dyes.

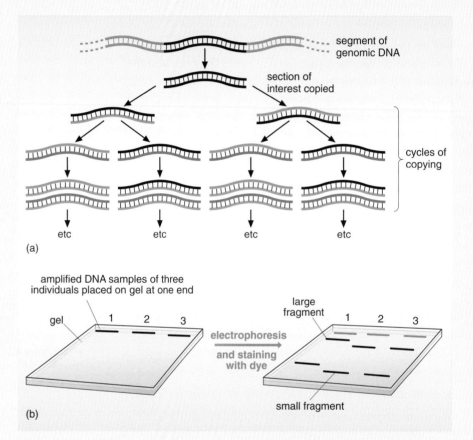

(a)

(b)

Figure 13.1   Analysing DNA for the presence of variants. (a) A section of an individual's genomic DNA that is of interest (black) is copied to give a short fragment. Each new strand is shown in green. This is then copied many times over in a process similar to DNA replication, which preserves the sequence of nucleotides in the original genomic DNA. Note that with each round of copying, each strand of a fragment is copied at each stage, and thus the number of fragments doubles with each 'cycle' of replication. (b) The technique of gel electrophoresis. The DNA fragment amplified by PCR from cells is placed onto one end of the gel (left). (In this example the DNA amplified from three individuals is used.) An electric current is applied to the gel, and the fragments separate according to their size. When stained, the fragments of DNA can be visualised (right). In this case, the fragments are of differing lengths, indicating that the section of DNA in the original genomic DNA differed in length. Smaller fragments move further down the gel than the larger fragments.

The process is rather like replication, in that each strand of the duplex is copied, the duplex split apart and the copying repeated over and over again. Any portion of an individual's genome can be amplified in this way, and as the process is like replication, the code or order of bases is preserved.

Now that we have a section of DNA amplified, how is the DNA analysed? Well, if the process of mutation has added or removed nucleotides, the amplified fragments will actually be of slightly different lengths and this can be easily visualised.

The many billions of copies of an amplified DNA fragment are placed on one end of a thin rectangular-shaped gel (jelly-like substance) on a supporting plate (Figure 13.1b, left) and separated according to their size, by the technique of *gel electrophoresis*. This technique involves an electric current being passed through the gel from one end to the other. The DNA fragments move towards the other end, at a rate that depends on their size.

Large fragments move through the gel with difficulty, but smaller fragments of DNA move more easily and thus move faster. Therefore, large fragments remain close to the end at which the DNA was placed and small fragments move to the opposite end of the gel (Figure 13.1b, right). Once the separation between the fragments is achieved the current is switched off, the DNA is visualised using special dyes and the image captured by camera.

Using the PCR technique it is possible to amplify any gene, even from small numbers of cells and, by analysing it further, to tell whether it is the normal and/or the disease allele. You saw how this was achieved if the fragments of normal and mutant alleles are different lengths (Fig 13.1b, right), but what if they differ only by the sequence of bases? In this case, the base sequence can be determined using the technique of DNA sequencing. Although this technique is beyond the scope of the course and will not be assessed, it is described in Appendix 1 if you are interested.

In Figure 13.2 the DNA has been extracted from cells of eight individuals (numbered 1–8) and two fragments have been identified: fragment N corresponds to the normal allele and fragment M corresponds to the mutant (CF) allele.

What can we learn from Figure 13.2? The first point is that there is gene variation amongst the eight individuals. For each person there are either one or two fragments that represent the two alleles, one corresponding to the normal allele (N) and the other corresponding to the mutant (CF) allele (M). Recall that the common mutation in CF is the loss of three nucleotides, hence this allele is shorter in length and moves further in the gel. The individuals can be grouped into three categories in terms of the fragments present. Look at the fragments amplified for individuals 1, 2 and 3. Remember that each person has two copies of the CF gene, one on each of their copies of chromosome 7. Person 1 has just a single fragment, which corresponds to the mutant allele. So, person 1 has only the mutant allele for this gene; this single fragment on the gel represents the amplified DNA from each of his chromosomes. As they are both mutant alleles they are both the same length, three nucleotides shorter than the normal allele. Person 2 has also just a single fragment, but here it corresponds to the normal allele. Again, this represents the amplified DNA from both his chromosomes. In contrast, person 3 has both fragments and hence has both alleles.

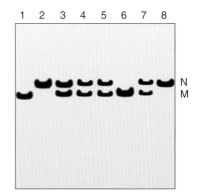

Figure 13.2 Visualising pieces of DNA from eight individuals that contain a specific gene — in this example, the gene for cystic fibrosis. The DNA segment that has been amplified is the region of the cystic fibrosis gene that contains the three missing nucleotides. The fragments that can be seen represent the normal allele (N) and the mutant (cystic fibrosis) allele (M).

■ Using Figure 13.2, group the eight people into three groups (I–III) in terms of the fragments and hence alleles that each has: group I, mutant allele only; group II, normal allele only; group III, both alleles.

☐ Group I: individuals 1 and 6 have only the fragment for the mutant allele.
Group II: individuals 2 and 8 have only the fragment for the normal allele.
Group III: individuals 3, 4, 5, and 7 have both, and hence both alleles.

The individuals in group III have been identified as having two different alleles of the gene for CF.

■ What is the term used to describe this genotype, in contrast to that of individuals in groups I and II?

☐ Group III individuals are said to be heterozygous, in contrast to members of groups I and II, who are homozygous.

A further significant point is that as CF shows a recessive pattern of inheritance, the disease-causing mutant allele is recessive.

■ Which individuals will exhibit the disease symptoms, and why?

☐ Individuals 1 and 6 would be expected to exhibit disease symptoms, because they have only the mutant allele. Only individuals who are homozygous for the disease-causing, mutant allele, show a recessive disease (Section 6.3).

We can explore further this question of which individuals will exhibit the disease, and why, by relating the genetics of CF to events at the level of the protein coded for by the gene, and consider how the *CF* normal allele and the *cf* disease allele of the gene and their protein products are operating. The gene for CF codes for a protein embedded in the cell membrane (Figure 13.3). This protein, which is called the cystic fibrosis protein (CFP), is involved in the transport of salt and accompanying water in glands that produce mucus (such as those in the tubes of the lungs and nose), or digestive enzymes (such as the pancreas) or sweat (in the skin). The normal allele codes for a normal CFP with normal function, whereas the *cf* allele codes for defective CFP with greatly reduced salt transport activity.

Figure 13.3 A schematic representation of cells with the cystic fibrosis protein (CFP) in the cell membrane from individuals of three genotypes: (a) normal *CF CF* homozygotes; (b) *cf cf* homozygotes with cystic fibrosis disease phenotype; (c) *CF cf* heterozygotes with normal phenotype.

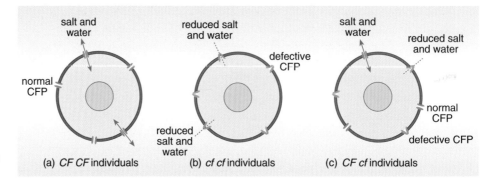

Cells of individuals who are homozygous *cf cf* synthesise only the defective CFP (Figure 13.3b). The transport function of CFP in their cells is significantly reduced. The failure to transport effectively salt and the water that accompanies the salt, leads directly to the accumulation of thick mucus within the lungs and other organs.

Secretions in the tubes of the lungs and other organs become sticky for the simple reason that not enough water flows out of the cells. It also explains why the sweat of CF patients has excess salt; the salt is more concentrated due to insufficient water. There is a very obvious link between the disease-causing mutation, the protein CFP, and the actual effect in the lungs and other organs. In contrast, individuals who are homozygous for the normal allele synthesise non-mutant CFP, which functions normally (Figure 13.3a).

Heterozygous individuals, however, have both alleles, *CF* and *cf.* In these individuals both forms of the CFP are produced in roughly equal amounts and embedded in the cell membrane (Figure 13.3c). Yet these people do not exhibit the disease symptoms because they still produce sufficient normally functioning CFP to ensure transport of salt and the accompanying water.

This example shows that the terms 'dominant' and 'recessive' can be better understood at the level of the functioning protein, rather than at the level of the gene. In the CF example, the dominant normal phenotype represents the presence of normally functioning CFP and the recessive phenotype represents CFP with significantly reduced transport activity. The heterozygote makes *both* proteins, yet the individual has the phenotype associated with the normally functioning CFP; the activity of this normal protein in heterozygotes is sufficient to result in a normal phenotype.

So far, we have assumed that the CF phenotype is the result of only one particular disease allele. This is indeed the case for 70% of patients who carry the same disease allele that has three consecutive nucleotides deleted. However, 30 different mutations account for another 20% of patients, and the remaining 10% of patients have been found to have one of over 900 *different* mutations, all affecting the same gene. Each of these mutated genes has a different change in the nucleotide sequence, and more different mutations are still being found. It is possible that others have escaped detection at the DNA level because of technical limitations. Each one of these different mutated versions of the CF gene results in a defective CFP protein that cannot carry out its correct function in the body. This genetic variability contributes to the phenotypic variability between CF individuals. For example, not all individuals have a blocked pancreas, a small percentage produce normal sweat, and a very small percentage are fertile.

Examples such as CF show how information in genes — the genotype of a particular gene — is converted into the phenotype. This is illustrated in Figure 13.4. This figure summarises the sequence of events from the normal allele of the gene for CF to the development of the normal phenotype, and, for comparison, shows the sequence of events from the mutation in the gene for CF to the development of the disease phenotype.

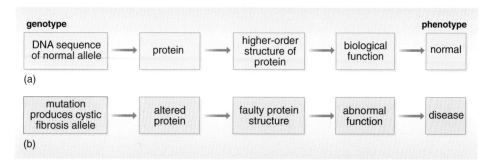

Figure 13.4   The sequence of events from genotype to phenotype: (a) from the normal allele to the normal phenotype; (b) from the mutant allele to the disease phenotype. Note that 'higher-order structure' refers to its three-dimensional shape.

13.2   Huntington's disease

A different form of DNA mutation event occurs in several human neurological diseases, including the dominant disorder Huntington's disease (HD). HD (introduced in Section 6.2), first described by George Huntington in 1872, is a degenerative neurological disorder that begins in adult life.

The gene involved in HD is called the Huntingtin gene and it is located at the tip of the short arm of chromosome 4. (The chromosome can be seen in Figures 3.1 and 3.2). The mutations that occur within this gene occur at an unusual sequence of bases. In a normal copy of the Huntingtin gene, the stretch of DNA at this particular site consists of the three nucleotides, CAG, in the non-template strand and the complementary three, GTC, in the template strand, repeated over and over again. Hence it is described as a *triplet repeat*.

■   What is the corresponding mRNA codon?

☐   Codon CAG.

In individuals without the disease, this stretch of DNA is made up of between 11 and 34 repeats of the triplet CAG. So the DNA sequence in the normal allele varies from individual to individual, some having a run of 11 CAG triplets in the middle of the gene, others having 34 CAG triplets, and yet others having a number anywhere between these two extremes. In those individuals with HD the unusual sequence of the gene is made up of between 40 and 100 repeats. So the DNA sequence also varies between individuals with an allele that causes Huntington's disease.

■   With reference to Table 11.2, for which amino acid does the mRNA codon CAG code?

☐   The CAG codon codes for the amino acid glutamine (Gln).

■   What would be the effect on the structure of the protein of the additional CAG codons in the disease-causing allele?

☐   The protein will be longer, owing to the additional glutamine amino acids.

How is the effect of this mutation eventually converted into the HD phenotype? The gene for HD is 'switched on' or made active in nerve cells (Section 11.7). The normal protein has a number of functions including transport of other proteins within nerve cells. For reasons not yet understood, in individuals with HD, the longer protein is toxic to the nerve cells causing them to die. This leads to neuro-degeneration (breakdown of the nerves) which in turn results in jerking limb movements. Crucially, this toxicity kills the nerve cells even in the presence of the normal protein, and hence the disease-causing *HD* allele acts in a dominant fashion and HD is a dominant disease.

Intriguingly, the strength of the toxicity to the cells shows a direct relationship to the number of additional glutamine amino acids: repeats that are over 60 CAG codons in length almost always result in the earlier death of the affected individual. The measurement of the length of repeat in an individual's DNA forms the basis of a direct DNA test for the presence or absence of the *HD* allele, as is shown in Figure 13.5. In this case, the amplified DNA fragment contains the section of the CAG triplet repeat.

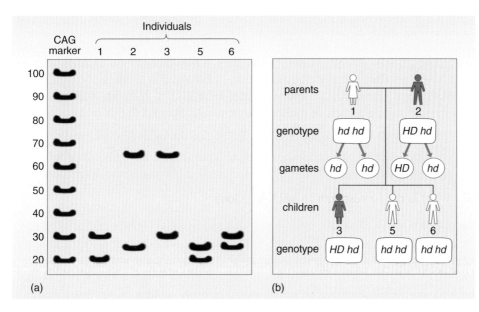

Figure 13.5   Visualising pieces of DNA from five individuals from a family affected by Huntington's disease. (a) The DNA segment carrying the CAG repeat has been amplified and the fragments separated on a gel, alongside a series of marker fragments that contain a known number of CAG repeats from 20 to 100. Individuals 1–6 were shown in Figure 6.2. (b) Using the CAG markers, determine approximately how many CAG repeats are present in each of the alleles in each individual and gamete.

■   Take a look at Figure 13.5(a). What do the different sizes of the amplified DNA fragments indicate?

☐   The amplified fragments or bands, move at different rates along the gel and are therefore of different lengths. The differing lengths are due to the differing number of CAG triplets in each DNA fragment being analysed.

■   The family analysed in Figure 13.5 is the same as the one you saw in Figure 6.2. Use the CAG marker on the gel to determine how many CAG repeats represent that individual's genotype and each gamete. You should look back at your answers on Figure 6.2 as to who inherited the *HD* and *hd* alleles.

☐   You should be able to determine that the mutant allele (*HD*) has about 65 CAG repeats and it is clearly passed on from individual 2 to individual 3. The three normal *hd* alleles contain approximately 20, 25 and 30 CAG repeats and are inherited in a normal manner.

As you can see from this example, the use of these types of DNA tests is very clear and simple to follow in a family pedigree. For the HD test, however, there is one additional piece of information that this test result reveals.

■ Can you recall what this test reveals about the likelihood of disease development in the individuals who test positive for the *HD* allele?

☐ As the allele that is present contains over 60 CAG repeats, it encodes a protein that includes over 60 glutamine amino acids. This is associated with an earlier onset of disease in many cases.

We have seen how mutations in the gene for CF and the gene for HD lead to disease. By far the majority of mutations in disease genes result in the production of an impaired protein with a loss of function (as in CF), and only infrequently an abnormal protein with a gain of function, i.e. an additional function (as in HD).

For many disorders it has taken years to locate and identify the gene involved and, in turn, to determine the gene product, and for many disorders the gene and gene product have yet to be identified. An understanding of the function of the protein will ultimately lead to the development of treatments, a point we return to later in the course. For those genes that are mutated in disease, we have seen that direct testing of an individual's DNA can be used as an accurate diagnostic test. But next, in Chapter 14, we describe how the Human Genome Project led to the generation of the first human genome sequence, take an overview of what sequences are present in our genome and also look at how obtaining the sequence of the genomes of other organisms has helped our understanding of human genes.

 Activity 13.1   After the genome – Part 1

Now would be a good time to view this video sequence, which covers material from the course so far. It will help you revise many of the essential course concepts in a different context.

Question 13.1

Explain, with reference to the CFP, why the cystic fibrosis allele is recessive to the normal allele in a heterozygote.

Question 13.2

Jane, 2 years of age, is not developing as she should. Although she has clinical symptoms of cystic fibrosis her sweat appears normal.

(a) Would a DNA analysis be useful in this case?

(b) If she does not have the usual *cf* mutation, does this disprove she has cystic fibrosis?

13.3   Summary of Chapter 13

A primary aim for medical genetics is to understand the link between the defective protein and the symptoms of the disease. Studying disease alleles and their gene products can also help us to learn about the function of the normal protein, and this may ultimately lead to the development of treatment.

The terms 'dominant' and 'recessive' can be better understood at the level of the functioning protein, rather than at the level of the gene.

Variability in the symptoms of a disease phenotype between individuals may be a consequence of different disease-causing alleles of the gene.

Direct testing of DNA using simple laboratory techniques can be used as diagnostic tests for many diseases.

Chapter 14
Sequencing and interpreting the human genome

Research on the human genome has being going on for over 100 years since it was shown that genes govern the inheritance of characters and that the inheritance of genes and characters follow the same patterns in many organisms. (These patterns were discussed in Chapters 5 and 6.) This research began its ultimate stage in the form of the **Human Genome Project** (HGP), the goal of which is to determine and understand every detail of our genome. This genetic knowledge is a valuable starting point for biological and medical research. The most important application is in the diagnosis of genetic disorders and a better understanding of how genetic variation influences our health.

The previous chapter showed that the first step in understanding the symptoms of a genetic disease and developing treatments is to identify the mutant genes that specify the defective proteins. As our ability to analyse the cell's DNA and proteins increased, the huge challenge of deciphering the complete human genome developed in the form of the HGP. The HGP was a large international project, with several aims, the main two of which were:

- To discover all the genes, their position and order along each chromosome.
- To determine the DNA nucleotide sequence of the human genome, and to understand and interpret fully all the details of the sequence.

Other aims included research into the ethical and social issues raised by knowledge about the human genome. Central to progress of the HGP was the sequencing of the genomes of organisms such as bacteria, yeast and fruit-fly, which allowed the development of genome-sequencing techniques.

We begin this chapter by describing how the HGP achieved its goals and where human genome analysis has ventured since its completion. Then we look at the various categories of DNA within the genome and review the genomes of other organisms that have either been completed or are underway. Finally, we will examine what we have learnt about how the human genome sequence varies between individuals and how the knowledge of other genomes can inform research in human health. This chapter builds on knowledge from earlier chapters, particularly the structure of DNA (Section 10.1), DNA replication (Section 10.2), the processes of transcription and translation (Sections 11.2–11.5) and mutation as a source of genetic variation (Chapter 13), and you may need to refer back to these sections at some points.

14.1   Deciphering the human genome sequence

By describing the HGP in the historical setting of the scientific and technical background of the time, we can explore the key steps in the project's development. These important and influential milestones in the research of genes and genomes are illustrated in Figure 14.1.

	2009	First draft of Neanderthal genome
	2008	Complete sequence of African and Asian individual genomes Complete sequences of cancer genomes
	2007	Complete sequences of Craig Venter and James Watson genomes New human genome map of 3.1 million DNA variants
Many other genomes sequenced	2005	Chimpanzee genome published First human genome map of 2 million DNA variants published Human gene count between 20 000 and 25 000
	2003	Human sequence pretty much complete First draft sequence of chimpanzee genome
	2002	First draft sequence of mouse genome
	2000	First draft sequence of human genome: 85% sequenced
	1999	First human chromosome sequenced: chromosome 21
	1996	Yeast genome sequenced
	1995	Genomes of two species of bacteria sequenced
Many human genes isolated	1994	HGP achieves first genetic map of the human genome
	1991	HGP begins
	1989	Cystic fibrosis gene isolated from all other DNA sequences
	1984	Gene for Huntington's disease located to chromosome 4
	1983	First major database for DNA sequencing established
	1982	Automation of DNA sequencing technique developed
	1975–77	Methods for DNA sequencing developed
	1973–74	Methods for molecular cloning developed
	1966–68	Restriction enzymes discovered
	1966	Genetic code deciphered
	1956	Chromosome number in humans identified as 46
	1953	Model of DNA determined by Watson and Crick
	1936	Genes for colour blindness and haemophilia located to the same chromosome in humans
	1924	Inheritance of human ABO blood groups follows same pattern as characters in other organisms
	1907	Inheritance of eye colour in humans follows same pattern as characters in other organisms
	1900	Segregation of genes recognised in a number of organisms

Figure 14.1 The significant steps in the development of the Human Genome Project and other important milestones in the research on genomes up to and including 2009. Note the increase in the pace of discoveries and achievements. (See text later in Chapter 14 for explanations of new terms.)

The HGP was a product of the development of genetics since the turn of the 20th century. By 1950, it was known that the genes were located along the chromosomes, and that the genetic material was DNA. Figure 14.1 shows that it was not until 1953 that the double helix structure of DNA was discovered by Watson and Crick. Deciphering the genetic code was accomplished in the 1960s.

It will help here to review the scale of what scientists were attempting to achieve when the HGP was first envisaged. So far we have described the human genome as comprising 3 000 000 000 base pairs (Chapter 1) but in fact, each human cell contains twice this amount! The 23 *pairs* of chromosomes (Sections 3.1 and 4.1.1) actually represent two *copies* of the human genome. Thus each cell contains around 6 000 000 000 base pairs of DNA, packaged into the 23 pairs of chromosomes. Recall from Section 10.1 that the term base pair refers to complementary pairs of bases that sit within the core of the double helix (Figure 10.5). Base pair is usually abbreviated to **bp**, and you may see this abbreviation from now on. Each chromosome can be considered as a very long DNA molecule, ranging from over 200 million bp to about 33 million bp arranged in a linear sequence (Figure 10.7).

The ability to analyse such large amounts of DNA was a result of several techniques that had been developed over several decades of genetics research (Figure 14.1). First, in the late 1960s a number of enzymes that can cut DNA into fragments were discovered. These enzymes allowed researchers to cut the DNA down to a size that is manageable to work with in the laboratory. Second, the techniques to determine the sequence of base pairs in a fragment of DNA were developed in the 1970s — techniques that were automated in the 1980s (we describe them in Appendix 1). Third, the first database was set up in 1983 for the storage of DNA sequence information. Finally, in the 1980s many human genes were identified and their sequences determined, such as the gene for cystic fibrosis, and it was recognised that this was the way forward for genetics.

From the 1980s, the HGP became established, achieved funding from many public charities and government agencies and by the summer of 2000 the first draft sequence comprising 85% of the genome was announced (as described in Chapter 1). The scientists involved formed the international Human Genome Consortium, which included 16 institutions in France, Germany, Japan, China, the UK and the USA. The total cost for the production of the first draft was estimated at about $300 million worldwide. In a related announcement, Celera Genomics — a privately funded company and one-time rival of the Human Genome Consortium — based in the USA, declared that it had also completed its own first assembly of the human genome sequence. A draft sequence covering 90% of the human genome and an initial analysis of the sequence were announced jointly by the two groups in February 2001.

The early draft sequences were far from perfect, containing hundreds of thousands of gaps and many errors, but by 2003 very few of these remained in the then published sequence. Since then, much of the ongoing work has been devoted to completing the missing segments and producing a complete catalogue of all the genes, and how their products interact in the development and maintenance of a human being, *Homo sapiens*. In 2005, researchers deciphered the very first 1 million bp of DNA sequence from the extinct Neanderthal.

The completion of the first *individual* human genome sequences (the original HGP studied a pool of DNA from several individuals) in 2007 included the genomes of James Watson (who had co-discovered the structure of DNA in 1953) and Craig Venter (who had headed the Celera Genomics project). These achievements marked the development of newer and cheaper technologies for DNA sequencing and subsequently, in 2008, the full first genomes of an African and an Asian individual were published. (Prior to this all sequenced genomes had been from Caucasian individuals.) Notably, the price to obtain a completed sequence in 2008 had shrunk to less than $0.5 million dollars and by 2009, the new techniques allowed the first draft of the entire Neanderthal genome to be deciphered.

One of the original aims of the HGP had been to make the sequence of the human genome freely available to everyone, so the data has to be stored in such a way as to be accessible to scientists all over the world. Sophisticated computer programs can then be used to analyse the sequence, for example to identify gene sequences in the mass of data. The huge amount of human genome sequence data and the relevant computer programs to analyse it are held on large computer databases, accessible to anyone through the internet.

The nucleotide sequence of four letters, A, C, G and T, has had to be analysed and interpreted to reveal, for example, which parts correspond to genes. The sequence will be valuable not only for what it tells us about our genes, but also because of what it tells us about the organisation of our genome. It is beyond the scope of this course to explore the entire human genome, but to give you some idea of the structure of the genome as a whole, such as how much of the DNA codes for proteins, we will take an overview in the next section. Some results of a more detailed analysis of the sequence and how genes are arranged along each DNA molecule are briefly described in Chapter 15.

There is a summary of the techniques used to decipher the human genome sequence in Appendix 1. You do not need to study this; it is for your interest.

14.2   DNA roles and genome organisation

So far in this course we have considered only DNA sequences that correspond to genes, but we now consider two other important questions:

- How much of our genome corresponds to genes?
- How are these genes organised within the genome?

Figure 14.2 illustrates the overall composition of the human genome as a pie chart. Each coloured slice represents an amount of DNA of a particular category — the relative size of the slice indicates the amount as a proportion of the total.

■ What is the most striking feature about Figure 14.2?

□ Only a very small part of the genome corresponds to gene sequences, that is, codes for proteins.

The majority of the genome appears to be nothing to do with genes! As we will see, however, although only a small proportion of the genome actually codes for proteins, a sizeable component serves to support the genes in their function.

14.2.1   Genes and supporting sequences

Figure 14.2 shows that 27% of the genome supports gene structure and function. This includes sections of DNA that are required to ensure that genes are activated in

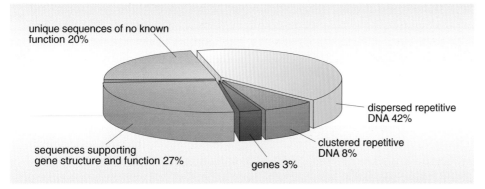

Figure 14.2 A pie chart illustrating the relative proportions of the different categories of DNA sequences in the human genome.

the correct cells and at the correct time. Recall from Section 11.7 that cells become specialised because some genes are activated or 'switched on' in them and other genes are 'switched off'. Therefore the sections of DNA responsible for controlling gene activation have a critical role in cell specialisation and cell function.

Other DNA sequences that are included in the proportion of DNA that supports gene structure and function actually occur within genes themselves. In Chapter 11 we examined the precise relationship between the base sequence of DNA in a gene and the linear sequence of amino acids in a protein. However, the information for making proteins in the great majority of genes is *not* an uninterrupted sequence of DNA bases. Rather, most genes are 'split' into separate parts by intervening non-coding sequences, as shown in Figure 14.3.

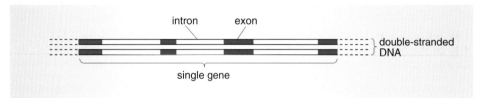

Figure 14.3 A sketch of a hypothetical split gene, consisting of four short exons (protein-coding regions) and three larger, intervening, introns (non-protein-coding regions).

■ Consider a protein with a sequence of 300 amino acids. Approximately how many mRNA bases and hence how many DNA base pairs would you expect to code for this protein?

☐ Each mRNA codon is a triplet of three bases, which codes for one amino acid, so 900 mRNA bases and hence 900 DNA base pairs would be expected to code for this protein.

You may be surprised to learn that genes vary considerably in size from around 2000 to over 100 000 base pairs in length. For example, for many proteins of average length of around 300–400 amino acids, each gene contains 100 000 base pairs — about 100 times the number that is apparently needed! What, then, is the relationship between all these extra DNA base pairs and the final protein sequence? The rules that we learnt in Chapter 11 apply, in that, for example, 900 DNA base pairs would be needed to code for a protein of 300 amino acids. However, only a relatively small number of base pairs within such a gene actually code for amino acids in the protein: such protein-coding DNA sequences are termed **exons** (Figure 14.3). Within the DNA sequence of a gene the exons are interspersed with non-protein-coding regions termed **introns** (Figure 14.3). A large proportion of the base pairs of a gene comprises introns, the sequences of which do not 'appear' in the final protein product of the gene.

A gene with exons and introns is described as a *split gene*.

As Figure 14.3 shows, usually there are relatively long intron regions interspersed with relatively short exon regions. However, the split gene shown in Figure 14.3 is a very simple, indeed hypothetical, example with only four exons. Many genes that have actually been identified and characterised are much more complicated than this. For example, the cystic fibrosis gene is very large, comprising 250 000 base pairs including 26 introns.

■ From Figure 14.2, what is the total percentage of the genome that corresponds to genes and their supporting sequences?

☐ Together they amount to 30% of the total genome: 3% corresponds to protein-coding gene sequences and 27% corresponds to sequences that support gene structure and function.

In addition to finding genes, the HGP aimed to *map* these genes within the genome. Just like any other map, the map of the human genome provides information about the location of features (genes) and their position relative to each other. As described in Sections 3.1 and 5.2, each chromosome contains many genes. Hence the human genome map identifies the genes and their exact location and order along each chromosome. Projects are ongoing to characterise all the sequence elements that support the genes.

If all the genes and their supporting sequences together amount to only about 30% of the human genome, what features make up the remaining 70%? We examine the remaining DNA sequences in the next section.

14.2.2   Other DNA sequences

Examination of the remaining 70% of DNA shows that it falls into one of three categories. Most of these sequences have no known function or significance. One of these categories is called *unique sequences* because each sequence is present only once in the genome.

The remaining DNA is called *repetitive* DNA, because sequences are repeated a number of times over. Repetitive DNA can be divided into two classes according to its distribution along the chromosomes: one class shows a *clustered* distribution, that is, many copies are grouped together consecutively at one location (each repeat is usually 10–25 base pairs long); the other class is found *dispersed* throughout the genome, i.e. at many places along each chromosome (each repeat varies in length, usually from hundreds to thousands of base pairs).

How are genes and the various other categories of DNA organised along a chromosome? A simplified picture of the distribution of each category along a 'typical' chromosome is shown in Figure 14.4. Although most of the highly repetitive DNA sequences have no known function, some of the clustered repetitive DNA, in blocks of a million or more base pairs, is found at specific locations on the chromosomes. One such clustered repeated sequence is known to be associated with the centromere, and thus appears to have a role in chromosome structure (Figure 14.4).

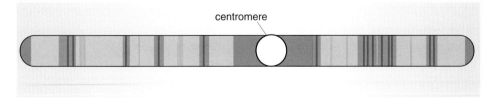

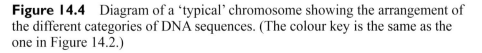

Figure 14.4   Diagram of a 'typical' chromosome showing the arrangement of the different categories of DNA sequences. (The colour key is the same as the one in Figure 14.2.)

A second kind of clustered repetitive DNA is found at the tips of each chromosome. This DNA sequence is important in maintaining the overall chromosome length by protecting the tips during DNA replication. It also serves to anchor the chromosomes to the nuclear membrane at the growth phase of the cell cycle (Section 2.2) when the chromosomes are not visible. It has proved impossible to sequence fully much of the clustered repetitive DNA, and it is likely that much of the sequence 'missing' from the recently published drafts is this kind of DNA.

14.3   Beyond whole genome sequencing: identifying genetic variation in the human genome

As the initial human genome sequence was being assembled, it became apparent that the actual sequence of bases in some stretches of a chromosome was not always the same. Recall that the original sequence was actually obtained from a sample of DNA that was pooled from several individuals. Hence, as individual DNA fragments were decoded and the sequence of a chromosome generated by stitching together smaller pieces, the final sequence actually represented a mixture of the DNA sequences present in the donors of the DNA samples.

■ Based upon what you have learnt about human genes, what do you think these differences represent?

☐ They represent variation in the DNA sequence that is present in each of the individual donors.

■ Can you think what the origin of these differences is?

☐ It is the process of mutation, whereby the DNA code of bases changes, either through DNA synthesis errors or through the action of mutagens (Chapter 12).

So the first human genome sequences were actually not representative of any one individual; they were a composite of several people. It was not until 2007 that we saw the complete genome sequence from just a single individual determined, in this case for two of the scientists who most influenced the HGP; James Watson and Craig Venter (Figure 14.1). In these cases, the sequences obtained represented the unique genomes of those persons with all their own DNA variants.

■ Why would identifying differences in the DNA code be useful for studying human health?

☐ As you saw in Chapter 13, differences in DNA sequence underlie differences in gene function and some will be associated with disease.

By identifying differences between individuals, we can catalogue all of the variants that exist within the human genome and this will allow scientists to determine which are associated with specific diseases or which can influence our health.

In order to examine DNA variation, therefore, scientists set out to record and locate along each chromosome, as many variant DNA bases as possible. In 2005, the first 'map' of 2 million 'common' DNA variants was published, based upon looking for differences between 280 people of different ethnicities from around the world. Two years later, another 1.1 million had been added (Figure 14.1).

The term 'common' means that these are DNA variants that are present in over 1% of people examined. In actuality, a total of over 20 million differences in the sequence of the human genome had been identified by the end of 2009. These data suggest that any two individuals differ by over 1 million bases. Whilst this might seem like a large number, it means that we are in fact over 99.99% identical at the DNA level. We will take a closer look at variation in one human gene in the next chapter.

14.4   Other genome projects

In parallel with the study of the human genome, scientists have been sequencing the genomes of many other organisms and storing the information in electronic databases. Once the details of a genome begin to emerge, they can be compared with those of the genomes of other organisms. Recall from Chapter 2 that humans consist of large numbers of different kinds of cell, almost all of which have a nucleus containing identical genetic information. This is also true of other organisms, whether animal, plant or fungi (although some organisms consist of single cells). Bacterial cells, however, differ from other organisms in that their DNA is not enclosed in a nucleus. Each type of organism, including bacteria, has a genome made up of DNA.

14.4.1   Size of genomes of other organisms

Let us begin by comparing the size of the genomes of some of these organisms. Table 14.1 shows that there is considerable variation in the sizes of the genomes among the organisms listed. Note the small size of the bacterial genome. One reason for this is that introns (Section 14.2.1) are absent from bacterial genomes, so each gene is much smaller than those in other organisms. Another reason is the almost total absence of repetitive sequences of DNA in bacteria. Now look at the sizes of the genomes of the other organisms listed in Table 14.1.

Table 14.1 Genome sizes of representative organisms. Sizes given are either height or length, whichever of the two is the larger dimension of that particular organism; all sizes are approximate. An asterisk indicates that the organism is so small that a microscope is required to see it.

Group	Organism	Size of organism/cm	Genome size/bp
vertebrates	human	180	3 000 000 000
	mouse	10	3 000 000 000
invertebrates	fruit-fly	0.2	170 000 000
	locust	5	6 000 000 000
fungi	yeast	*	12 000 000
bacteria	*Escherichia coli*	*	4 000 000

■ Do smaller animals have smaller genomes than larger animals?

☐ No. For example, if you compare the sizes of the human and mouse genomes, you can see that the mouse genome is of similar size to the human genome, although the mouse is a much smaller animal. Similarly the locust, an insect about 5 cm long, has a genome that is twice the size of the human genome.

We can make another observation from Table 14.1. The organisms are listed in a series of decreasing body complexity. By 'complexity' we mean having features such as larger nervous systems, more complicated organs and a greater number of cells and types of cell.

■ Is there any indication that complex organisms, i.e. vertebrates, have larger genomes than the fungi represented in Table 14.1?

☐ Genome size does coincide to a certain extent with the complexity of the organism. For example, yeast has a smaller genome than vertebrates.

■ Vertebrates are more complex organisms than invertebrates. Do all vertebrates have larger genomes than invertebrates?

☐ No. As noted above, the locust genome is twice the size of the human genome.

Thus, the correlation between complexity and genome size is not precise. Is the genome size related to the total number of genes present? This is actually a hard question to answer because we don't have a complete genome sequence for all of the organisms listed in Table 14.1, but from available data, it would seem not always to be the case. In general, however, more complex organisms have a greater number of genes.

The differences in the number of genes, however, account for only a small proportion of the differences between the sizes of genomes. The bulk of such differences is due to repetitive DNA. The general rule is that the larger the genome the greater the number of repetitive sequences of DNA. The yeast genome, for example, contains very few repetitive DNA sequences, and the locust genome contains a significantly greater proportion of repetitive DNA than the human genome.

14.4.2   Relevance of other genome projects

Figure 14.1 shows that three genomes were sequenced by the mid 1990s: two species of bacteria, and yeast used in bread and beer making. Why are these events listed there? At the time when the HGP was conceived, it was considered important to undertake the sequencing of the genomes of several other organisms. By 2009, more than 1600 genomes of different species had been sequenced (many of which were those of bacteria and viruses) and might have also been included in Figure 14.1. Why expend considerable resources, expertise and time on these apparently insignificant organisms? Within the context of the HGP and human health there are a number of reasons.

First, many gene sequences in one species have been found to be very *similar*, but not *identical*, to those of another species. This is because all species are related to each other through the process of *evolution*. Many genes in different organisms have similar nucleotide sequences. They are not usually identical because genes undergo different changes by mutation. Let's take, for example, the nucleotide sequence of the haemoglobin gene. The sequence in the mouse is similar to the sequence of the human haemoglobin gene. Such sequences are said to be **conserved**. Scientists working on the HGP realised that similarities between human gene sequences and those of other organisms could speed up the process of isolating human genes, particularly those associated with disease.

A second reason for sequencing the genomes of other organisms is that humans do not make ideal experimental animals. From a genetic and ethical standpoint, a researcher cannot set up specific breeding experiments, and the human generation time is far too long! Several species have been adopted as 'model' organisms, because they are easy to keep in the laboratory and have a short life cycle. Discoveries made with them give important clues to *human* biology and *human* genes, making the study of these organisms important to biological and medical research. Many biological processes, influenced by genes, such as the activities of living cells, are controlled in these organisms in the same way as in humans. So conclusions about biological processes drawn from experiments using mice, for example, can often be applicable to humans. Furthermore, understanding the genes and the organisation of a genome, starting with bacteria, the simplest of organisms, reveals how the whole genome functions to direct the development of that particular type of organism.

A third reason why so much effort has been devoted to study of the genomes of model organisms is that many of these studies provided a means of developing and fine-tuning the procedures used in the sequencing of the human genome. Much of the ability to complete the drafts of the human genome sequence was due to technical advances made and tested while sequencing genomes of other organisms. As studies in themselves they also provide a wealth of information for biologists who study those organisms.

The final reason is that a large number of the decoded genomes represent organisms that affect human health. The genomes decoded include those of many viruses, bacteria and other pathogens that infect humans and cause disease. Knowledge of these genomes helps accelerate research into vaccines and drug treatments to combat these pathogens.

This chapter has examined the different categories of DNA, how the sequence of bases of the human genome was determined, and other genome projects. In the next chapter we examine the other main aim of the HGP, to discover all the genes and their order along each chromosome. In doing so we will focus on several areas of the human genome and illustrate how much variation there is and how comparison with other organisms helps us understand gene function.

Question 14.1

Complete the sentences below by inserting the most appropriate of the following words and phrases: exon, intron, repetitive DNA, conserved gene sequence.

(a) An _____ is a non-coding sequence of bases within a split gene.

(b) _____ describes the similarity between gene sequences in different types of organism.

(c) _____ is a DNA sequence that is repeated many times in the genome.

(d) An _____ is a coding region of bases within a split gene.

Question 14.2

List the reasons for sequencing the genomes of organisms other than humans.

14.5   Summary of Chapter 14

The HGP was an international scientific undertaking established to study the human genome, with the ultimate goal of working out its entire nucleotide sequence.

Only a small proportion of the genome corresponds to genes and sequences that support genes. Many human genes are split genes, containing exons, which code for proteins, and introns, which do not. The majority of the human genome is composed of unique sequences of unknown function and of two types of repetitive DNA sequence, dispersed repeats and clustered repeats.

Genome sequencing projects have generated an enormous amount of information, which is stored on electronic databases and analysed by sophisticated computer programs, and is accessible via the internet.

There is no consistent relationship between the size of an organism and the size of its genome. Genome size does correlate to a certain extent with the complexity of the organism, but the correlation is not precise. The larger the genome the greater the proportion of repetitive DNA that is present.

Genome research involves not just the study of the human genome; the genomes of many other organisms are under intensive study. This work is of pivotal importance to identifying human genes and understanding the role of other processes common to life, such as how the activities of the living cell are controlled.

Chapter 15
Analysis of the human genome sequence

In this chapter we explore some of the scientific findings about our genome. Over the past 40 years or so, thousands of genes have been isolated, (i.e. identified to the precise location within the genome and sequenced), of which many hundreds are associated with disease. However, only a small proportion of the total DNA in our genome actually corresponds to genes (Section 14.2). This raises a number of intriguing questions about the organisation of our genome. Is the distribution of genes similar along each chromosome? Are the genes arranged according to their functions, or some other criteria?

We answer these questions, beginning with an examination of the gene content, gene distribution and the repetitive DNA content along one particular chromosome, chromosome 21. Chromosome 21 was actually one of the first chromosomes for which the complete DNA sequence was obtained, primarily due to it being the smallest. Having explored the organisation of genes and DNA sequences on chromosome 21, we then compare it with the rest of our genome.

The amount of variation in the human genome results in many millions of base differences between each individual, but where is this variation? We examine a gene that plays a major role in the development of human eye colour and see how variation across the gene can affect the function of the gene.

One of the important outcomes of the HGP was the availability of the sequence for each human chromosome in electronic databases, easily accessed from anywhere around the world over the internet. We move on to examine how these electronic databases are accelerating the discovery of new disease genes. Isolating disease genes, such as the cystic fibrosis gene (Section 13.1), is one important goal for medical research because the links between a gene, its gene product and associated phenotype can then be determined. Hence we can learn about the function of the normal and abnormal protein products within the body, and this may ultimately lead to the development of a treatment for a disease.

We conclude this chapter by looking at the unexpected and remarkable discovery that large sections of the human genome sequence are duplicated within our chromosomes, and look at the possible consequences of these duplications for human health.

This chapter builds on knowledge from earlier chapters, particularly genome organisation (Section 14.2), DNA variation across the genome (Section 14.3), gene conservation between species (Section 14.4), and you may need to refer back to these sections at appropriate points. In order to illustrate underlying principles about our genome we present a lot of data, such as the total number of genes, the number of base pairs in a specific chromosome and the number of variant DNA bases in a gene, but you are not expected to remember these.

15.1   The genetic organisation of chromosome 21

Now that all our genome has been fully sequenced, many times over, it is of interest to understand how the genes and other DNA sequences, such as repetitive sequences, are arranged and organised within the genome. To address this, we will look at the DNA sequence of chromosome 21. In order to appreciate the size of chromosome 21 relative to other chromosomes in our genome, look at the karyotypes in Figures 3.1 and 3.2.

■ How does the size of chromosome 21 compare with the size of other chromosomes in the genome?

☐ Chromosome 21 is of similar size to chromosome 22; other than the Y chromosome, they are the smallest chromosomes in the genome.

Considering the huge size of the human genome, it is not surprising, therefore, that one of our smallest chromosomes, comprising about 47 000 000 bp, was actually the first to be completely sequenced and reassembled (in 1999). Another reason for the intensive research on chromosome 21 is that it is involved in a relatively common mutation (Section 12.4). Occasionally, three copies of chromosome 21 are present in the karyotype of an individual instead of the usual two copies.

■ What is the phenotype of individuals with three copies of chromosome 21?

☐ Down's syndrome (Section 12.4).

We can ask a number of questions about chromosome 21:
• What genes does it contain?
• What is the distribution of the genes?
• How are the repetitive sequences of DNA distributed along the chromosome?

15.1.1   The gene content of chromosome 21

The analysis of the sequence of chromosome 21 reveals that it contains 294 genes. How were these genes identified within the genome sequence? Over 150 of them had already been identified by geneticists before the sequencing of chromosome 21 was completed. This large proportion of genes reflects the fact that chromosome 21 had been intensively studied in order to determine which particular genes might contribute to the production of the Down's syndrome phenotype. Another way to identify genes is to use the similarities between human gene sequences and those of other organisms (Section 14.2.2). Recall that scientists use computer programs to search the human genome sequence databases for matches to conserved gene sequences in the databases of other organisms. Researchers have also used computer programs that can identify sequences in the human databases that might correspond to a gene. Such programs recognise potential genes in the genome by looking for essential structural features, such as start and stop codons (Section 11.4) at the beginning and end of each exon (Section 14.2.1).

By mid-2009, the functions of most of the proteins encoded by the 294 genes were known and several had been found to be involved in diseases, including a form of hereditary deafness and a particular form of leukaemia. The function of the remainder is still unknown. This highlights that much work remains to be done before we can understand fully the functioning of our genome.

15.1.2   Distribution of genes along chromosome 21

A simplified picture of the distribution of each category of DNA, including DNA sequences corresponding to genes and repetitive DNA, along a 'typical' chromosome is shown in Figure 14.4. The 294 genes on chromosome 21 are distributed along the length of the chromosome, although their arrangement varies between regions. For example, in one region there are only seven genes in a stretch of over 7 000 000 bp. There are several other stretches in which genes are even scarcer, and in total these add up to one-third of the length of the chromosome. Other regions of the chromosome are described as 'gene-rich', but even here, the arrangement of genes varies.

In order to appreciate these differences, let us compare the number of genes in two sections, each of about 900 000 bp, from different regions of chromosome 21. These are shown in Figure 15.1.

■   How does the number of genes compare between the two regions (a) and (b) of chromosome 21, shown in Figure 15.1?

☐   Region (a) has 11 genes compared with 36 genes in region (b).

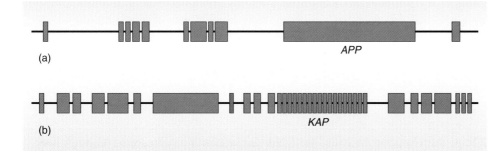

Figure 15.1   The distribution of genes in two regions (a) and (b) of chromosome 21, each about 900 000 bp in length. Each purple bar represents a gene.

In fact, region (a) has above the average *gene density* for the entire chromosome, while the density in region (b) is well above average. Gene density is the number of genes within a defined number of bp, for example 1 000 000 bp. The size of the genes themselves also varies enormously, as shown in Figure 15.1; some genes are over 70 times bigger than others. Most of the differences in size can be accounted for by the differences in the number and length of introns. The gene *APP* (an abbreviation for amyloid precursor protein) in Figure 15.1a, is a large gene that has been explored in some detail. Mutations in this gene are associated with a form of Alzheimer's disease, characterised by progressive dementia. The gene itself spans 290 000 bp of chromosome 21. The APP protein is encoded in 19 small exons scattered across this region. The mRNA product of the *APP* gene is only 2900 bp in length. Hence, about 99% of the *APP* gene is DNA that does not code for APP protein. Some of this DNA functions as supporting sequences (Section 14.2.1) that determine the activation of the *APP* gene in specialised cells in the brain; the remainder makes up introns.

Whilst, in general, genes are not grouped along the chromosome, several small groups of genes tightly linked together are known to exist. The remarkable property of these groups is that each gene within a group is a copy of each other gene in the group. Hence, they are described as a *gene family*. Notice the group of genes labelled *KAP* (<u>k</u>eratin <u>a</u>ssociated <u>p</u>roteins) in Figure 15.1b. Keratin proteins are a predominant component of skin cells. *KAP* is a gene family of 18 multiple copies of a gene tightly grouped together.

■ Would you expect all copies of the gene to encode the same protein?

☐ Yes, since the DNA sequence of each copy is the same.

A detailed examination of genes with a known function reveals that chromosome 21 contains genes with a variety of biological functions. For example, some genes code for membrane proteins and others code for enzymes. Thus not all of the genes that code for proteins of similar function are situated in close proximity within our genome. For example, genes that code for membrane proteins are found scattered throughout the genome. Nor are the genes that are active or 'switched on' (Section 11.7) in one cell type or tissue type, grouped together on the same chromosome.

In summary, human chromosome 21 contains genes with many different functions that are 'switched on' in a variety of cell types. There is no overall systematic pattern to the distribution of genes along the chromosome; there are areas in which genes are less densely packed than others. Thus, equivalent lengths of the genome contain different numbers of genes.

15.1.3   Repetitive DNA in chromosome 21

Recall from Section 14.2 that the DNA sequences that correspond to genes and supporting sequences represent only 30% of the human genome. About 50% of our genome consists of repetitive DNA sequences (Figure 14.2). How is repetitive DNA distributed along chromosome 21?

■ What are the two types of repetitive DNA in the human genome?

☐ Clustered repeats and dispersed repeats (Section 14.2.2).

In fact, the proportion of repetitive DNA in chromosome 21 is higher than for the genome as a whole. One reason for this is that the chromosome is very small and the centromere, which contains a very large block of clustered repetitive DNA sequences, makes up almost 25% of the chromosome's length. The centromere is of similar size in all chromosomes so the proportion of clustered repeat sequences is much smaller in larger chromosomes.

In a similar way to the distribution of genes along the chromosome, dispersed repetitive DNA is also unevenly distributed. For example, there are regions that contain a high density of repetitive DNA, whereas other regions have far fewer repeats. About 30% of chromosome 21 is composed of dispersed repetitive DNA. About two-thirds of these sequences are repeated many tens of thousands of times along the chromosome, whilst most of the remaining dispersed repetitive DNA consists of sequences present between only 10 and 100 times on the chromosome. As described in Section 14.2.2, these repeats appear to have no biological role. At present we can, therefore, only observe their presence.

15.2   A snapshot of the genetic organisation of the human genome

The human genome is divided into chromosomes which vary in length as shown in Figures 3.1 and 3.2. Examine these figures and answer the following question.

■ Which chromosome is the longest?

□ Chromosome 1 (by definition, since chromosomes are arranged in the karyotype according to size, starting with the longest).

■ Approximately how many times longer is chromosome 1 than chromosome 21?

□ Approximately five times.

Analysis of the sequence of the total human genome sequence suggests that the most likely number of protein-coding genes is between 20 000 and 25 000. The final count will have to await confirmation that each gene sequence is functional, that is, it produces a protein. How are these genes distributed throughout the genome? Does the number of genes on a chromosome correspond to the size of the chromosome? Is there such a thing as a typical human gene?

15.2.1   The distribution of genes within the genome

We start our exploration of the organisation of the genome, by examining whether there is a relationship between the size of a chromosome and the number of genes it contains. Comparison between the two similarly sized chromosomes, chromosome 21 and chromosome 22, reveals that the latter chromosome contains 574 genes, almost twice as many genes as chromosome 21 (294). Figure 15.2 shows the distribution of genes along these two chromosomes for comparison. Not surprisingly, though, our largest chromosome — chromosome 1 — has the largest number of genes, with a total of 2579 genes scattered along its entire length of 247 000 000 bp.

Figure 15.2 Pictorial representation of chromosome 21 and chromosome 22 showing the distribution of genes in each chromosome on one side of the centromere. Genes carried on the other side, i.e. the short side, shown here above the centromere, are not given. The purple bars to the right of each chromosome indicate numbers of genes. The length of a particular bar represents the number of genes present in the corresponding chromosome region against which the bar aligns (see scale, bottom right). On chromosome 21, the relative positions of *APP* and *KAP*, discussed in Section 15.1 (Figure 15.1), are shown.

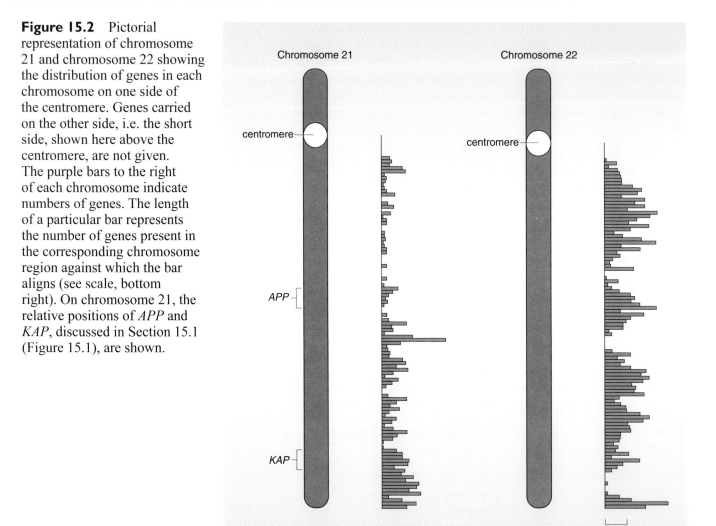

Table 15.1 The gene density per 1 000 000 bp for six human chromosomes.

Chromosome number	Number of genes per 1 000 000 bp
1	10–11
13	4–5
19	25
21	6–7
22	12–13
Y	2.3

We can compare the gene density of each chromosome in terms of the number of genes per 1 000 000 bp. These are shown in Table 15.1 for six chromosomes.

The gene density of chromosome 21 is the average for the genome as a whole, i.e. 6–7 genes per 1 000 000 bp. Looking at Figure 15.2 and the data in Table 15.1 should convince you that gene density varies widely between chromosomes.

■ How does the pattern of gene distribution for the genome as a whole compare with the pattern of gene distribution we observed for chromosome 21?

☐ The pattern of gene distribution we observed on chromosome 21 holds true for the entire genome: some sections of the genome of equivalent length contain more genes than others.

There are large stretches throughout the genome that are completely free of genes, similar to those we described in chromosome 21 (Section 15.1.2). These stretches vary in length, the largest being over 3 000 000 bp long.

Many gene families exist, rather like the *KAP* gene family on chromosome 21 (Section 15.1.2). Outside of these families of genes, however, there is no apparent clustering of other types of genes on specific chromosomes or regions of chromosomes, such as those 'switched on' in specific cells or tissues. As far as we can tell, therefore, our genes are not arranged in any particular order throughout the genome.

15.2.2   The structure of human genes

Is there such a thing as a 'typical' gene? On average, a human gene spans a region of approximately 30 000 bp, but genes come in all sizes, even on the same chromosome. Examining the entire human genome reveals even more variety than we saw on chromosome 21, as is illustrated by the following examples.

The gene for one of the largest human proteins, titin, found in muscle cells, has the greatest number of exons in the human genome. The gene is located on chromosome 2 and is made up of 234 exons that span 281 000 bp, which encode over 26 000 amino acids. The gene for a type of muscular dystrophy (a progressive muscle wasting disease) called Duchenne muscular dystrophy is one of our largest genes. It consists of 76 exons covering a length of 2 300 000 bp of the X chromosome. In contrast to these two examples, the smallest human genes are less than 1000 bp in size, and many of them have only one or two exons. For example, the *TSH2B* gene is a single exon. It codes for a protein of 126 amino acids, which is found bound to DNA forming part of the structure of chromosomes. There does not, therefore, appear to be a 'typical' human gene.

15.2.3   Repetitive DNA sequences across the genome

Recall from Chapter 14 that repetitive DNA sequences make up 50% of the genome (Figure 14.2). Some repetitive DNA sequences are repeated only a few times in the genome whereas others are repeated many hundreds of thousands of times.

The amount of clustered repetitive DNA forming centromeres totals about 2% of the genome. However, the sequence of the DNA repeat in the centromere of each chromosome is not the same, and this allows researchers to use a probe that recognises and sticks specifically to visualise centromeres of specific chromosomes, as shown in Figure 15.3.

The uneven distribution of dispersed repetitive DNA sequences that is found on chromosome 21 also occurs throughout the entire genome. For example, 90% of a region of 525 000 bp on the X chromosome is composed solely of dispersed repetitive DNA sequences. In contrast, some regions of the genome are virtually devoid of dispersed repetitive DNA sequences. For example, a region of 100 000 bp on chromosome 2 contains only 2% dispersed repetitive DNA sequences. It is not clear why there is such variation in the distribution of dispersed repetitive DNA sequences throughout the genome.

Figure 15.3   The centromere of a specific chromosome can be located by means of a technique using DNA probes labelled with dyes. Here the DNA probe is complementary to the repeat sequence of the centromere of the X chromosome and hence can form base pairs with it. The probe is labelled with a dye that is yellow against the red chromosomes.

15.3   Sequence variation across the human genome and its effects

The fact that if we look at many individual human genomes we can find many tens of millions of variant bases (Section 14.3) immediately raises several questions. Where are they in the genome? Do they affect genes? Do they affect the phenotype of an individual? If they do affect the phenotype, does this affect the individual's health?

To try and answer these questions, we will look a little closer at one particular gene called *OCA2*. This gene is one of several genes that play an important role in determining human eye colour because the protein it codes for helps determine how much brown pigment is found in the iris (the coloured portion of the eye), in the light-sensitive portion of the eye and also in hair and skin.

The *OCA2* gene occupies approximately 350 000 bp of the DNA of chromosome 15, and it is found just below the centromere. The portion of the gene that codes for the protein is split across 24 exons scattered along the gene (Section 14.2.1). By examining a database for the DNA sequence of chromosome 15, where all the variant bases are also recorded, we can see that there are many different versions of the gene. Each of these versions carries a different base at one position in the gene and there are almost 70 common versions of this gene. Figure 15.4 shows a summary of where all of the variant bases lie along the 350 000 bp. It is important to realise that this drawing is a representation of the gene in many thousands of people; most of us would only have one or possibly two of these variants. If you had one of the variants, you would still share the other 349 999 bases in common with everyone else.

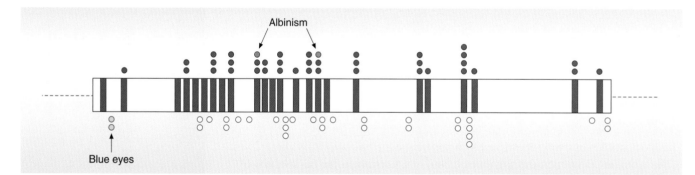

Figure 15.4   The human *OCA2* gene contains many variant bases scattered along its sequence, some (top) lie within the protein exons and others (below) lie in the non-protein coding segments. Several of the variants affect the phenotype of the individual when present as two copies; causing either a form of albinism or blue eyes.

If you look at Figure 15.4, the locations of DNA variants that are located in the protein-coding exons are shown above the gene. Below the gene are the locations of variant bases that are in the interrupting segments, called introns (Section 14.2.1).

■   Consider the different bases that are found in exons. What might be the effect of these differences in bases on the protein?

☐   As exons carry the protein-coding portion of the gene, the code for which amino acid is incorporated into the protein may be altered (Chapter 11).

Several of these variants in exons do indeed lead to alterations in the amino acid that is added to the OCA2 protein. We show two such variants, highlighted in yellow, in Figure 15.4. These variants lead to amino acid changes that completely destroy the function of the protein. Individuals that have two versions of the *OCA2* gene (one on each copy of chromosome 15) with this type of change develop a form of albinism that results in them having light-coloured eyes that contain no brown pigments at all, but they also have light brown hair and creamy white skin, suggesting that this gene also affects pigment production in hair and skin. The lack of pigments in the eye can lead to vision problems.

■ An individual that inherits one copy of the variant coding for a defective protein and one version encoding a function protein has normal coloured eyes with pigment. What can you say about the inheritance pattern shown for this type of albinism?

☐ It shows recessive inheritance; that is, an individual needs to inherit two copies of the variant coding for the defective protein to show the phenotype.

Rather like we saw with cystic fibrosis (Section 13.1), the function of the protein allows us to see why a particular trait is recessive. The cells of a person with only one copy of the gene that gives a functional protein will produce brown pigment.

As we mentioned at the start of this section, the *OCA2* gene plays an important role in determining *normal* human eye colour. First, we should say that human eye colour is actually determined by several genes, but *OCA2* appears to be one of the most important. Brown coloured eyes tend to be dominant over blue coloured eyes in most cases, but other genes can interfere with this simple pattern of inheritance. One particular DNA variant that is found near the start of the *OCA2* gene, outside of protein coding exons, is present in many individuals having blue eyes, but only when they have two copies of the variant (Figure 15.4).

■ As this variant is not within a protein-encoding portion of the gene, can you suggest how it might exert its effect and lead to blue eyes?

☐ The most likely effect is by affecting how much of the gene is copied into RNA and therefore how much protein is made (Chapter 11).

The most likely explanation is that, as blue eyes have little brown pigment, the variant DNA base causes much less of the OCA2 protein to be made. Hence, having just one copy of this variant with another that does allow protein to be made will result in the individual having brown eyes. Only when two copies of the variant is present will only a small amount of OCA2 protein be made and blue eyes result.

From this short description of the *OCA2* gene, you can see how sequence variation within a single gene has no effect in most cases, although it can give rise to a normal variant (eye colour) or cause a disease (albinism). As of writing (2009), several projects are underway to obtain the sequence of thousands of individual human genomes. As more individual genomes are sequenced, we will eventually arrive at a full list of all the different versions of genes that exist in the human population. How will this help us to understand human disease? In the next section we explore how the knowledge of the human genome sequence allows the genes that influence our health to be identified.

15.4   Identifying the genes that cause genetic diseases

When you think of the huge number of genes in the human genome and the variable pattern of their distribution across our chromosomes (Section 15.2.1), you might ask: how is it possible for geneticists to determine exactly which one of the 20 000–25 000 genes goes wrong in any particular genetic disease? The details of how this was done are beyond the scope of this course, but what is important to understand is the complexity of the task, the large amount of laboratory resources required (including staff time) and the length of time taken. To find disease genes, researchers use an approach that involves three steps:

1   Using DNA that has been collected from members of families and from individuals with a specific disease phenotype, they first localise the gene to a particular chromosome location.

2   Once this is achieved, the next step is to hunt for the genes within that specific chromosome location (which might be millions of bp in length). This is achieved by identifying the genes using the genome database. These are what are termed 'candidate' genes as they are likely candidates to be causative of the disease.

3   Finally, the sequences of these candidate genes are obtained from individuals with the disease and compared with those without disease.

■   What features of the human genome are likely to influence the success of this approach in identifying the gene that causes the disease?

☐   There are two major factors that influence how rapidly you would be able to identify the disease gene; the number of candidate genes and the amount of variation in the DNA sequence in the genes.

As you saw in Table 15.1, the gene density varies immensely between chromosomes, and even along a chromosome (Section 15.2.1). If the region identified as containing the disease gene has only one gene within it, then it is likely to be far easier to study than a region with 100 genes. As we saw with the *OCA2* gene, the number of DNA variants in and around a gene can be quite high (Section 15.3), identifying which of the differences between diseased and non-diseased individuals might also be difficult. By obtaining the DNA sequence of a gene in many individuals with a specific disease and from unaffected individuals, it is possible to identify variants that are associated only with disease. This is one reason why the databases containing all the known human DNA variants are important as they allow disease-causing mutations to be more rapidly identified.

This is, indeed, how many disease genes are now being identified. For example, since its completion, the database containing the X chromosome sequence has enabled researchers to identify more than 50 genes that are involved in medical conditions including a form of night blindness, susceptibility to obesity and susceptibility to cleft palate.

15.5   Duplicated regions in the human genome

Analysis of the human genome sequence has led to a surprising and remarkable discovery about the structure of certain regions of the genome. When assembling the genome sequence, long segments on one chromosome appeared to be identical to regions elsewhere in the genome. Such regions are called *segmental duplications*. These duplicated segments are complete copies of entire segments of DNA sequence: genes, repetitive and unique sequences all perfectly duplicated, as the example shown in Figure 15.5 illustrates.

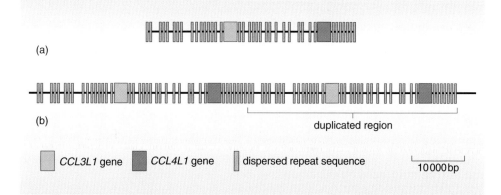

Figure 15.5   (a) A representation of a segment of chromosome 17. (b) A representation of two copies of the segment (a), showing that the entire segment, including genes and dispersed DNA, is copied to form a segmental duplication. (Details about gene *CCL3L1* can be found in the text.)

Such segmental duplications are sometimes on the same chromosome and sometimes on another chromosome. In some cases, the segments of duplicated DNA are very large, being several hundreds of thousands of bp in length. In fact almost 5% of the human genome is made up of this type of duplication. Another unexpected observation is that some segments are not simply duplicated but are present as three or even more copies. At present, we know very little about how or why these segmental duplications have arisen.

However, another truly remarkable and very unexpected discovery has been revealed about the human genome. The number of copies of such duplicated segments can vary between individuals. To appreciate the significance of this finding, consider the following important example. A small segment of 37 000 bp of chromosome 17 is one such duplication (Figure 15.5). The number of copies of this segmental duplication can vary between individuals from one copy to seven copies per copy of the genome. However, in the case of this particular segment, all the copies are found on chromosome 17 adjacent to one other. Within each copy of this segmental duplication is a gene called *CCL3L1*, which codes for a protein that performs many different roles in the body. One remarkable role it seems to have is to block the infection of cells by HIV, the virus that causes AIDS (acquired immunodeficiency syndrome).

■ If up to seven copies of the *CCL3L1* gene are present in one copy of the genome, what is the largest number of copies that is possible within each cell of an individual?

☐ As each cell has two copies of chromosome 17, the largest number of copies the cell could have is 14. (Recall that each cell contains two copies of the genome, Section 14.1.)

Indeed such individuals, although fairly rare, do exist. As you might expect, the amount of CCL3L1 protein produced is related to the number of copies of the gene present in an individual, i.e. more CCL3L1 protein is produced in individuals with a large number of copies of the segmental duplication than is produced in those individuals with a small number of copies. Individuals infected by HIV gain some protection against the development of AIDS if they are fortunate enough to have a large number of copies of this particular segmental duplication because of the increased amount of CCL3L1 protein compared with individuals with a small number of copies. We do not know how many similar stories might emerge in the future.

This example illustrates that in addition to the duplication of whole chromosomes, as in the case of Down's syndrome (Section 12.4), human health can also be influenced by duplicated *segments* of a chromosome.

In conclusion, as the functions of all of the genes on each chromosome are determined, the goal of a complete registry of all the genes and all the variants in each gene across the human genome will be reached. Which of these genes play a role in human disease can then be identified. In contrast, a full understanding of the function of all the proteins that are coded for in the human genome and how they interact with each other will take many decades to unravel.

As these discoveries take place over the next few years, the impact of this knowledge will be considerable. One of the areas of medicine that will particularly benefit is that of cancer, which is the topic of the next chapter.

Question 15.1

Which of the statements (a)–(g) is incorrect?

(a) The centromere is composed of dispersed repetitive DNA.

(b) Some genes that are identical copies of each other are grouped together to form a family.

(c) The genes that are active or 'switched on' in one cell type are not all located on the same chromosome within the human genome.

(d) The distribution of dispersed repetitive DNA along chromosome 21 varies between different regions along the chromosome.

(e) Some regions of chromosome 21 contain genes that are less densely packed than those in other regions.

(f) DNA variants are found only in protein-coding portions of genes.

(g) Segments of DNA sequence are duplicated within the genome, sometimes more than once.

15.6   Summary of Chapter 15

The distribution of both genes and repetitive DNA along human chromosomes is uneven. Some genes are present as a family of multiple copies in a tightly linked group.

Genes are of different sizes and do not appear to be distributed across the genome in any particular order.

A comparison of the DNA sequences of individual chromosomes reveals that the density of genes differs by over five-fold.

Variants in human genes are found in both protein-coding and non-coding sections. Most variants within a gene do not have any effect, whilst others within the same gene can affect normal phenotypic variation or health.

The identification of all the genes in the human genome and the variants that are found within them will greatly speed up the search for genes associated with particular diseases.

Some segments of the human genome are duplicated to form segmental duplications, and this can result in a range of numbers of copies for particular genes between individuals. Variations in the numbers of copies of a gene due to segmental duplications might influence human health.

Chapter 16
Cancer: somatic mutation and cellular disease

Cancer is essentially a genetic disease of cells. So the focus of this chapter will be on individual cells and the genes within those cells. In Chapter 15 we learnt how our increasing knowledge of the human genome is accelerating the isolation of disease genes, including those genes involved in the production of cancer. What makes cancer such a challenging disease for scientists to understand is the fact that it is not a single illness, but a wide variety of diseases that can affect any tissue of the body. However, all types of cancer are formed by the same basic process of uncontrolled growth and division of cells, and the capacity of cells to spread to other sites within the body. A great deal is already known about the genes involved in cancer, but there is still an enormous amount to learn. It is important to do so, since cancer is one of the most common and severe medical problems in developed countries, where it accounts for more that 20% of all deaths, and is responsible for a large proportion of the total cost of medical care.

The underlying cause of cancer, like other genetic diseases, is gene mutation (Chapter 12). Most genetic diseases (Chapters 6, 8 and 13) are caused by mutations of DNA that are inherited from parents via their gametes. However, for the most part, cancer is caused by *somatic* mutations, i.e. genetic changes that occur in somatic cells, and the mutant alleles are not passed on to the offspring. Recall from Section 4.1 that somatic cells are all the cells in the body, other than cells of the ovaries and testes that give rise to gametes. Every human somatic cell (with the odd exception) contains the same genes, and each cell has the potential to form a cancer. Hence, cancer gives a unique insight into the importance of somatic mutation. In a few cases, a mutation that may contribute to the production of cancer takes place in the gamete-producing cells and is passed on to succeeding generations. Environmental factors are also implicated in that they can increase an individual's risk of developing cancer.

In this chapter we examine the relationship between genes and cancer, and describe the roles of genes in causing cells to become cancerous. We also analyse the relationship between cancer and environmental factors. Since cancer is caused by an interplay between genes and environmental factors, it is an example of a multifactorial disease. This chapter integrates many concepts introduced earlier in the course within the single topic of the genetic disease of cancer. You may find it useful to refer back to these; appropriate references are provided in the text.

16.1   Somatic mutations

Every cell in the body (with the odd exception) contains a copy of the same genetic material as a result of the process of mitosis (Section 2.2.1). In adults, only some cells continue to divide by means of mitosis to produce replacement cells. Whether a cell continues to divide or not is normally under the strict control of genes within each cell. Cancer results from the breakdown of this genetic control of the cell cycle in an individual cell as a result of mutations occurring in the genes within that cell. One of the most widely studied areas of genetics is the control of the cell cycle, which involves the processes of cell growth and cell division (Section 2.2), and it is known to involve the products of at least 100 different genes in a complex series of interactions.

Cancer results from the accumulation within one cell of a small number of independent mutations that can take place over a long period of time. In fact many years may elapse between one mutation occurring and the next. The production of cancer starts with a single mutation in a cell which transmits it to all its progeny cells. Subsequently, some generations of cell division later, a second mutation occurs in one of these cells which transmits it to its progeny and so on, as shown in Figure 16.1. Here only four cell generations are shown but in reality mutations accumulate randomly over a large number of cell generations. Mutations in *at least* five or six different genes have to accumulate within a cell before it becomes cancerous. If only one or two mutations occur in a cell then no cancer develops. If you look back to Figure 14.1, you will see that the first completed sequence of an entire 'cancer' genome was achieved in 2008. In this case, researchers obtained the entire sequence of an individual's 'normal' genome by obtaining the sequence from DNA isolated from a small sample of skin cells. This DNA sequence was then compared with the sequence obtained from the cancer cells (from a form of leukemia) of the same individual. This comparison identified 10 DNA bases that were mutated in the cancer cells. These mutations must have arisen over the 50 years of this individual's life before the leukemia became apparent.

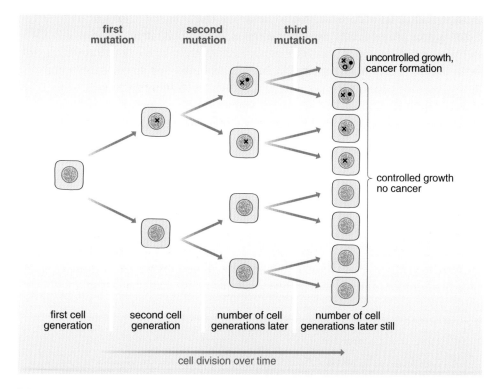

Figure 16.1   Over time, a few independently acquired mutations accumulate in one cell and can lead to the development of cancer. For simplicity, only four cell generations are shown, but it takes many more cell generations for a sufficient number of mutations to accumulate in a cell to produce cancer.

Some mutations may be unimportant to the functioning of the cell, but others may be threatening, particularly those that occur in genes that keep the processes of cell division and cell growth in check. These mutations can give the cell a 'growth advantage' over cells carrying non-mutated genes. Thus the cell divides more quickly and the relative proportion of the mutated cells in the body increases. The increased cell division leads to the production of a *tumour*, which is a localised abnormal growth. More mutations occur, each resulting in more aggressive growth, which eventually produce cancer. You can now see why detecting cancer early is important. The larger the tumour becomes, the more likely it is to accumulate other mutations, and hence the quicker the tumour will grow and cancer develop.

The development of cancer is a multi-step process.

In some cases it takes many more than 10 years for sufficient mutations to accumulate in a cell and give rise to cancer, which is why the incidence of cancer increases with age. In the West more than 80% of cancer cases occur in people who are older than 55. The risk of getting cancer at the age of 75 is five times higher than at the age of 55, and a hundred times higher than at the age of 20.

16.2   Genetic change and cancer

We will now consider which types of gene are involved in the development of cancer. It is recognised that there are three: *oncogenes, tumour-suppressor genes* and *DNA repair genes*.

Unmutated oncogenes are called proto-oncogenes. In the *normal* cell, proto-oncogenes promote cell growth and cell division. Their action is counterbalanced by tumour-suppressor genes that suppress or block cell division, as shown in Figure 16.2a. We do not know the total number of proto-oncogenes and tumour-suppressor genes in the genome, but many of each type do exist.

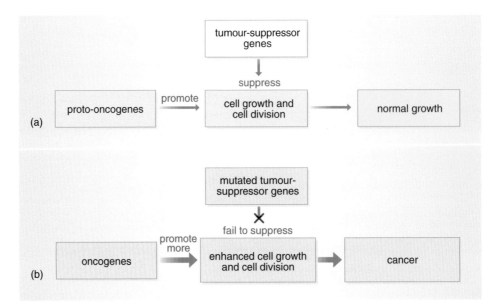

Figure 16.2   Scheme to show the role of oncogenes and tumour-suppressor genes in cells. (a) Normal cell growth is controlled by the products of proto-oncogenes and tumour-suppressor genes. (b) Cancer is the result of mutations in both types of gene.

For cancer to develop, mutations in a number of proto-oncogenes and a number of tumour-suppressor genes are required to accumulate in the same cell. Figure 16.2b summarises the contributions of oncogenes and mutated tumour-suppressor genes to the production of cancer in a cell: oncogenes promote *enhanced* cell growth and division; mutated tumour-suppressor genes lose their capacity to suppress or block cell growth and division.

The third type of gene, DNA repair genes, promotes stability of DNA by correcting errors as they arise. If DNA repair is reduced, more mutations will accumulate in a cell, and the more likely that proto-oncogenes and tumour-suppressor genes will be damaged.

We will discuss just one example of each of these three types of gene.

16.2.1 Oncogenes

We will take as our example of an oncogene a gene called *RAS*. What is the difference between a cell with a mutant allele of the gene, i.e. an oncogene, and a cell with a proto-oncogene?

The *RAS* proto-oncogene codes for a protein that promotes cell division. The protein lies in the cell membrane, just like the CFP that is involved in the transport of salt and water across the cell membrane (Section 13.1). The RAS membrane protein, however, carries out a different kind of role: it receives signals from outside the cell that tell the cell to prepare to divide. Hence the protein plays a crucial role in the control of cell division, a role that depends on a remarkable property of the RAS protein itself. The protein can change its shape from an inactive form to an active form, and only the active form signals the cell to divide. By switching between these two forms the protein is able to control cell division, as shown in Figure 16.3a.

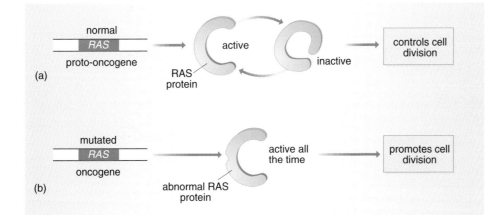

Figure 16.3 The *RAS* gene and the RAS protein: (a) in a normal cell; (b) in a cancer cell.

A comparison has been made between the DNA sequences of the *RAS* gene in normal cells and the *RAS* gene in cancer cells from a number of different patients. This revealed that the normal cells in all patients had an unmutated *RAS* gene but the gene in cancer cells of the patients had an altered nucleotide sequence, i.e. it was mutated.

■ What effect would a change in the sequence of nucleotides have on the protein product of the gene?

☐ A change in nucleotide sequence leads to changes in the amino acid sequence of the protein (Section 12.2).

The effect of the change of amino acid sequence on the RAS protein was to disrupt its normal function (Section 12.2). In fact the defective RAS protein was locked permanently in the active form (Figure 16.3b). As a result, the protein constantly signals the cell to prepare to divide, which is why it promotes enhanced cell division.

Various proto-oncogenes have been identified within the genome. Like all genes they are present in two copies, so, for example, there are two copies of the *RAS* gene in each cell. A mutation in only one copy is sufficient for the gene to promote cell division.

■ From what you have just read, are oncogenes dominant or recessive to the proto-oncogene, i.e. the normal copy of the gene?

☐ They are dominant since the presence of the one mutated oncogene is sufficient to promote cancer.

It is important to note that mutations in a number of different oncogenes are required to change the cell into a cancerous one. This is because the process of cell division and cell growth, as mentioned above, is under the control of many proto-oncogenes and tumour-suppressor genes, the products of which interact in a complex way.

16.2.2   Tumour-suppressor genes

Recall that the products of proto-oncogenes promote cell growth and cell division; the products of tumour-suppressor genes normally suppress or *block* these processes (Figure 16.2a). We have seen that oncogenes behave in a dominant fashion.

■ Tumour-suppressor genes contribute to cancer only when *both* copies of the gene are mutated. What can you conclude about the relationship between the normal allele and mutant allele of a tumour-suppressor gene?

☐ The mutant allele is recessive to the normal allele of a tumour-suppressor gene.

The role of the tumour-suppressor gene is to suppress cell division. It is only when its function is *absent* that cancer develops, i.e. cell growth and division are no longer blocked (Figure 16.2b).

A notable example of a tumour-suppressor gene is the retinoblastoma gene, which is associated with susceptibility to a tumour of the retina — a layer of tissue at the back of the eyeball that is sensitive to light. A retinoblastoma tumour is exceedingly rare, occurring in only 1 in 100 000 children. Treatment usually involves removal of the affected eye(s), although small tumours can be removed by radiation treatment.

There are *two* types of retinoblastoma: familial and sporadic. The same gene is involved in both types, and both require two distinct alterations — one in each of the two copies of the retinoblastoma gene in a cell in the retina.

The familial type, shown in the pedigree chart in Figure 16.4, is passed on from generation to generation thus demonstrating that in these families there is an inherited predisposition to retinoblastoma (RB). Individuals inherit one normal allele *RB* from one parent and a mutated retinoblastoma allele *rb* from the other parent. They are heterozygous *RB rb*. One normal allele *RB* is sufficient to direct normal growth. A second mutation — this time a somatic mutation — in the normal copy of the gene in a cell of the retina can occur during development of the eye. Once both copies of the gene are mutated in a cell, uncontrolled growth begins leading to a tumour, as shown in Figure 16.5a. The occurrence of the second mutation is a matter of chance. However, it seems that there is a high probability that the single normal allele will undergo somatic mutation in at least one of the million or so cells that give rise to the retina.

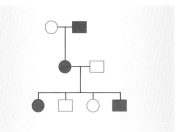

Figure 16.4   A pedigree chart of familial retinoblastoma.

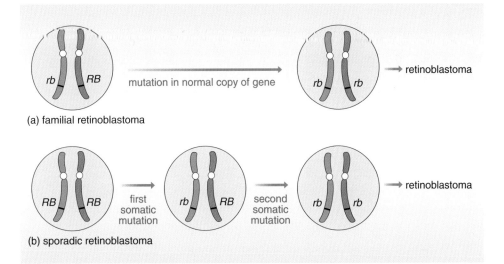

(a) familial retinoblastoma

(b) sporadic retinoblastoma

Figure 16.5   The events involving the retinoblastoma gene that lead to the development of retinoblastoma: (a) familial retinoblastoma; (b) sporadic retinoblastoma. For cancer to develop, mutations in other genes are also required.

Now compare the pedigree chart of the familial form of retinoblastoma (Figure 16.4) with one for the sporadic form (Figure 16.6). Around 60% of all cases of retinoblastoma are not passed on from generation to generation since there is no inherited predisposition; they appear sporadically, without warning, in an otherwise healthy family, as shown in Figure 16.6.

■   Can you suggest how the sporadic form of retinoblastoma arises?

☐   This type of retinoblastoma arises when *two* somatic mutations occur, one in each copy of the retinoblastoma gene in a cell in the retina.

These two steps towards the development of retinoblastoma are shown in Figure 16.5b. We have considered mutations only in the retinoblastoma gene, but

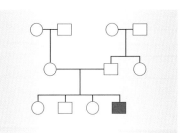

Figure 16.6   A pedigree chart of sporadic retinoblastoma.

it is important to remember that for a cancer to develop, mutations in other genes are also required.

The retinoblastoma gene is only one example of many tumour-suppressor genes in the human genome, which all share the function of blocking or suppressing cell proliferation. Retinoblastoma shows particularly clearly that the same mutations can occur both in gamete cells that give rise to gametes and in somatic cells. The example of familial retinoblastoma clearly illustrates that some individuals have a genetic predisposition to cancer.

16.2.3   DNA repair

A third type of gene that contributes to cancer production is genes that are normally involved in repairing errors in DNA. Recall from Section 12.3 that the majority of spontaneous errors that may occur during DNA replication are eliminated by remarkably efficient repair enzymes. Each of these repair enzymes is a protein (Section 9.2) and is therefore the product of a gene, which itself may have a mutation. A mutation in a DNA repair gene can lead to a defective enzyme, which is unable to repair damaged DNA.

■   What would be the consequence to cells of a defective DNA repair enzyme?

☐   Errors would go uncorrected and so mutations would accumulate in cells.

The more mutations that accumulate in a cell, the more likely that proto-oncogenes and tumour-suppressor genes will be damaged. This is seen in certain hereditary disorders, the best investigated of which is xeroderma pigmentosum. This is a recessive disorder that results from mutation in both copies of a gene that codes for an enzyme that repairs DNA damaged by ultraviolet light. Individuals with the disorder tend to suffer from skin cancer because DNA in their skin cells that is damaged by exposure to sunlight goes unrepaired.

To summarise this section, we recognise three types of genetic alteration that can lead to cancer: oncogenes (mutated proto-oncogenes), which actively encourage cells to multiply; mutations in tumour-suppressor genes, which fail to stop unwanted cell division; and mutated DNA repair genes, which fail to repair damaged DNA so that mutations accumulate. The ability to examine the DNA sequence of 'cancer' genomes will eventually lead to the identification of all proto-oncogenes, tumour-suppressor genes and genes involved in repairing damaged DNA. This in turn will lead to the development of better treatments.

Activity 16.1   Somatic mutation and cancer

This activity requires you to write a summary, and explains how to set about doing this.

16.3 Environmental factors

Cancer, like many multifactorial characters, is caused by a complex interplay of many environmental and genetic factors. (This idea was introduced in Chapters 7 and 8.) Clearly, we cannot prevent ourselves growing older and accruing more and more mutations; however, we do have some control over environmental factors that increase the risk of us developing cancer. Many cases of cancer in the UK are related to our physical environment and lifestyle. In fact, it has been estimated that at least 50% of all cancers can be attributed, at least in part, to environmental factors.

Recall from Section 12.3 that environmental agents known as mutagens can produce mutations. These environmental agents, such as ultraviolet light, which we considered in the previous section, can cause somatic mutations, which in turn cause cancer. It is important to note that ultraviolet light damages DNA in all of us, and we rely on enzymes to repair the damage. However, exposure to too much sunlight might mean that the damage exceeds the amount that our enzymes can repair and so causes cancer.

As early as 1954, Doll and Hill, working in the UK, showed conclusively that lung cancer is linked to smoking. Deaths from lung cancer in men are now falling in the UK and USA as the numbers of smokers decline, but deaths in women continue to rise because women took up smoking decades after men did in these two countries.

Individuals vary in their risk of succumbing to environmental factors. Consider tobacco smoke and lung cancer. Tobacco smoke contains several chemicals (hydrocarbons) that can be converted by the body into substances that promote cancer. So why is it that some people smoke and yet don't get lung cancer? There are a number of variants of genes that affect the way the body handles hydrocarbons. (The idea of different genes interacting with different risk factors in disease was introduced in Section 8.2.) Some individuals are much better than others at converting chemicals in tobacco smoke into forms that can easily be removed from the body by means of excretion. Hence, some people smoke and don't get lung cancer. In contrast, other people convert the chemicals in tobacco smoke into substances that promote cancer in cells of the lungs and other tissues, such as the lining of the mouth.

One striking line of evidence for the link between cancer and environmental factors comes from comparisons between the same populations in different environments. The incidence of specific types of cancer differs in various parts of the world. (*Incidence* is the number of *new* cases arising in any given period, such as a calendar year.) For example, breast and colon cancer, which are among the major types of cancer to affect the Western industrialised countries, are rare in Japanese people in Japan, but not among Japanese people living in the USA, who have become as vulnerable to the disease as Americans.

■ What do these observations about Japanese people suggest?

☐ That something in the environment affects the incidence of breast and colon cancer in these people.

Although such comparisons can never prove the cause of cancer they can give us powerful clues. In such cases, scientists suspect that diet is the factor, but it is difficult to pinpoint which aspect of diet. However, there is general agreement that fruits and vegetables contain chemicals that act in some way to protect DNA from mutations. For example, the low consumption of fruits and vegetables has been associated with high incidence of cancer: the quarter of the population in the USA with the lowest dietary intake of fruits and vegetables has roughly twice the rate for most types of cancer.

Consider a specific chemical in our diet, folic acid. (You can identify this nutrient on the table of contents on some cereal packets, for example.) Folic acid has a protective function, protecting cells from succumbing to mutations that might lead to cancer. Thus a deficiency of folic acid may be a risk factor for the development of cancer, and recent research shows this to be the case. However, some individuals are more susceptible than others to the danger of a low intake of folic acid because of their particular genotype. This example shows how intimately our genomes are affected by our environment.

A better understanding of the interplay between environmental and genetic factors will be an important consequence of the HGP. We know that environmental factors, such as diet and smoking tobacco, are important causative agents in the production of cancer. But we also know that there are a large number of variants of genes with different levels of susceptibility to cancer. Once gene variants susceptible to cancer have been determined, geneticists will be able to research which environmental factors interact with which gene variants. But for now we can reduce our risk of cancer by staying out of the sun, eating a healthy diet with lots of fruit and vegetables, and not smoking tobacco.

To conclude this chapter, we have seen that the process of somatic mutation is important. However, genes transmitted in gametes can also influence individual susceptibility to a particular cancer, such as the retinoblastoma gene and xeroderma pigmentosum gene. In addition, certain genes play a role in individual susceptibility to environmental agents that promote cancer, such as the chemicals in tobacco smoke.

> Although cancer can be described as a genetic disease, its development is a result of a series of interactions between environmental and genetic factors.

We have touched only briefly on the very complex subject of cancer, just enough to give you a flavour of what is already known.

Question 16.1

Summarise the roles of proto-oncogenes and unmutated tumour-suppressor genes in the normal cell.

Question 16.2

Explain why someone who has an inherited predisposition to defective DNA repair is more prone to cancer.

Explain why not everyone who smokes gets lung cancer.

16.4   Summary of Chapter 16

Cancer is essentially a genetic disease of cells caused by somatic mutations that result in uncontrolled cell growth and cell division. At least five or six mutations have to accumulate within a cell before it becomes cancerous.

Three types of gene are involved in the development of cancer: oncogenes (mutated proto-oncogenes), which promote cell growth and division; tumour-suppressor genes, which normally constrain cell division; and DNA repair genes. Oncogenes act in a dominant fashion; mutated tumour-suppressor genes are recessive to the normal allele. The ability to obtain the DNA sequence of entire 'cancer' genomes will help speed up the search for these genes.

The more mutations that occur in a cell as a consequence of defective DNA repair enzymes, the more likely that proto-oncogenes and tumour-suppressor genes will be damaged.

An individual may inherit variants that increase their susceptibility to a particular cancer, such as those of the retinoblastoma gene and the xeroderma pigmentosum gene.

Cancer is caused by an interplay between many genes and environmental factors, and as such is a multifactorial disease. Examples of environmental factors include ultraviolet light, the chemicals in tobacco smoke and dietary factors such as folic acid deficiency.

Chapter 17
Genes and populations

We have confined ourselves so far to a discussion of the inheritance of genes within families, but in order to understand more about the distribution of variants of genes around the world we must turn to look at wider groups within countries and continents. This is because the genotype of individuals, including those with genetic disease, is a reflection of the population to which they belong. Why is it, for example, that cystic fibrosis (CF) affects mainly people of northern European ancestry (Section 6.3), whereas a disease of the blood called sickle cell anaemia affects those from tropical regions of the world?

The focus of this chapter is on **population genetics**, the study of factors that influence the frequencies of variants or alleles in populations. Here we are using the term **population** in a biological sense, that is, a group of individuals among whom mating occurs more often than with members of other populations. We begin by examining differences in the frequencies of alleles between some geographically distinct populations of the world, and explore the factors that bring about these differences. We conclude the chapter by considering human genome diversity. This chapter builds on knowledge from earlier chapters. You may find it helpful to refer back to these chapters; appropriate references are provided.

17.1   Differences between populations

In order to understand the present-day genetic structure of human populations we need to look at our evolutionary history. A common genetic origin for *all* modern humans lies in Africa, over 100 000 years ago, from where migration across the globe occurred. About 10 000 years ago humans were spread over wide areas of the planet, but the population size was at least 3000 times smaller than it is today (Figure 17.1). At this low population density, breeding populations were

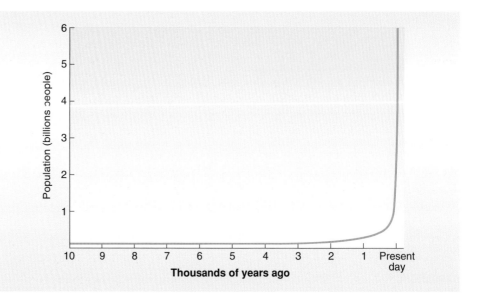

Figure 17.1   World population growth over the last 10 000 years. Present day population numbers have arisen from relatively small numbers of individuals.

relatively isolated from each other and evidence suggests that most of the major genetic differences between geographically distinct present-day populations must have arisen before population growth increased contact between the previously separated groups. The populations we see today are considerably larger (Figure 17.1), but, importantly, the 6 billion people that constitute today's population are genetic descendents of the same small pool of early humans.

We have seen in Section 7.4 that there are differences between populations in genes that influence height, for example. Humans in all parts of the world share the same set of genes. Populations differ only in the *frequency* of alleles or variants of these genes.

■   How do variants arise?

☐   Variants arise as a result of DNA mutation.

Recall from Section 12.2 that mutations essentially occur at random. Some variants are very largely restricted to members of a certain population, most likely because they only arose within that population, but, more often than not, the same variants are present in most populations, with different frequencies in different populations. For example, the frequency of the CF disease allele is high in Europeans, and the *B* allele of the ABO blood group system is common in Asians but absent in native Americans. Skin colour is a multifactorial character (Chapter 7) involving at least three or four genes, and the frequency of alleles of these genes varies throughout the world. The variant *OCA2* gene that results in blue eyes is found at higher levels in Europeans but at only low levels in Africans and Asians, where brown eyes predominate.

A large amount of DNA sequence information is now available from the collection of entire genome sequences, and the frequency of gene variants has been studied between populations. Differences in allele frequencies between populations do exist, and these can potentially trace an individual's likely geographic origin. These differences can be detected when the allele frequencies for one or a small number of genes are analysed. However, when many loci are considered (including gene sequences and other categories of DNA sequences (Section 14.2)), few differences in the rest of the genome between populations are found. Any two individuals within a particular population have a similar number of genetic differences to any two people chosen at random from any two populations in the world. Put another way, the number of DNA differences that exist between a white European and a black African are not significantly different from those that exist between any two white Europeans or between any two black Africans. These similarities reflect the common origin of us all from that small population of African modern humans that existed over 100 000 years ago.

We can examine these genetic differences more closely at the level of DNA sequence. On average, any two individuals differ by one in every thousand base pairs (0.1%). This means that if we were to compare two people chosen at random, they would differ by about 3 million bp (0.1% of 3 billion bp). In Section 15.3 you saw how DNA variants were distributed across one gene. Over the entire genome, however, the majority of the differences occur within introns (regions, within genes, that do not code for proteins) and within repetitive DNA, rather than within exons (protein-coding regions) (Section 14.2.1). Most of the total variations that exist between all individuals can actually be found within a very small regional population of several million people, such as that found in a large city.

In summary, the basis for genetic differences between populations is mutation, and populations differ from each other in the *frequencies* of alleles or variants for a small number of genes. The question of what factors bring about these differences in the frequency of genes and their alleles has been addressed by examining the frequencies of disease-causing alleles, because these can easily be counted or detected, but the same principles apply to an allele of any gene. We will examine in turn two processes that together explain why frequencies of alleles or variants vary in different parts of the world:

- natural selection, and

- chance or random events.

17.2   Natural selection in action

The theory of natural selection was proposed by Charles Darwin to explain how organisms change over time, i.e. how they evolve. The theory recognises that individuals vary in characters, i.e. they have different phenotypes and genotypes. Those with advantageous characters have a greater probability of survival, and therefore of reproducing. Provided that such characters are inherited, individuals with the more advantageous phenotype will become more common over successive generations because they are more likely to survive and leave more offspring, i.e. they have more *reproductive success*. This process of differential reproduction between different genotypes is known as *natural selection*.

We can view the process of natural selection as a driving force by which the frequencies of certain alleles change over time; mutations that have a detrimental effect upon the individual are 'weeded out', whereas mutations that increase the ability of individuals to survive and reproduce are favoured. We will examine the evidence that natural selection is working today to change the frequency of alleles by considering the best understood case, that of sickle cell disease and the haemoglobin gene.

More is known about haemoglobin and its variants than about any other human protein. Recall from Section 9.2 that haemoglobin is present in red blood cells and has the crucial function of carrying oxygen from the lungs to all the cells of the body. People with normal blood contain a type of haemoglobin called haemoglobin A. One of the variants of this molecule, called haemoglobin S or sickle cell haemoglobin, is common only in regions of the world where there is (or once was) a high prevalence of malaria. (*Prevalence* is the total number of people with a particular character at a given time.)

This unusual haemoglobin causes the red blood cells to assume the 'sickle' shape that gives the disease its name. To appreciate this difference in shape, compare in Figure 17.2 the normal red blood cells with the sickle cells in the blood from a person with sickle cell trait, discussed below. Sickle cells are more fragile than normal red blood cells. They split open readily and consequently are rapidly

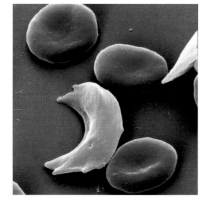

Figure 17.2 Red blood cells from a person with sickle cell trait. Compare the sickle cells with the normal red blood cells.

destroyed — hence the disease, anaemia. (Anaemia is a deficiency in the quantity and quality of red blood cells.) The anaemia causes heart failure and physical weakness. Furthermore, the abnormal sickle cells, unable to squeeze through narrow blood vessels, cause failure in blood supply and hence oxygen delivery, which in turn can lead to brain damage and kidney failure.

The genetics of sickle cell disease are as follows. The gene that codes for haemoglobin is designated Hb. A person with normal haemoglobin A is homozygous for the allele Hb^A and so has the genotype $Hb^A Hb^A$, and a person with sickle cell disease is homozygous for the mutant allele Hb^S and so has the genotype $Hb^S Hb^S$.

Many people in the world die each year from sickle cell disease, most of them in childhood.

■ According to the theory of natural selection (outlined in the first two paragraphs of this section), would you expect the mutant allele Hb^S to increase or decrease in the population?

☐ You might expect that natural selection would lead to its gradual disappearance, since it clearly reduces the reproductive success of people with sickle cell disease.

The Hb^S allele remains common, however, and in some parts of the world, such as East Africa, it is present at a frequency of 20%. (In other words, 20 out of every 100 haemoglobin alleles in the population are Hb^S instead of Hb^A.) Why is the Hb^S allele so common if it has such a devastating effect on reproductive success? Why has it not been eliminated by natural selection? The answer to this puzzle becomes clear when we look at individuals who are heterozygous.

■ What is the genotype of people who are heterozygous for the sickle cell allele?

☐ $Hb^A Hb^S$.

The alleles Hb^A and Hb^S do not show a simple dominant/recessive pattern; rather, both are said to show *incomplete dominance*, which is similar to the codominance shown by the genes determining the ABO blood groups (Section 5.4). The result of this is that the heterozygous phenotype is intermediate between the two homozygous phenotypes. Heterozygotes are described as having the *sickle cell trait*. These $Hb^A Hb^S$ individuals are anaemic, but only slightly, because only a proportion of their red blood cells become sickled (Figure 17.2). This, of itself, is not sufficient to explain the high frequency of the Hb^S allele in human populations, however. (This frequency of the Hb^S allele is the sum of that in homozygotes $Hb^S Hb^S$ and that in heterozygotes $Hb^A Hb^S$.) Of much greater signficance is the fact that heterozygotes have a major advantage over *both* kinds of homozygous individual; they are better able to withstand malaria. There are several lines of evidence to support this conclusion. Here we will consider three. One line of evidence comes from comparing the geographical distribution of the Hb^S allele with that of a particularly severe form of malaria. Look at Figure 17.3.

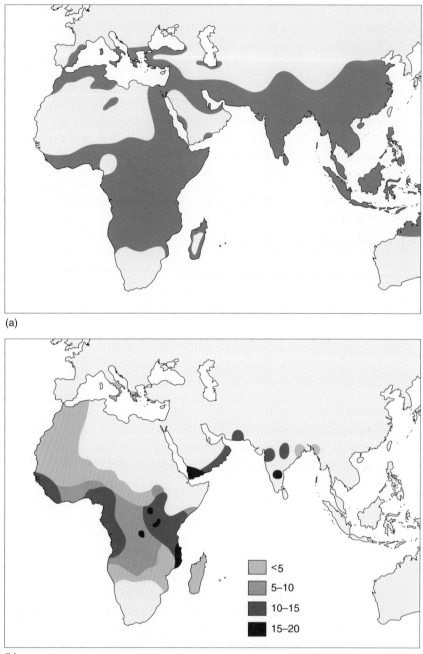

Figure 17.3   (a) The distribution of malignant malaria (a particularly severe form of malaria) in Africa and southern Asia. (b) The distribution, or frequency, of the Hb^S allele (per cent within the human population), which causes sickle cell disease in the homozygous condition.

■   What is the relationship between the two distributions?

□   They are similar. Most of the areas that have a high incidence of the sickle cell allele are areas where there is malignant malaria, such as India and tropical Africa.

People who are heterozygous for the sickle cell allele are less susceptible to malaria than either of the homozygotes. Consequently, natural selection actually favours the heterozygotes in those areas of the world where malaria is prevalent.

The second line of evidence for the association between malaria and sickle cell disease comes from a detailed look at the organism responsible for malaria, called *Plasmodium*. This single-celled animal lives in the blood, within the red blood cells, and is not able to survive and reproduce as well in sickled red blood cells as it does in normal ones. When red blood cells collapse because they contain haemoglobin S, they no longer provide a home for the *parasites*, which are released into the blood fluid where they are destroyed.

A summary of the phenotypes associated with each genotype of the Hb^A and Hb^S alleles is given in Table 17.1.

Table 17.1 Genotypes and phenotypes of the Hb^A and Hb^S alleles.

Genotype	Phenotype
$Hb^A Hb^A$	normal homozygotes: at risk of dying from malaria
$Hb^S Hb^S$	sickle cell disease homozygotes: at risk of dying from sickle cell disease
$Hb^A Hb^S$	sickle cell trait heterozygotes: some resistance to malaria, some symptoms of anaemia

Let us look at how the process of natural selection is working in relation to the three genotypes listed in Table 17.1. In regions of the world where there is a high incidence of malaria, heterozygotes Hb^AHb^S suffer from mild anaemia, but this adverse influence on their reproductive success is more than offset by their greater resistance to malaria, in comparison with Hb^AHb^A homozygotes. This means that many more of them survive to reproductive age, have children, and so pass on both Hb^A and Hb^S alleles to the next generation. This explains why the Hb^S allele is not lost from the population, but is present in unexpectedly high frequency. Some of the Hb^S alleles will be 'drained off' from the population through early deaths of Hb^SHb^S homozygotes, but this is offset by the 'topping up' of Hb^S alleles in the population through the success of the Hb^AHb^S heterozygotes.

For a third and final piece of evidence that the Hb^S allele confers some resistance to malaria, we can look at a population genetically related to those in tropical Africa, who became geographically separate in a part of the world where malaria is absent. About 15 million indigenous Africans were transported to the Americas as slaves in the 18th century, taking the sickle cell disease allele with them.

■   If sickle cell disease provides an advantage only in those regions of the world where malaria is rife, would you expect the frequency of the mutant Hb^S allele to have decreased, increased or stayed the same in the present-day black population of the USA?

☐   Since sickle cell homozygotes Hb^SHb^S rarely leave descendants, and heterozygotes Hb^AHb^S would no longer be at an advantage compared with normal homozygotes Hb^AHb^A, the frequency of the mutant Hb^S allele would be expected to decrease in these populations.

In fact, the frequency of heterozygotes in the African-American population that is descendent from the slave population has decreased to 1 in 500 of the population, compared with 1 in 25 in parts of present-day equatorial Africa. This is because the character, sickle cell trait, is only advantageous in environments where malaria is present. This illustrates the important point about natural selection that a character may be advantageous only in certain environments, and thus will be selected for only in those environments. In this case, the non-mutant form of the gene (Hb^A) can be considered the advantageous allele.

The example of sickle cell disease shows clearly how natural selection acts to change the frequency and distribution of a particular allele Hb^S in a population.

The high frequency of CF might result from a comparable situation. Carriers of CF who are of northern European descent have some resistance to bacterial infections of the gut that cause cholera, one of the symptoms of which is diarrhoea. Individuals infected with cholera, particularly children, are at risk of dying from dehydration. Carriers of the CF mutation may have some resistance to dehydration because they have reduced salt and water transport across cell membranes. Hence the mutation may have remained at a high frequency in earlier centuries when such infections often occurred in these populations.

Activity 17.1   Sickle cell disease: a lethal advantage

This activity requires you to view this video sequence, which broadens the discussion of sickle cell disease by putting into a social context.

17.3   Chance or random events

So far, we have considered one of the two processes that affect the frequency of variants in different parts of the world, natural selection. We now examine the other process, random or chance events.

Human populations that are geographically close to each other, or who are descended from a recent common ancestor, usually share some of the same alleles. There is, however, an important exception to this, which occurs when a population lives in relative isolation from other populations. The inhabitants of the island of New Guinea provide a number of remarkable examples of this. Until relatively recently, isolated populations lived in separate valleys unaware of each other's existence. These populations had their own distinctive genetic abnormalities, such as premature ageing in one valley, delayed puberty in another, and one population had the highest known incidence of profoundly deaf individuals in the world. Such effects suggest that a different ancestral disease mutation became prevalent in each isolated population. The change in the allele frequency of each of these isolated populations between one generation and the next was due to *chance events*. Natural selection would not be responsible because none of the disorders enhances reproductive success.

In large populations, such chance events are unlikely to have a great effect because chance differences in reproductive success between individuals will tend to even themselves out when a large number of individuals are involved.

■ Why in small populations can chance events have a strong effect?

☐ Because if only one individual happens, by chance, to produce more children than the others, his/her characters and associated alleles will become more common in the next generation.

Similarly, a particular character can easily disappear from a small population by chance events.

To summarise Sections 17.1–17.3:

Genetic variation between individuals, introduced by the random process of DNA mutation, is present in the human genome. Natural selection and chance events are the mechanisms by which differences in the frequency of variants or alleles between populations arise.

17.4 Human genome diversity

We learnt at the beginning of this chapter that genetic data do show differences, albeit small, between populations. However, these differences are rapidly being lost as a consequence of migration between populations. With the invention of technology for global travel, human populations have begun to intermarry, leading to the gradual 'homogenisation' of language, culture and genes. This is in contrast to natural selection and chance events, which lead to *differences* between populations in the frequency of variants (Sections 17.2 and 17.3). As populations mix, so will their genes. For example, Welsh-speaking Welsh have a higher frequency of certain alleles than English-speaking Welsh, and vice versa, but these differences will gradually disappear as the two groups intermarry. Even the most isolated of populations, such as Yanomami Indians of the Amazon rain forests, are disappearing. Disease and assimilation with Westerners threaten their genetic integrity. Society, which was once based on small groups with little migration, is now changing with an increased movement of peoples and increased matings outside local groups.

■ How do you think the exchange of genes between formerly separate populations might affect the frequency of recessive genetic disorders?

☐ They will decline in incidence, because the chance of a carrier of the recessive allele mating with another carrier will go down.

As we have seen, recessive genetic disorders — such as CF and sickle cell anaemia — are usually associated with particular populations. Increasing rates of intermarriage between people from different populations will tend to reduce the incidence of any recessive genetic disorders that either population experiences. So, with increased movement and intermarriage between populations, the chance of children being born with two copies of recessive disease genes will decrease.

Before the differences between populations are completely blurred, researchers are using relatively isolated populations to identify disease genes or genes that render people susceptible to disease, by following phenotypes, family pedigree charts and DNA sequences. An example of a relatively isolated population is a group of islanders, such as those who live in Newfoundland. There, the 550 000 individuals are descended from just 25 000 English, Scottish and Irish settlers who colonised the province between the 17th and 19th centuries.

■ How will the genetic diversity of Newfoundlanders compare with that of the people of 21st century Britain and Ireland?

☐ Newfoundlanders will be more similar genetically to each other than the people of 21st century Britain and Ireland are to each other.

The important point here is that the more similar a group of people's genes are, as in the case of an isolated population, the more prevalent disease alleles might become due either to natural selection (sickle cell disease, Section 17.2) or to chance events (profoundly deaf individuals, Section 17.3). Any variants, either within genes or within other DNA sequences in the genome, that appear consistently within a population, can help to locate disease alleles and disease susceptibility alleles.

One commercial company that was established in Iceland, deCODE, had the added advantage, in addition to family pedigree charts, of a central database that included the health or medical records of all individuals in Iceland going back to 1915 when the Icelandic National Health Service began. Until about 60 years ago, the population was almost completely isolated from immigration by other populations. This approach to discovering genes is proving to be very powerful. For example, using the database and DNA samples from the 270 000 individuals who currently live in Iceland, deCODE researchers took only ten weeks to find a gene for a disorder called familial essential tremor. Since its foundation, using a genetic analysis of the DNA from this population, mutations that cause several diseases have been found, including a gene involved in stroke (brain haemorrhage), a multifactorial disorder. The company also used this approach to home in on regions of the genome containing genes associated with osteoarthritis, asthma, diabetes, heart disease, Alzheimer's disease and other disease phenotypes. These early successes led to the formation of several other population-based genetic 'biobanks' around the world, each hoping to identify the genes that are mutated in diseases common to those populations and to also consider their interaction with population-specific environments.

The debates and ethics surrounding these types of biobanking genetic projects are considered in the final section of the course.

Question 17.1

Summarise the evidence supporting the hypothesis that $Hb^A Hb^S$ heterozygous individuals are better able to withstand malaria than are homozygous $Hb^A Hb^A$ individuals.

Question 17.2

Attempt to explain the distribution of each of the following diseases in terms of natural selection or chance events: (a) porphyria and (b) thalassaemia, both of which are described below.

(a) The dominant genetic disorder porphyria is rare in most parts of the world but is relatively common in South Africa. The gene normally has little effect, but its carriers have a severe, and sometimes fatal, reaction to barbiturate drugs. About 30 000 Afrikaners carry the disease allele today, which we know they all inherited from a couple from Holland who arrived in South Africa in the 1690s.

(b) Thalassaemia is a recessive genetic disease, prevalent in Mediterranean countries, the Indian sub-continent, Malaysia and the Far East and in parts of Central and West Africa. Affected homozygous individuals have anaemia and other associated blood problems, and fail to survive without continual medical support. The disease is associated with loss of part of the haemoglobin molecule. Its distribution overlaps part of the area where malaria is currently or was once prevalent.

17.5   Summary of Chapter 17

The basis for genetic differences between populations is mutation. Differences in allele frequencies between different populations arise by means of natural selection and chance events.

The example of sickle cell disease shows how the frequency of a particular allele in populations is influenced by natural selection. The sickle cell allele is maintained at high frequency because it confers a reproductive success in the heterozygous condition.

The change in the frequency of an allele that does not confer an effect upon reproductive success, in a small or a relatively isolated population, is due to chance events.

Studying relatively geographically restricted or isolated populations can be useful to increase the rate of discovery of disease causing genes and many projects are now underway around the world.

Chapter 18
What will a knowledge of the sequence of the human genome do for us?

Genes on their own, strictly, don't *do* anything. An isolated human gene, if you had one laid out in a dish, would just be a tiny filament of DNA. Even if you added all the other human genes — however many there finally turn out to be — the whole lot would still be as inert as fish on the fishmonger's slab.

Genes can only do their work in the right surroundings. As we have seen, those surroundings matter at several different levels. In the first place, the human genome must be enclosed within the nucleus of a cell, and the cell has to be equipped with all the right machinery for transcribing and translating, regulating and replicating, the genetic information stored in the DNA sequences.

One cell, in turn, is part of a vast community of cells — some tens of trillions — which make up an adult human. In that community, it knows what kind of cell it is, and where it is, whether it should reproduce, and for how long, and which genes it should keep active, which it should switch off (Section 11.7).

Also, as we discussed in Chapters 7, 8 and 17, the environment combines with genetic factors to shape a phenotype and, ultimately, the course of a human life.

However, that is only one way of looking at the surroundings of the cellular community that makes up a human being. A human is also a person, who has a family — more or less complex depending on its history. The family in turn is part of a wider society and culture (as shown in Figure 1.4). That society has ways of regulating its affairs, its laws and customs. High income countries have a host of complex institutions — like hospitals and health services, or insurance companies. A person, as the owner of a particular human genome, will interact with these institutions and the level of health provision available is likely to affect how their genetic information is used. (Section 12.1 explains that each of us has a different DNA sequence in our particular genome.) In low-income countries, where access to, and provision of health care is often more limited, the ability to examine personal genetic information or the prospect of utilising this information to influence health care is unlikely to be an option. As a citizen, each person may wish to influence how their national laws are adapted to deal with genetic information, or how their various medical and national institutions cope with these laws.

Beyond this, each individual country is part of a global economy, in which health care is vastly better resourced in some parts of the world than others. Both government-funded medical research and commercial development of drugs and other therapies are overwhelmingly geared to the diseases of the relatively affluent. If genetic technologies (discussed below) ever advance significantly in the direction of phenotypic enhancement — 'improving on the normal' — rather than therapy (Section 20.2), then the questions of justice and equity posed by current health disparities are likely to become still more complex.

This last section of the course shifts from the science of human genetics to discussing the health, social and ethical issues emerging as our knowledge of human genetics expands. Recall that an issue can always be considered from more than one point of view or perspective (Chapter 1). As you read the remaining chapters, you need to bear in mind whose interests are being represented by each perspective, e.g. the individual, the medical profession, pharmaceutical companies, or society in general. Chapter 19 looks at genetic testing, and some of the problems that it poses for individuals and families. Then in Chapter 20, we look at the prospects for improving medical treatments on the basis of increased understanding of genes arising from the increased availability of human genome DNA sequence information.

Finally, in Chapter 21, we consider how health services may need to respond to wider changes in medical practice that put more emphasis on the importance of genetic information. These chapters assume knowledge about genes and their inheritance covered earlier in the course. You may find it helpful to refer back to these concepts; appropriate references are provided.

Chapter 19
Genetic testing

When most people encounter *genetic testing* today, it is usually in a medical context. In high-income countries, a clinical practitioner or family doctor may refer us to a regional genetics unit at a local hospital, or we may approach our doctors, asking for genetic tests because we suspect something about our family history. In these cases, testing is likely to be supported by extensive discussion about health matters and family history, as well as about the implications of the results of any test being performed. We might also encounter advertisements in the media offering genetic testing 'over-the counter' through postal or internet based services.

In this chapter, we look at the issues and problems facing individuals and families when confronted with genetic testing. We will look at broader institutional issues, such as how and where the testing gets done, and how the availability of testing varies across the world in Chapter 21.

This chapter looks at three different uses of genetic testing: prenatal diagnosis, childhood testing and adult testing. Such tests provide genetic information in the form of a predictive diagnosis, hence they are described as **predictive tests**. Prenatal diagnosis uses techniques such as amniocentesis to test fetuses in the womb. For example, it is commonly offered to women over 35 years of age to test for Down's syndrome in many high-income countries, such as the UK (Section 12.4). Childhood testing involves testing children for genetic diseases that may not become a problem until they grow up, and adult testing is aimed at people at risk of late-onset disorders, which do not appear until middle age. In addition, we address some of the issues involved in carrier testing, another predictive test. This involves the testing of people from families with a history of genetic disease, to find out who carries the gene, and who therefore might pass the disease on to their children even though they themselves are unaffected. Here the aim is to enable couples to make informed choices about whether or not to have children, and if so whether they might have a genetic disease.

■ Can you recall the meaning of the term carrier?

☐ A carrier is a person who is heterozygous for a recessive disease, and thus does not suffer from the disease themselves (Section 6.3).

The technologies that make genetic testing possible range from chemical tests for gene products in the blood, through examining chromosomes from whole cells (Section 3.1), to identification of the presence or absence of specific, defined DNA sequences, such as the presence of mutations within a gene sequence (Chapter 13). The last of these is becoming much more common in the wake of the publication of the complete human genome sequence. The technical details of particular tests are changing fast and they are becoming much more accurate. But the important point is that it is possible to test for more genes, and more variants of those genes, using very small samples of material. For an adult, a cheek scraping these days provides ample cells for most DNA testing.

At this stage, we should distinguish testing from *genetic screening*. Genetic testing is used with individuals who, because of their family history think they are at risk of carrying the gene for a particular genetic disease or are of a particular age when genetic conditions are more common, such as for Down's syndrome. Screening (Chapter 21) covers wide-scale testing of populations, to discover who may be at risk of developing a genetic disease.

All these different kinds of test can bring benefits, but all three, i.e. prenatal diagnosis, childhood testing and adult testing, have also been noted as requiring careful management because of personal and *ethical* issues that can arise from the kind of information they provide. We are confronted with moral choices here, for example, who gets that information and under what circumstances, what they do with it, and who decides what to do with it, are all important issues. Even finding out what people would like to know is not necessarily straightforward. (Is telling someone they can have a test for Huntington's disease (HD), say, the same as telling them they may be at risk of the disease?) Here we are not primarily concerned with the technologies for testing, but with the ethical context within which testing takes place; a context framed by issues such as informed consent, individual decision-making and confidentiality of genetic information. Before looking at any of these questions in detail, though, a few words about the context in which they most often occur — genetic counselling.

19.1   Genetic counselling

In countries that offer genetic testing through their health services, it is usually the accepted practice to offer such testing only after patients have undergone **genetic counselling**. This is defined as the provision of information and advice about inherited disorders, and includes helping people to:

- Understand medical facts;
- Appreciate the way in which inheritance contributes to the disease in question;
- Understand the options for dealing with the disorder;
- Choose the course of action with which they feel most comfortable — or least uncomfortable.

The advice-giver may be a doctor, a specialist genetic counsellor or, perhaps, a nurse with special training in genetics. We will discuss the potential demand for such advice in Chapter 21.

The core value of genetic counselling is often taken to be *non-directiveness*; it is not the counsellor's job to tell a patient what to do, but simply to help them to make an informed decision. Thus genetic counselling is 'not about making wise decisions, but about making decisions wisely'. Counsellors should not even advise people whether to take a test or not, nor should they recommend a particular course of action should the patient opt for testing. Despite the long tradition of non-directiveness in genetic counselling services that have developed over many years, such as those in the USA and Europe, there are still debates about it in a medical setting. One problem is how to assess the success of a counselling service. How can one measure 'effective communication', and 'good decision-making'? For example, should prenatal diagnosis be assessed in terms of the number of tests carried out and pregnancies terminated (which is an option if a prenatal test indicates an affected fetus)? This would provide administrators with useful numbers, but has been criticised as forcing counsellors to see success in terms of only one output — and hence encouraging directiveness. Simply providing genetic counselling and the option of prenatal testing might make some individuals feel that they have to have a termination if the prenatal test indicates problems.

Another aspect of genetic counselling is the provision of **carrier testing** for families whose history makes them suspect that they may have a genetic disorder. This means identifying those individuals who, although not suffering from the recessive disorder, do carry one version of the faulty gene and could pass it on to their children. Although carrier testing does not involve the emotional challenges of telling patients that they, or their child, have a genetic disorder, it does involve issues such as risk to future children, and whether partners should be tested to see if they too are carriers.

The point about this brief discussion of genetic counselling has not been to provide clear-cut answers, but to show that even in the case of a practice that has been developed for decades, there are still a large number of issues that are hard to settle. Thus we should not be surprised to find that when we look at more recent developments in genetic technologies — such as testing for multifactorial diseases (discussed in Section 19.4.2) — clear-cut answers and easy predictions about how people behave and what services to offer are also in short supply.

■   What skills do you think a genetic counsellor has to develop?

☐   Genetic knowledge, empathy, communication skills, and patience are all likely to be valuable.

19.2   Prenatal diagnosis

The type of genetic testing that the majority of us are most likely to come across is still **prenatal diagnosis** (PND). This involves testing a fetus during pregnancy, to see whether it is likely to suffer from a number of different disorders — some genetic, some not. While recent developments allow tests for certain multifactorial genetic diseases (such as spina bifida), prenatal diagnosis has been available since the 1960s to test for Down's syndrome.

■   How could a Down's syndrome fetus be identified?

☐   The cells of the fetus would contain three copies of chromosome 21 instead of the usual two (Section 12.4).

Most cases of Down's syndrome are the result of a new mutation arising in the gamete-producing cells. This contrasts with childhood diseases, such as cystic fibrosis (CF), which result from the fetus inheriting two recessive mutations because the parents are carriers. Here prenatal diagnosis has removed much of the uncertainty about the risks of genetic diseases. In a family who know that both parents are carriers of CF, either because they already have a CF child (Figure 19.1) or as a result of carrier testing, prenatal diagnosis allows the

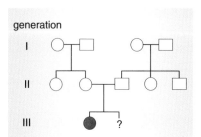

Figure 19.1   The pedigree chart of a family with a child with cystic fibrosis. Will their second child be affected?

conversion of a probable risk of the disease affecting an unborn child to nearer a certainty that it will or will not be affected.

■ What is the probability of a child born to two carriers being affected with CF?

☐ The probability is 1 in 4 (Box 6.2).

■ Look at Figure 19.1; if one child is already affected by CF, is the chance of the second child being affected reduced?

☐ No; the outcome of any fertilisation is independent of any other (Box 6.2).

Prenatal testing might then change the probability from 1 in 4 to near certainty that the fetus is or is not affected. However prenatal diagnosis cannot be used to rule out all possible birth defects, or all genetic disorders, because suitable tests do not yet exist to detect them. Nor is it foolproof even for those diseases that it can generally detect, such as CF (Section 13.1).

Box 19.1 overleaf outlines the techniques for prenatal diagnosis of fetal abnormalities early in pregnancy.

As more prenatal testing is performed, we may see an increase in abortions since there may be no treatment for the particular disease detected. Yet this is obviously a difficult decision to make, not only in terms of the very public debates that surround abortion, but also with regard to the difficult private decisions that women (and their partners) face in these circumstances.

Supporters of prenatal diagnosis point out that as the accuracy of the tests improve, there should be fewer abortions. At present, they argue, a substantial proportion of post-test abortions are normal pregnancies because the tests are not always accurate and decisions are based on estimated risk.

To others, selective abortion of affected fetuses is always morally objectionable, and especially so when the disorder might not be life-threatening, as in many individuals with Down's syndrome. However, fewer than five per cent of all prenatal diagnoses are, in fact, positive. So for the vast majority of prospective parents, prenatal diagnosis serves ultimately to reassure them that the unborn baby is not affected by the disease in question.

The tensions and ambiguities that surround fetal testing have given rise to what has become labelled the 'tentative' pregnancy. Some women, who know that they are due to have an ultrasound scan or other prenatal test, may refuse to regard themselves as 'properly' pregnant, in case the test indicates a problem and they are faced with the decision of whether to abort or not. As we saw in the section on genetic counselling, merely offering testing and termination might be seen as implying that these choices should be taken up. Yet this suggests that a pregnant woman who agrees to prenatal diagnosis should have made a prior commitment to terminate the pregnancy if she is carrying a fetus with a genetic (or other serious) disorder.

Box 19.1 Techniques for prenatal diagnosis of fetal abnormalities

There are a number of techniques available for prenatal diagnosis, and these are listed in Table 19.1 along with the abnormalities or diseases they can be used to detect.

Table 19.1 Techniques for prenatal diagnosis and abnormalities/disease detected.

Technique	Abnormality/disease detected
non-invasive techniques	
maternal serum screening: determination of fetal protein levels	spina bifida
ultrasonography	organ abnormalities of nervous system, kidneys, heart, gut and limbs
invasive techniques	
fetoscopy	organ and limb abnormalities, skin disorders, blood disorders
amniocentesis:	
chromosome analysis	Down's syndrome
DNA studies	many genetic disorders
determination of fetal protein levels	spina bifida
chorionic villi sampling	genetic disorders (e.g. muscular dystrophy, cystic fibrosis, Huntington's disease)

Maternal serum screening tests the mother's blood for the presence of proteins produced by the fetus; both it and *ultrasonography* are non-invasive with no known risk to the mother or fetus. The development of such non-invasive tests is likely to increase and will possibly include analysis of trace amounts of fetal DNA that circulate in the mother's serum. *Fetoscopy* has the advantage that the fetus can be visualised directly by inserting a very fine optical telescope (fetoscope) through the abdominal wall into the uterine cavity. *Amniocentesis* involves the removal of a small amount of amniotic fluid, which bathes the developing fetus and contains fetal cells. The fluid can be analysed for its protein content, which may be abnormal in spina bifida, or chromosomes can be counted or the DNA analysed for certain genetic abnormalities. Another common approach is *chorionic villi sampling*, which is the removal of cells from the edge of the placenta. Most of the placenta is fetal tissue, so it is genetically identical with the cells of the fetus. This yields a greater amount of DNA than the sampling of amniotic fluid. These sampling techniques for prenatal diagnosis are associated with a small increase in the risk of spontaneous abortion, compared with the risk in pregnancies not screened by these methods.

■ Aside from offering the possibility of termination, what other purposes might a prenatal test serve?

☐ A couple might wish to be forewarned of the birth of a child with special needs, so they could prepare to care for their baby.

■ What sort of factors might influence personal decisions about abortion?

☐ Moral, religious, financial, experience of knowing a family with the disease, and having an affected child already.

In combination with in-vitro fertilisation (IVF) (Section 4.2), it is also possible to perform tests upon the early developing embryo before it is re-introduced into the reproductive tract. This technique, termed **pre-implantation genetic diagnosis** (PGD) involves the removal of one or two cells from the developing embryo. DNA is then isolated from these cells and genetic tests performed to detect the presence of disease-associated alleles. PGD is technically very demanding, but has the advantage that it avoids the risks and issues associated with fetal testing at later stages using amniocentesis or chorionic villi sampling and it allows selective re-implantation of embryos that do not carry the disease-associated allele. It has been used successfully to select embryos after IVF from parents carrying various disease-causing genes.

■ Whilst PGD clearly removes the issue of the abortion of a fetus, what other factors would influence the acceptance of PGD?

☐ Moral and religious issues surround the status of the embryo, especially the storage or destruction of embryos tested that do carry the disease-associated alleles and the storage or disposal of 'spare' embryos.

PGD also raises issues as to whether this technique, rather than being used as a way of ensuring that disease alleles are not inherited by the embryo, could be used to select embryos that have desirable features, such as transplantation compatible organs or bone marrow. We will return to this topic in Chapter 20 when we discuss 'designer babies'.

Activity 19.1   Personal and medical issues of prenatal diagnosis

Now would be a good time to do this activity, which requires you to read an article and to consider the issues it raises.

19.3   Genetic testing of children

Within clinical genetic services, a difference has grown up between the testing of children and the testing of adults (Section 19.4). Sometimes the genetic testing of children is relatively uncontroversial. For example, the genetic test may simply be to confirm a medical diagnosis that has been made on clinical grounds. So a three-year-old with low weight, blocked lungs and poor digestion may be given a genetic test to see whether they have CF or not (Section 13.1).

There are other cases where a test is used predictively for a disorder which may affect the child soon and which needs observation. For example, in a family where the dominant disorder familial adenomatous polyposis coli (FAP) is present, there is an increased risk of bowel cancer. Medical surveillance for tumours (Section 16.1), which can be removed if diagnosed early, is often started at about 10 years of age. **Pre-symptomatic testing** of children to determine whether they carry the FAP gene, and hence need to be monitored, makes sense.

But we can contrast such a straightforward case of predictive testing with genetic tests for a disorder like HD, a late onset (over 40 years of age) neurological disorder, for which there is no cure, and only limited treatment.

Now that a test for the gene responsible for HD is available, should children be tested?

■   What do you think are some of the arguments against testing a child for HD?

☐   Some that you may have thought of are as follows: (i) testing a child prevents them making a future decision for themselves when they are an adult; (ii) confidentiality, important in the case of adult genetic test results, will be automatically overridden in the case of a child brought in for testing by his or her parents; (iii) family knowledge of the test's result might lead to a child being treated differently by his or her parents and siblings, because they might be brought up with lower expectations of themselves.

Adult uptake of the HD test has been far lower than predicted. When asked hypothetically if they would take the test, a clear majority of at-risk adults said 'yes': now that the test is available, only 10–15% have actually gone for testing. Hypothetical decisions about genetic testing, either for oneself or (by extension) one's children do not seem adequately to represent real attitudes to tests when they are offered.

When people request genetic testing for their children, they usually make assumptions about what the child would want if they were older, and that the information gained from a test will be of benefit to the child concerned. On the basis of previous testing programmes, neither of these points seems valid. The bottom line is that problems in adult testing for HD seem to arise not in the context of testing, but that of the counselling session, the provision of information and the comprehension and implications of risk estimates. These problems are going to be magnified in the case of testing children.

19.4   Genetic testing of adults

HD is a good example of a late-onset disorder because it is fatal, non-treatable, relatively frequent and has a strong genetic element that can be tested for. There are others that fall into a similar category, i.e. mainly relate to a single gene, such as adult polycystic kidney disease. The issues surrounding late-onset multifactorial diseases, such as diabetes and breast cancer, will be dealt with separately. To date, relatively few diseases that fall into both these categories can be tested for, but with the increasing knowledge that we obtain from population studies and genomic DNA sequencing of individuals, the number of tests available will increase.

19.4.1   Late-onset single-gene disorders

An individual might know that a late-onset disease such as HD is present in their immediate family and that they might have inherited the disease gene. The problems of genetic testing for HD (Section 13.2) revolve around the fact that it is *pre-symptomatic* (Figure 19.2).

One dilemma is the long delay between testing positive and developing the clinical symptoms of the disorder in middle age. Is it better not to know and live in hope, or as one individual cried 'get it over with, I'm so tired of wondering?' Of course, a negative test result (i.e. the person does not carry the gene for HD) could be a huge relief, but for those who are told that they do carry the HD gene, there are huge psychological and practical problems.

■ Look at Figure 19.2. HD is a dominant disorder. What is the probability of inheriting the disease, if one parent manifests it?

☐ The probability is 1 in 2 (Box 6.1).

■ What is the DNA test for HD?

☐ The test directly measures the length of the CAG triplet repeat in an individual's DNA (Section 13.2).

One of the core issues in adult testing for single-gene disorders such as HD is getting informed consent from the patient to carry out the test. One problem is what counts as 'informed'. How much does the patient need to know about the science of genetics to make a considered decision concerning a genetic test? But there are also examples of attempts to procure a genetic test for HD without the knowledge of the patient concerned. Sometimes this involves getting children tested (see Section 19.3), but cases have been reported where psychiatrists, social workers and lawyers have tried to get a test carried out on an adult without the permission of the person concerned. There can also be strong pressure on individuals who, although they are aware they are undergoing testing, might not be exercising their own best judgement. An example is the family pressure that can force prospective parents to be tested so that they can make 'responsible' decisions about having children.

A related problem is that even though someone may opt out of testing for HD, they may unwillingly discover their status through a member of their family going for a test.

■ Within a family, who do you think should be told the results of a genetic test and why?

☐ There is no right answer here.

Do the individual's brothers and sisters have the right to information that relates to them? If a parent knows she or he is at risk and refuses to get tested, how would they feel if their adult son goes for a test for his own peace of mind and finds out he (and therefore his parent) carries the gene? Genetic information tells us about our families, whether we want to know or not.

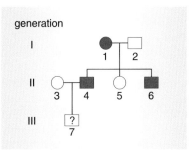

Figure 19.2   The pedigree chart of a family with Huntington's disease. Will individual 7 manifest the disease?

■ Outside the family, who might be interested in the results of the test?

☐ Employers and insurance companies. (We take up this point later in the chapter.)

19.4.2   Late-onset multifactorial disorders

It is becoming clear that many, if not most, of the common diseases that affect the high income countries of the world are multifactorial disorders with some inherited genetic component (Chapter 8). Some of the genes that render individuals susceptible to diabetes, coronary heart disease, hypertension and many cancers, including breast cancer, have been identified and can be tested now for the presence of mutations. Multifactorial disorders present a real challenge for genetic medicine. For example, while it may be true that there is a strongly inherited component to the form of diabetes which usually occurs during adolescence (type 1 diabetes), it is not at all clear what purpose genetic testing for such a component would serve in terms of health. This is because, currently, there is no way to stop the development of the disease.

In terms of some disorders, for example heart disease and cancer, **susceptibility testing** might allow doctors to advise particular patients to change their diet and lifestyle, to counteract the effects of their increased genetic risk. (The idea of 'susceptible' disease alleles interacting with different environmental, or risk, factors was introduced in Section 8.2.) Unfortunately, what evidence there is suggests that the results of a genetic test may fix in a patient's mind that they are going to develop the disease anyway, no matter what changes they make. This 'genetic pessimism' means that giving individuals the results of tests may be counter-productive.

Communicating the results of such tests is difficult, in any case. Susceptibility tests only indicate the risk of developing a particular disorder, either in terms of the odds of developing the disorder over a lifetime, or as a relative risk in comparison with those people who do not carry the mutation. These tests are *not predictive* in the sense of definitely telling people whether they will get a disease or not. If we think back to the complexities and difficulties that surround genetic counselling in single-gene disorders such as HD, then the added problems of a multifactorial disorder should give us pause for thought (Section 19.1).

Activity 19.2   Personal and medical issues of genetic testing

Now would be a good time to do this activity, which requires you to read an article relevant to this topic.

19.5   Commercial interest and genetic testing

Beyond the obvious personal issues related to testing for late-onset disorders — either single-gene or multifactorial — there are also broader issues to do with how other groups in society deal with genetic information.

19.5.1   Insurance companies and employers

One possible use of genetic tests is by insurance companies and employers to restrict the people to whom they offer insurance policies or jobs. In some countries, insurance companies have drawn up specific codes in agreement with governments on how they will use the results of *adverse* predictive genetic tests. For example, in the UK, the government's Genetics and Insurance Committee (GAIC) approved the use of a predictive genetic test of the *HD* gene in cases where an applicant is applying for life insurance over £500,000; that is, individuals who have a positive result for the mutation should inform their insurance company. The UK insurance industry has agreed a voluntary moratorium until 2014 on the use of tests for two genes associated with the development of breast cancer, BRCA1 and BRCA2. It is worth noting that people can disclose negative (non-adverse) results for tests that GAIC has not approved, if it would get them a lower premium than would otherwise be the case based on an adverse family history. This is most applicable with the BRCA tests for which most (greater than 90%) test results are negative. Critics of the insurance industry claim that support for this policy with regard to all genetic tests is only a little way off, and that regulation is required to formally restrict insurers' access to test results.

■ Why might insurers worry if people know the results of their genetic tests and don't tell?

☐ An applicant could apply for more insurance than they otherwise would, and cost the insurer more money than predicted.

In other countries, specific legislation has been introduced in an attempt to directly regulate the use of genetic information. For example, the USA enacted the Genetic Information Discrimination Act (GINA) in 2008, which specifically protects people from discrimination by health insurers and employers on the basis of personal DNA information. However, this law does not cover life or long-term care insurance.

We will further illustrate the issues of employment and genetic testing with two examples. In the UK, only one employer, the Ministry of Defence, is known to test for a genetic disorder. They test for carriers of the sickle cell mutation, i.e. for people who have the sickle cell trait (Section 17.2), on the grounds that such carriers may pass out at high altitude and therefore should not become fighter pilots. This is controversial because sickle cell trait is common among people of West African origin, and thus a testing programme could be seen as racially motivated (a similar ban was lifted in the USA following public protests in the 1970s).

As genetic tests become more available and as the cost decreases, the chance of employers using such tests to select their workforce increases. In 2002, before GINA was enacted, one railway company was prosecuted by the US Equal Employment Opportunities Commission and fined $2.2 million for secretly testing employees for a gene thought to be linked to an increased risk of developing repetitive strain injury (RSI), presumably with the aim of avoiding employing those at risk in jobs where this condition might be triggered.

Could it ever be right to test employees? Perhaps you might agree with certain types of workers being tested if it means protecting the public. Would, for example, it be acceptable to test airline pilots or train drivers for gene mutations that suggest they might have sudden cardiac failure? What about testing professional athletes such as football players to identify those with genes that might make them faster runners or stronger players?

19.5.2   DNA: who owns what?

There are more problems to do with commercial interests and genetic testing that relate to ownership. To develop genetic tests scientists need the help of patients and families who suffer from the disorders concerned, and there are any number of cases where the test for a particular disorder was made possible only through families donating time, money and genetic material, in the form of blood samples (Section 15.3 and Section 17.4). Yet often, one of the first results of the identification of the gene 'for' a disease is the patenting of that gene sequence by the research team involved.

A *patent* is a legal agreement that gives an inventor exclusive rights over his/her invention for a period of time (usually 20 years). The inventor can then develop the invention or license it to other people, in return for money. One controversy is whether a naturally occurring thing — such as a gene — can be viewed as an invention, and hence be patentable.

Patenting is often justified on the grounds that the way to develop a usable genetic test is to get pharmaceutical companies interested, which will happen only if they know that their research cannot be 'poached' by competitors — hence the protection of the patent. Yet patients' groups have reacted angrily when it is revealed that the gene for which they provided the raw material has been commercialised, and that they may have to pay for the genetic tests that they helped to develop.

In 2001, a patients' group in the USA began legal action to sue the hospital and doctor who patented the gene for Canavan's disease, a rare disease of the central nervous system, which the families and sufferers helped to identify by donating DNA. The patients' group objected to the royalty payment that the hospital took from each test, and the limits placed on the number of free tests that individual medical centres could carry out. The case was settled out of court in 2003, with researchers being able to use the test for free, but clinical testing is still being charged.

In a broader sense, this case can be seen as an example of 'biosociality' or 'genetic citizenship'. First coined in 1995, by the anthropologist Paul Rabinow, biosociality describes the process by which people with particular genetic conditions (and their families), in addition to support groups and activists, begin to redefine their social status in terms of 'their' particular gene, identifying themselves with other people who have a condition caused by the same genetic error. For example, in the case of HD, sociologists have noted a range of new social practices emerging around the HD test, which relate to decisions about whether to take the test or not, who in one's family to inform of one's decision, and the responsibility of those at risk of HD to learn as much as possible about the condition. The result is people who regard themselves as 'responsible-genetic subjects' with a range of life strategies and a social context that has developed out of their being at risk of a genetic condition. It is not that these new social categories will replace traditional ones such as race and class, but they will cut across them, perhaps eventually redefining them along genetic grounds. One consequence of this is the way in which patient groups have become involved in encouraging, funding and even participating in genetic research.

Question 19.1

Suppose that a new DNA test becomes available, which can indicate susceptibility to the common disorder of coronary heart disease. List the major benefits and problems that such a test could have for an individual.

Question 19.2

Distinguish between each of the following: prenatal testing, susceptibility testing, pre-symptomatic testing and genetic counselling.

19.6 Summary of Chapter 19

A number of types of genetic test are available to families for predictive diagnosis of genetic diseases: prenatal diagnosis (where there is either a likelihood that the fetus has Down's syndrome or a known history of a predisposition to a genetic disorder); carrier testing (to identify those who might pass the gene on); and pre-symptomatic testing of both children and adults (where individuals in a family may have inherited a disease such as HD). Susceptibility testing identifies mutations in genes that indicate the risk of developing a multifactorial disease.

Genetic counselling gives information to couples and individuals to assist them in making decisions about inherited diseases, genetic testing and the consequences of a positive result; but there is still much debate over how it is carried out. The problems and major ethical considerations of these types of genetic test are related to abortion, informed consent to testing, respecting patients' rights to make their own decisions following testing, and disclosure of information revealed by genetic testing (e.g. to other family members, insurance companies and employers).

Commercial interests in DNA sequences and DNA tests raise questions about ownership.

Chapter 20
Genetic medicine: dreams and realities

We have seen how genetics can be used in medicine to confirm a diagnosis, make a fresh one, or predict a disorder likely to occur in the future. At the moment, that is often all that can be done. The so-called 'diagnostic therapeutic gap' is one immediate problem for us to deal with. When the only options on offer after a genetic test are to terminate a pregnancy, or prepare to deal with the disease as best you can, some of the dilemmas of new genetic knowledge are sharper.

Genetic testing is only the beginning of the effect of genetics on medicine. What about treatment? This chapter looks at various ways in which the new knowledge of the human genome will affect how illnesses are treated. These treatments are already getting underway. We look at the one that gets talked about most — gene therapy — but also at other possibilities, which may be more important in the short term. These include using information about a person's genotype to prescribe drugs more closely tailored to their body chemistry. Finally, we discuss how the media report these possibilities, and the effects that this may have on how the public views genes. As genetic explanations for disorders and characteristics become more widely accepted, how does that affect ideas about what good health — or disease — consists of? This, in turn will be one of the influences on the future development of genetics in health services, and on the regulation of genetic technologies, the topics that we discuss in the final chapter.

20.1   Gene therapy

Gene therapy is often reported to be one of the most hopeful fields of medicine to arise from our understanding of how deficits in certain genes cause human disease. If we know so much about all these genes, surely we can use this knowledge to try to treat some diseases in which genes are involved at a fundamental level? But what exactly is gene therapy, and where is the work heading?

Just looking at the two words coupled in the phrase 'gene therapy' raises an important ambiguity.

■   From what you have learnt so far, what might gene therapy mean?

☐   It could mean treatment that involves correcting genes that are involved in causing an illness in an individual. Or, it could mean using genes to treat an illness caused in some other way.

It turns out that it means both. Most of the public debate has been about the former meaning, i.e. correcting or repairing genes, but early applications have focused on the latter meaning. These applications involve using 'designer' DNA to tackle diseases that are not inherited — by using altered viruses designed specifically to attack cancer cells, say. Here, the DNA is working more or less like a drug. In fact, many 'gene therapy' trials approved so far have been attempts to treat a variety of cancers.

Here, though, we will focus on the first of the two meanings of gene therapy, correcting genes. Some genetic diseases can be tackled by modifying the phenotype, without worrying about how DNA might be involved. Most simply, a multifactorial problem like a cleft palate can be corrected surgically. But for many diseases, such as cystic fibrosis (CF), non-genetic treatments can help to alleviate some symptoms, but so far that is all. So in a single-gene disorder such as CF, the theoretical focus is now on the gene and its product. We begin by focusing on gene products, i.e. proteins, and then consider genes.

If the product, that is a particular protein, is abnormal, can it be corrected? If it is missing altogether, can it be supplied? Sometimes, the answer involves **genetic modification** of other organisms. This technique is described in Box 20.1.

Box 20.1 The technique of genetic modification of organisms to aid human health

The technique of genetic modification of organisms relies upon our ability to isolate the gene or genes of interest from human DNA and insert them into bacterial cells. Once inside the bacterial cells, if the human gene is active or 'switched on' then the bacteria behave like 'living factories', manufacturing large amounts of the human protein encoded by the gene (Figure 20.1). This can be extracted and purified from the bacterial cultures, ready for use by humans.

The use of genetic modification has enabled unlimited quantities of certain human proteins to be produced more easily and less expensively than was previously possible. Problems exist with this approach, however, as proteins must fold themselves up into very specific structures to have a biological effect (Section 9.3). Often this doesn't happen very effectively in bacteria. In order to overcome this problem, the cloned human DNA has been introduced into sheep. In this case, the human protein is secreted into the milk, allowing for a continuous process of production (Figure 20.1). Alternatively, the cloned human DNA can be used for gene therapy by direct intervention in the individual's DNA (Figure 20.1 and Box 20.2).

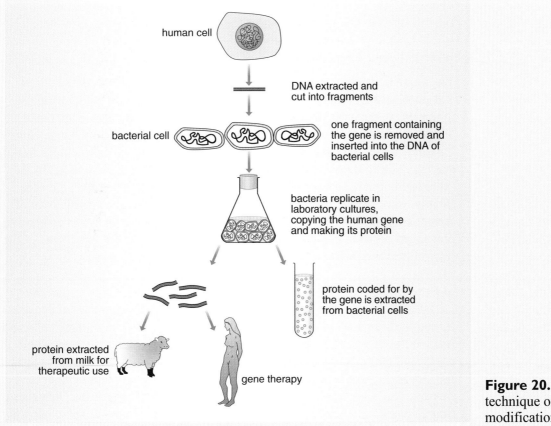

human cell

DNA extracted and cut into fragments

bacterial cell

one fragment containing the gene is removed and inserted into the DNA of bacterial cells

bacteria replicate in laboratory cultures, copying the human gene and making its protein

protein coded for by the gene is extracted from bacterial cells

protein extracted from milk for therapeutic use

gene therapy

Figure 20.1　The technique of genetic modification of organisms.

Human clotting factor, the protein used to treat haemophilia (Section 12.1), can be made by splicing the human gene into bacteria (Figure 20.1). Insulin, which is used to treat diabetes, can be produced by sheep in their milk. Then you can supply the missing gene product to the patient like any other medicine.

The methods of using either bacteria or sheep, like others involving production of genetically modified organisms for food, have been controversial in their way. Much of the technology involved in making genetically manipulated or modified organisms, involves doing the same sort of thing — inserting DNA into cells — as involved in gene therapy (as shown in Figure 20.1).

■   However, this technology is not gene therapy proper. Why not?

☐   All that happens is that the protein is extracted and given to patients, usually by injection on a regular basis, so the gene is not being corrected or repaired.

Suppose you could inject the gene instead — to provide *direct* intervention in the individual's DNA.

■   Even if you could get a new gene into a human, what else would be needed to make sure it worked as a therapy?

☐   The gene would need to be active — get transcribed into mRNA and translated into protein (Section 11.7). And it would have to enter the right cells.

There is no point making haemoglobin in skin cells, or in producing in blood cells the protein that CF patients need in the lining of their lungs. And ideally it would have to go on working, perhaps in the cells' descendants, otherwise repeat treatments would be needed.

The idea of, in effect, treating the genotype, has been around from the 1960s. Since the new technologies of genetic modification came into widespread use in the 1980s, many trials of gene therapy have been carried out on humans. Despite high hopes, few have yet shown clear benefits to patients. At the turn of the millennium, it looked as though gene therapy would be more complicated, and take longer to deliver, than was thought 10 or 20 years previously. On the other hand, it may turn out that the techniques now being tried are superseded by more successful ones as our knowledge increases. The remarkable pace of technical developments suggests that it would be unwise to discount changes to human genes in the medium term. The rest of Chapter 20 considers some of the possibilities and problems to look out for.

20.1.1   Somatic gene therapy

Earlier in the course, you learnt about the distinction between somatic cells, those making up almost all of the body, and germline cells, which are the eggs and sperm and the cells that produce them (Section 4.1). **Somatic gene therapy** is the transfer of genes into the somatic cells of the patient, such as cells of the bone marrow, and hence the new DNA does not enter the eggs or sperm. The genes transferred are usually normal alleles that could 'correct' the mutant or disease alleles of the recipient (see Box 20.2).

Box 20.2 The technique of somatic gene therapy

The technique of somatic gene therapy involves inserting a normal gene into the appropriate cells of an individual affected with a genetic disease, thereby permanently correcting the disorder. Figure 20.2 outlines the simplest methods of getting genes into the person's cells using either viruses (which carry the human gene, in place of one of their own genes, into a cell) or liposomes (small fat-like molecules which can carry DNA into a cell). In some cells, the gene or genes become inserted into a chromosome in the nucleus.

The target cells might be bone marrow cells, which are easily isolated and re-implanted. Bone marrow cells continue to divide for a person's whole life to produce blood cells, so this approach is useful only if the gene you want to deliver has a biological role in the blood. Delivery of a gene that has a biological role in, say, the lungs, muscle, eyes, or liver would have to occur within those target organs. In many cases, accessing the appropriate tissue or, if the gene is required in multiple tissues (e.g. muscles throughout the body) ensuring it can be delivered where it is needed, is a major problem.

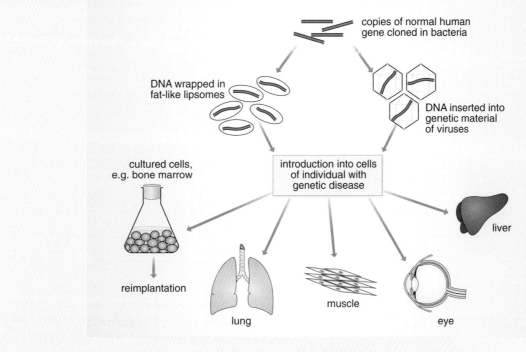

Figure 20.2 The technique of somatic gene therapy.

■ Will somatic gene therapy prevent the treated person from passing on the defective gene to their children?

☐ No, because the gene they receive in somatic gene therapy does not enter their gametes.

However, there are four major scientific hurdles that have to be overcome before somatic gene therapy is likely to work. The first is getting the human gene into the patient's cells (using viruses or liposomes, Box 20.2). Adverse results in several gene therapy trials, including the death of one patient, highlighted some of the risks of using viruses. In one trial that had initially seemed a success in terms of gene delivery and protein expression, a long-term effect was that the inserted DNA had damaged a cancer-related gene and a small number of individuals subsequently developed leukemia. Clearly, there is still some way to go with respect to safety of the techniques.

The second obstacle is getting the gene into the right cells. For example, for sickle cell disease (caused by defective haemoglobin in red blood cells, Section 17.2), the cells to choose would be the patient's bone marrow cells. For CF, application in the lungs and gut would be needed. The lungs might be accessible via an aerosol spray. Treating the gut would need some way to deliver genes in a package that the patient would swallow, and which would protect them from digestive enzymes (Section 9.2) until they could act.

The third obstacle is avoiding the body's natural immune response when the 'new' or 'corrected' protein is made within cells. In some cases, this protein may appear to be a 'foreign' protein to the body and the cells making it are attacked by the cells that are naturally present to protect against invading viruses or bacteria. In some areas of the human body, such as the retinal cells in the eye, a natural barrier exists that gives some hope that gene therapy might work very well for certain degenerative eye disorders.

The final obstacle is making sure the gene is active, that is, switched on in the cell to produce the protein that the patient needs. This means it must be under the control of the sequence of DNA that is responsible for switching the gene on (Section 14.2.1). The results do not have to be perfect to produce benefits. In cystic fibrosis, animal tests have shown that if the normal gene can be transferred to only five per cent of cells in the lungs, this restores some normal function.

The prospects for somatic therapy for single-gene diseases are still improving.

■ Why is gene therapy an unrealistic option for multifactorial diseases?

☐ Because a number of genes are involved, multiple gene therapy would be required (Chapter 8).

In general, current efforts to treat disease by somatic gene therapy do not pose any novel ethical issues, provided there is proper enforcement of informed consent in trials. There is concern, however, about where the successful development of techniques for germline gene therapy might lead.

20.1.2 Germline gene therapy

Now that in-vitro fertilisation — bringing eggs and sperm together outside the prospective mother's body — is an established technology, the possibility exists that genes could be altered in eggs or sperm, or in a very early embryo. The obvious advantages of **germline gene therapy** are that the cells are accessible (because they are outside the body), so gene delivery is less of a problem than it tends to be with somatic cells; and the inserted gene (or genes) would be present in all the cells of the person so treated because it would be transmitted to progeny cells during growth and development.

■   Would a person who had received germline gene therapy transmit the inserted gene(s) on to their children?

□   They would also pass it on, because it would be present in their germline cells as well as their somatic cells.

This might be poor business for gene therapy companies, but could be good for people with a genetic disorder.

Until recently, there was widespread agreement that germline gene therapy in humans should be ruled out and the genetic alteration of embryos is currently illegal in many countries, including the UK (2009).

Beyond legislation, there are many other issues raised by germline gene therapy. It is currently not possible to predict where in the genome a newly inserted gene might end up, and this poses unknown risks of causing new mutations, or otherwise disrupting normal gene functioning. Even if these hazards could be removed, there are new ethical problems that could appear with serious development of germline therapy. These include how to decide which genetic alterations to permit. Some would clearly be aimed at correcting harmful mutations, but others might be considered enhancements, rather than treatments, as we will now discuss.

20.2   Saviour siblings and designer babies?

We have already seen how pre-implantation genetic diagnosis (PGD) can be used to identify embryos free of disease-causing alleles, allowing them to be selectively re-implanted into a mother (Section 19.2). This technique can be used to test for diseases such as CF, HD and Duchenne muscular dystrophy. In 2008, the body responsible for overseeing applications of IVF in the UK, the Human Fertility and Embryology Authority (HFEA), after having consulted with the public, allowed PGD to be used for the selection of an embryo free of the BRCA1 mutation.

The value of using PGD for parents to have children that are unaffected by genetic disease and also free from the 'burden' for future generations is clear. Others, however, might ask where the application of such technology stops. For example, whilst some may see the value of using PGD to select a non-Huntington's disease embryo, is such technology suitable for selecting the sex of a child? Does choosing the sex of the child differ if you are trying to avoid an X-linked disease?

One area where this is a heated debate is in the use of PGD to identify embryos with suitable genetic factors so that newborns can act as a source of cells or tissues to treat a sibling brother or sister that already has a disease. In this case, a 'saviour' sibling would be selected by genetically screening embryos generated by IVF and a suitable embryo with matching genes suitable for transplantation selected and re-implanted.

If we identify genes that have effects on many other human characters, from appearance to, perhaps, intelligence, then developing techniques to identify such embryos using PGD or to use gene therapy in the womb on unborn fetuses or through germline gene therapy could, in principle, open the way to wider attempts to influence the phenotype of the next generation. Even if experiments in humans are ethically barred, commercial and medical interests are driving the technology forward in animals (remember those genetically modified sheep in Box 20.1).

So far, the vast majority of those working with these technologies have rejected the idea of such applications and dismissed fears about such 'designer babies' or of 'embryo enhancement', arguing that we know little about the genes involved in such features and because of a wariness of more immediate hazards of gene therapy such as the ones outlined above (Section 20.1.2).

In the last few years, though, arguments in favour of permitting some use of germline therapy have been heard more often.

■ What do you think the argument in favour might be?

☐ Disease alleles would be eliminated.

Although 'bad' genes might be eliminated, might 'good' genes be added, such as those that contribute to intelligence, appearance or personality? Might the technique lead to the reappearance of *eugenics*, the practice of applying selective breeding and forced sterilisation to human populations in the belief that this would improve the human condition, which was seen in the early decades of the 20th century? You might like to think about whether *you* would vote to permit doctors to alter germline cells by inserting a new gene or genes. Would you change your views if the gene or genes in question gave the resulting baby immunity to HIV, the virus that causes AIDS?

In the longer term, the advent of reliable techniques for altering human genes could lead to genuinely new ethical problems that are difficult to outline in conventional terms. Most generally, moral philosophers have nearly always argued about justice in terms of inequalities arising from social differences between individuals — such as wealth, class, education and so on. But if we have the ability to alter or 'correct' inherited characters, we might have to try to work out a theory of justice that covered what we have always regarded as natural differences between individuals.

Activity 20.1   Application of genetic technologies

Now would be a good time to do this activity, which requires you to practise explaining some science.

20.3   Designer drug therapy: pharmacogenetics and pharmacogenomics

Although gene therapy often steals the headlines, a great deal of research currently focuses on applications of genetics in the more conventional therapies of pills and medicines. If we do not need surgery when we get sick, the chances are that we will come away from the doctor with a prescription for a drug or drugs. Much of the time, we will have to go back for a different drug because the first choice does not work properly, or because of side-effects that only some patients suffer. Can the new knowledge of human genes help to avoid some of this waste and delay before we get real help with our symptoms? Many drug companies think it can. Their strategies for making this happen go under the general name pharmacogenetics. There is a strong possibility that it will be pharmacogenetics, rather than tests for genetic diseases, that will lead to genetic tests being used in common medical situations.

The discovery that people have different abilities to taste and smell chemicals and that these differences have a genetic basis was the first indication that there might be important genetic differences in responses to drugs used to treat diseases. **Pharmacogenetics** is the study of genetic variations that control people's reactions to drugs. Subtle differences in body chemistry mean that the same drug may do different things in different people. Drugs usually act on proteins (Chapter 9), and individuals have variant forms of many proteins because they have different variants or alleles of genes. In some individuals, a drug may treat symptoms, as expected. In others, there may be no effect. Even worse, a drug that helps some people can harm others. Scientists have known for over 50 years that reactions to pharmaceuticals can vary depending on people's genotype. But it is only in the past 10 years, with the advances in knowledge resulting from the completion of the human genome sequence, that pharmaceutical companies have been able to think about using pharmacogenetics in their drug design and testing.

We now know that the effectiveness of a number of different drugs depends on patients' particular genotypes. For example, up to 7% of the white population in the USA will get no pain relief from codeine, no matter how much they swallow. Their bodies do not produce the protein that converts codeine into morphine and hence gives it its analgesic effect. Important medical disorders where we know there is a genetically controlled response to certain drugs include asthma, heart disease, schizophrenia, ovarian cancer, breast cancer, and Alzheimer's disease. The development of future genetic tests to identify and personalise drug treatments is highly likely.

Moving from genes that make drugs ineffective to ones that lead to actual harm, it has been estimated that adverse drug reactions (ADRs) are the fourth biggest killer in the USA, after heart disease, cancer and stroke. Not surprisingly, there is much research into those genes that contribute to ADRs to different drugs. It remains to be seen what proportion of common ADRs are caused by genetic factors as opposed to simpler, and more soluble problems such as poor prescribing practice on the part of doctors and drugs interacting with other drugs.

So there are two general approaches to pharmacogenetics. The first involves identifying genes that are disease specific and that alter the effectiveness of a drug's action. The second approach is to identify those genes that predispose to ADRs when drugs are taken; these are often alleles of the gene for a protein called P450, which is produced in the liver.

Although there is a great deal of interest in pharmacogenetics from the pharmaceutical industry, no one is quite sure how it will be used and how many drug prescriptions might be affected by genetic information. There are a number of questions to deal with before pharmacogenetics becomes a common approach for the drug industry. Spend a few minutes thinking about what these might be before reading on.

How will regulators of the drug industry respond?

In most countries, governmental organisations are responsible for overseeing and regulating drug testing and prescriptions. At the moment, any drugs prescribed using pharmacogenetic data have already gone through the normal testing procedures: close scrutiny of documents recording results of animal tests and human trials of the drug in question; clinical trials testing the effectiveness of the drug compared with the existing drug of choice.

But, at some stage, companies will want to put new drugs forward for clinical trials, selecting the patients in the trial from a genetically chosen population. This may mean that drugs will only be licensed for use on a smaller number of potential patients, but at least the drugs will work more effectively and safely. But how will regulators deal with this kind of running trial? The first stage will be the development of a reliable and accurate genetic test to identify the gene variants that are associated with a particular response to drugs. There will need to be pilot studies to determine how drug regulations should change to incorporate pharmacogenetic approaches.

■ What benefits and drawbacks might there be to the pharmaceutical industry in introducing pharmacogenetics?

☐ Benefits might include quicker clinical trials, greater success rate in trials, and fewer ADRs with less bad publicity. Drawbacks include fewer people take a drug therefore lower profits, and expensive technologies.

Will certain groups be excluded?

Although most research into the economics of pharmacogenetics is currently educated guesswork, companies estimate that patient populations might be divided into two groups in the case of each drug. One group (say 60%) will be able to take a particular drug. It will not produce adverse reactions and their bodies will process it effectively. The other group, the remaining 40%, will not be prescribed the drug, either because they will suffer an adverse reaction, or because their body fails to convert the drug into an active form. The question then is, whether it will be profitable for the drug companies to develop products to cover the excluded 40%. Of course, there may already be alternative treatments that the minority can use, but there may also be cases where numbers of people are denied treatment on pharmacogenetic grounds.

Whilst many of the DNA variants that give rise to differing responses to a particular drug are likely to be present in most populations, the frequency of these alleles might differ (Section 17.1). As many drugs are initially targeted at individuals in high-income countries, the development of genetic screening tests for drugs to suit only those populations is a distinct possibility. This could lead to a failure to develop genetic screening and improved targeting of treatments tailored to populations in low income countries. Will efforts be made to produce drugs to fill these gaps?

■ There is a possibility that some pharmacogenetic reactions occur in groups according to their ethnic origin. What are the potential problems with this?

☐ The research may come across as racially motivated. If drugs are not available for certain ethnic groups on genetic grounds, *de facto* discrimination would be in place.

Education issues: do doctors and other health practitioners know enough?

In many high-income countries that offer genetic testing within health provision, the testing is usually provided by specialist genetics teams, but pharmacogenetics assumes the spread of such tests into more common-place medical contexts, such as your local doctors' clinic or health care centre. Are the staff involved in prescribing medicines adequately trained to provide testing for the presence of particular gene variants to check a patient's likely response to a drug or to advise what to do with the information? Some pharmacogenetic tests are like 'traditional' genetic tests, and therefore carry with them issues to do with genetic counselling and individual decision-making (Chapter 19) and also have implications for other family members.

DNA databanks

These are one of the resources that will be needed to develop pharmacogenetic approaches to disease. Databases match DNA samples, usually from blood cells, with anonymous medical records (Section 17.4). These will allow researchers to link particular genetic variants with medical phenotypic features, such as heart disease; but will also be useful for pharmacogenetic research, i.e. identifying genes that influence the effectiveness of drugs or predispose to ADR.

There are many issues thrown up by these databanks, such as the Iceland deCODE experiment (Section 17.4). In the UK, a national project entitled UK Biobank will hold data on 500 000 volunteers aged over 40 years and aims to follow these individuals through their life. One of its aims is to study the association of specific genes or gene variants with the development and progression of common diseases such as cancer, heart disease, diabetes and Alzheimer's disease. Questions can be asked about whether adequate informed consent can be gained from the donors to the databanks. Should pharmaceutical companies be allowed access to the databanks? What happens when they develop a product from the information and patent it?

■ If you would be happy for your own DNA to be held in a research databank, what are the issues that you would want to know more about before donating?

☐ Some issues that you may have thought of are the effectiveness of safeguards on identifying the source of individual samples; the control on access to the data; whether the purposes of the research are clearly defined when the sample is given, and whether they may change later on; how any commercially useful information derived from the database will be used.

Beyond current ideas about pharmacogenetics, where testing is used to prescribe drugs that have already been developed, there is the next step, *pharmacogenomics*. This uses gene and protein structure databanks to actively design drugs on the basis of genetic information. This is potentially a very powerful way of making effective new medicines, but many of the issues outlined above will arise here, too.

Thinking further into the future, along these lines, the topics of toxigenomics and nutrigenomics become possibilities. *Toxigenomics* focuses on those genes that render us susceptible to toxins in the environment (perhaps in a work setting). *Nutrigenomics* is the molecular requirements of nutrition, which seeks to tailor our diets to our genetic make-up and thus improve health. Recall, for example, that individuals vary in their susceptibility to a low intake of folic acid (Section 7.3). Whatever the likelihood of these disciplines actually entering into everyday life, they do present an interesting development in the way in which we see genetics — moving beyond genes to a view that accepts that genes and environment interact and acknowledges that a fuller understanding of human health requires a balance between the two. Of course, a more skeptical position would be to suggest that we do not necessarily need to spend billions of pounds on genomic research when quite simple interventions (better prescribing practice, tighter pollution regulation, more exercise) may well improve human interaction with drugs, environmental toxins and our food.

20.4   'Personal' genomics

Each of our genomes is, of course, personal to only us. Unless we are one of identical twins, the assortment and segregation of DNA variants that occurred during the generation of our parents' gametes (Section 4.3) mixed and distributed a unique set of genes. The idea, therefore, of creating a profile of our own personal set of gene variants and what that might mean for our health is initially rather attractive to many people. Direct genetic tests promoted over the internet, on TV and in the press promise a wealth of genetic knowledge to individuals, usually in return for a small saliva sample and a payment that can range from several hundred to several thousands of UK pounds.

First, we should distinguish the type of tests being offered by most of these companies from tests that are designed to detect the presence of disease-causing alleles we have discussed in relation to prenatal, childhood and adult-onset disease testing (Chapter 19). The genetic tests that are being provided in most 'over-the-counter' products offering a personal genome 'profile' are based upon testing for the presence of up to several hundred DNA variants in many different genes all at once. The variants being screened for are considered by those companies as being genetic risk factors for disease or illness; these tests are offering to identify susceptibility factors (Section 19.4.2) and, as such, come with all the uncertainties we have already discussed. Both genetic and environmental risk factors increase the overall risk of an individual developing a particular disease.

Those offering such genomic profiling services suggest that by providing these profiles, individuals can make lifestyle adjustments or modify their health screening. In many areas of medicine, however, the profiles have received a considerable amount of criticism. In addition to the issues we have already talked about around susceptibility testing, those against the use of such profiles have raised concerns as to the evidence linking certain DNA variants to specific estimates of risk for an individual, how reliable the tests being used are, how confidential the information is and whether the individuals receiving their profiles are suitably informed and capable of interpreting what they are told. We will return to discuss how such genetic information might be handled in Chapter 21.

Activity 20.2   Applications of new genetic knowledge

Now would be a good time to do this activity, which is concerned with issues raised in this section.

20.5   Expectations and prospects of genetics

The wealth of possibilities for medical applications of the new knowledge of human genes is one reason for the constant stream of publicity about the 'power' of genes, and the hope that they offer for people with various disorders. But this emphasis on genes may raise unrealistic expectations, as well as having more subtle adverse effects on people's ideas about themselves, their health, and even their society. We close this chapter by looking at some of the ways in which ideas about genetics influence the way that medical and other problems are dealt with, and whether these changes are always desirable.

We can start with something as routine and apparently innocuous as deciding what disease you have. For example, the discovery of the gene for CF made it possible to carry out a direct, genetic test for the disease (Section 13.1). This was a useful supplement to the more indirect indicators used in the past — like the 'sweat test' that measured the amount of salt in perspiration.

But identifying the gene has also affected the classification of the disease, which at one time was based solely on symptoms. CF symptoms include poor breathing, low weight and reduced fertility — or infertility in the case of the majority of males. When the gene for CF was discovered in 1989, it was revealed that all the symptoms stemmed from problems in moving salt and water across cell membranes. Recall from Section 13.1, that this leads to a build up of thick mucus in the lungs, digestive system and testes — hence the various symptoms.

One form of infertility in males is called congenital bilateral absence of the vas deferens (CBAVD) — the vas deferens are little tubes that are cut when a man has a vasectomy to block sperm transport. CBAVD is common in male CF sufferers, but also occurs in men who do not have any of the other symptoms of CF (particularly the lung problems). A number of these infertile, non-CF men have been found to carry a mutation in the gene associated with CF. (The particular allele or variant only seems to affect their fertility.) These men have now been reclassified by doctors as having a 'mild' form of CF (despite their lack of symptoms). This does nothing for their treatment, but is bad news otherwise. Their insurance status, for instance, has changed from being infertile to having a lethal genetic disease, which normally kills its sufferers by their mid-30s. What seems to have happened here is that by focusing on the genetic diagnosis of disease, researchers have moved medicine away from the idea that it should be about treating individuals, and their symptoms.

We know from earlier in this course just how complicated genes are, and how mistaken it is to think that genes operate on their own, outside of a cellular environment (Chapter 7). At the same time, when we want convenient examples, we still tend to focus on individual genes (the 'gene for heart disease' or the 'gene for Alzheimer's') and emphasise the way in which they will become involved in medicine. And '*a gene for …*' fits into a newspaper headline so much better than '*a gene which in some people is associated with a susceptibility to …*'! So are we running the risk of over-hyping genetics?

There is often a sharp difference between how genetics is portrayed in the media, and what is going on inside laboratories. Aside from 'genes for' headlines, we can see obvious examples of this in the metaphors often used to describe the Human Genome Project: 'biology's moonshot', 'the book of life', 'the human blueprint'. These are simplified or exaggerated representations of what the Human Genome Project tells us. Following the announcement of the draft sequence of the genome in June 2000, a number of scientists pointed out that the genome sequence should be seen as 'just the start', and that the public should not expect miracle cures as a result. This attempt to undercut the razzmatazz that surrounds the genome project may be in part to prevent a crisis of inflated expectations. The human genome continues to attract major headlines almost a decade after the year 2000 headlines (Figure 1.3).

There is also evidence that the effects of genes on individual diseases are reported in ways that over-emphasise their effects. There were more mentions in the British press of genetic links to breast cancer than environmental causes in the year or so after the discovery of a gene associated with breast cancer, *BRCA1*, even though this gene only accounts for a small proportion of cases of the disease.

More broadly, critics suggest that our fascination with genes and inheritance has led to the gene (and the double helix shape in particular) becoming a 'cultural icon'. Pictures and descriptions of the gene have spread widely in popular culture: from comics to films, to television programmes to how we talk down the pub. 'It's in the genes' we say when our poor spelling, or driving, or diet is pointed out. But critics worry that talking about genes in this way will lead to our relying on genes as explanations in inappropriate situations. An example often given was the prediction by the editor of the US journal *Science*, Daniel Koshland, that the sequencing of the human genome would lead to the end of homeless people sleeping on the streets (he didn't explain how). The idea that genes can contribute to a serious social problem such as homelessness assumes a very different chain of causes and effects than the suggestion that a gene causes, say, CF. And thinking of people's problems in terms of genes may obscure other causes, and make social solutions to social problems less likely.

■ Can you recall any examples in the media of the kinds of characters that have been attributed to genetic control, but where the story is almost certainly more complicated?

☐ Alcoholism, aggression, depression, religiosity, homosexuality have all been mentioned. There have even been media sightings of the couch potato gene!

At the individual level we have already seen, in the case of some diseases, that the result of a genetic test may lead patients to adopt an overly fatalistic view of their disorder (Section 19.4.2). Such a response could be dismissed as a result of a lack of understanding about how genes 'really' work. But the fact is that people do not always react in the most rational of ways to such information. One reason for problems such as these may be the power often ascribed to genes in popular discussion.

However, some detailed research on media reporting suggests that the evidence here is not clear-cut. Although it may be true that discussion of genetics is more common in the media now than in the past, analysis of these stories also suggests more sophisticated treatment than in the past. Genetics is represented as complex, and the role of environmental and social factors is often discussed, as, for example, for nutrigenomics (Section 20.3). Thus although we would do well to be aware of the dangers of the misrepresentation of genetics, we shouldn't assume that merely discussing genetics leads to overestimating the power of the 'master molecules'.

■ What kind of research could help to find out what the general public thinks about genetics?

☐ Questionnaires (which can cover large numbers but tend to get simple responses), interviews (which give more details but cover fewer people), group discussion ('focus groups').

Question 20.1

Define (a) somatic gene therapy; (b) germline gene therapy; (c) pharmacogenetics.

Question 20.2

Why is germline gene therapy currently banned in the UK (and many other countries)?

Question 20.3

Why do individuals vary in their response to drugs? (Write one sentence.)

20.6   Summary of Chapter 20

Gene therapy is now under development. Beyond treatment with 'genes as drugs', for fighting cancer, for example, it will involve altering cells' DNA to correct inherited defects. These may be body cells or reproductive cells, referred to as somatic or germline therapy, respectively. Somatic therapy poses few ethical problems, but germline therapy, if it comes, will raise profound new issues for future discussion.

The development of new genetic tests and their application to early embryo screening and PGD raise issues around future selection of desirable genetic features.

Before widespread use of gene therapy, the use of genetic information to 'fine-tune' drug prescriptions is likely to affect medical practice more. Many companies are investing heavily in pharmacogenetics, the study of how individual variations in genotype affect patients' responses to drugs.

As these technologies develop, it is necessary to consider how new genetic discoveries are reported and discussed in the media. Exaggerated depictions of the power of genes may lead to unrealistic expectations for rapid medical application, as well as encouraging restricted thinking about social problems.

As the application of genetic technologies increases, concerns have been raised as to whether low-income countries will be disadvantaged by development of drugs and screening targeted at populations in high-income countries.

Chapter 21
Genetics, public health and health policy

When someone in a high-income country visits their health care provider for a flu jab, to confirm a pregnancy, or to report an unexpected pain, they know that behind him or her stands a vast system for diagnosis, treatment or prevention of disease in the whole population. The details differ from country to country but, frequently tens of thousands of people and large amounts of taxpayers money come together inside a complicated network of institutions to try to achieve what Americans call 'health maintenance'. In contrast, in most low and middle-income countries, the health care system is often significantly smaller and the provision of genetic services might be non-existent.

So far, we have mainly discussed the effects of new genetic knowledge on people, individually or in groups. But the extent of those effects and the speed with which they come about will be set, in large part, by health services. The new technologies — for genetic testing (Chapter 19) or screening (discussed below), pharmacogenetics (Section 20.2) or gene therapy (Section 20.1) — will have to be used by health workers. Governments, or health insurers, will have to pay for these new technologies, and answer for their effectiveness. Policy-makers will have to decide, not just whether these new technologies can be used, but how they will fit in with existing organisations. Consideration must be made for how advances in genetic technologies can benefit those outside of the high-income health care systems, such as in the development of genetically tailored drug treatments. In this final chapter, we look at some of the issues that policy-makers will face.

21.1   Predictive medicine?

Some experts now suggest that new knowledge of human genetics is likely to transform medical practice. They propose three main possibilities:

- Genetics will lead to the classification of diseases on the basis of the underlying genetics or biochemistry, rather than by symptoms (Section 20.5).

- Genetic information will identify people who are likely to respond to drugs, or to be harmed by them (pharmacogenetics; Section 20.3).

- Genetic variation will be a new '*susceptibility factor*', or '*genetic risk factor*', permitting monitoring and early treatment or, perhaps prevention, of an increasing proportion of common, multifactorial diseases, such as coronary heart disease, hypertension, stroke, cancer, diabetes and Alzheimer's disease (Section 19.4.2 and this chapter).

The first two will be important for professionals, but less so for patients' experience of health care. The result of a consultation will still be a diagnosis, or a drug prescription. They may be more accurate or more effective than before, but can be dealt with in familiar ways. It is the third, often summed up as the advent of **predictive medicine**, which could imply much greater changes.

Predictive medicine, if it comes, will be based on a much wider use of genetic testing — for more people, and more disorders. At the moment, there is quite a big gap between the scenarios sketched for the future of genetics-based medicine by forecasters and what the health system is geared up to deliver. As with any new technology applied to health in the context of a complex delivery system, implementation is not going to be simple.

■ What kinds of thing can you think of that influence whether, and how quickly, a new health technology gets taken up?

☐ First, of course, there needs to be demand, from doctors, or patients, or both. Then, in the abstract, introduction of new technologies into health care also typically needs all of the following:

- Demonstration that they work, or are *clinically effective* — through statistically valid trials;

- Demonstration that they are *cost effective* — through economic analysis of trials and other data;

- Standardisation of technology, and *quality control* — through technical definition of standards and, for example, regulation of suppliers or laboratories;

- Allocation of *resources*;

- Recruitment and *education* and *training* (or retraining) for health workers — including specialists, GPs, nurses, counsellors and technicians.

■ What will determine whether the factors above will affect how well genetic technologies might be rolled-out or extended to include or encompass countries of low income?

☐ The most likely pressure will be that of the allocation of resources, as well as the education and training of health care workers in those countries. Of course, other factors will come into consideration as genetic technologies may not be the priority of the health care service possibly overwhelmed with poor nutrition and infectious disease.

In the case of genetic technologies for predicting common diseases, all this is likely to happen along with a move to rethink public health in terms of genetic information. But before discussing how that might come about, let us consider what we have learnt about implementation from the genetic technologies that have already found widespread use.

21.2   Population screening for genetic disease: the precedents

So far, in Chapter 19, we have discussed genetic tests for people who are already concerned that they, their children, or fetus, may be at risk of a particular disorder. But knowing about particular genes, or their effects, also permits **screening** — the search in a population for persons with certain genotypes that are associated with a particular disease for which they do not know they are at risk. Thus the test may be offered to one and all. Until recently, screening programmes have often focused on one gene at a time, or one disease at a time, in cases where a mutated gene poses serious health problems and *something* can be done for those who are found to carry the mutation. What that something is varies with the disorder. We will look first at two different examples, phenylketonuria (PKU) and cystic fibrosis (CF), before moving on to consider sickle cell disease (SCD) screening in Africa and what the outcomes of population screening could be in the long term.

21.2.1   Phenylketonuria

The classic example of population screening is testing new-born babies for PKU. Individuals with PKU fail to make a protein, a certain enzyme (Section 9.2), and develop mental retardation. The absence of the enzyme results in both an accumulation of phenylalanine, which causes the mental retardation, and a deficiency of tyrosine in the body, as shown in Figure 21.1.

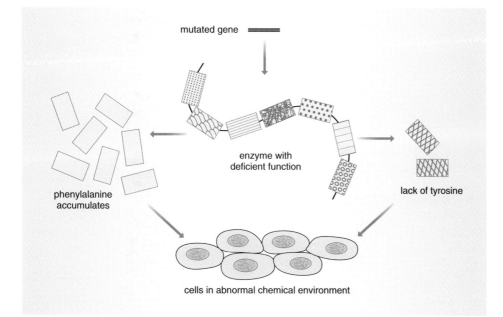

mutated gene

enzyme with
deficient function

phenylalanine
accumulates

lack of tyrosine

cells in abnormal chemical environment

Figure 21.1   A schematic representation of the biochemical consequences of the deficient gene product (enzyme) associated with phenylketonuria (PKU). This enzyme plays a role in the synthesis of amino acids, the building blocks of proteins. Specifically, the enzyme breaks down the amino acid phenylalanine into another amino acid, tyrosine.

■ Because both phenylalanine and tyrosine are constituents of a normal diet, in what way could mental retardation be prevented in babies born with PKU?

☐ By restricting the intake of phenylalanine in the diet.

PKU was the first disease for which treatment in the form of dietary restriction was successfully used. Most children are relatively free of symptoms when given such treatment, hence screening of new-born babies. The technique, first used in 1960, is not strictly a genetic test. No fancy DNA technology is involved, just a needle prick on the baby's heel to produce a blood sample (Figure 21.2). A cheap biochemical test then identifies children who have more phenylalanine than usual in their blood. Only some of these have PKU, and more tests are then needed to identify them more definitely. Babies who do have PKU are put on a phenylalanine-restricted diet, but this is harmful to those without the disorder.

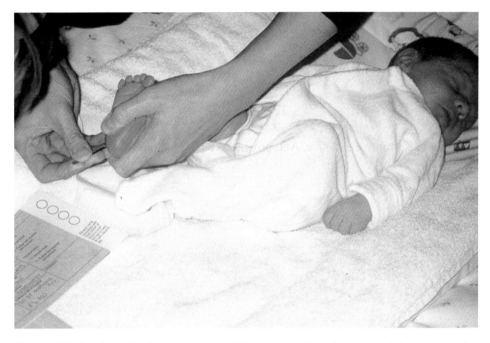

Figure 21.2   Blood taken by heel-prick, commonly called a Guthrie test, used for screening new-born babies for PKU and other disorders.

Not completely straightforward, then. As with all tests there is a possibility of misdiagnosis (of *false positive* results) from the heel-prick test. For those correctly diagnosed, the special diet is both expensive, and unappetising — not an ideal combination for child rearing. And a woman with PKU who bears children herself must also adopt a special diet when she is pregnant. On the whole, though, it works. Although PKU is fairly rare (around 1 in 15 000 live births), it used to account for roughly one per cent of profound mental retardation. Screening for PKU, which is common in most European, American and Australasian countries, has practically eliminated this.

As the test is so cheap, and long-term care of the disabled children so costly, universal screening is also seen as being cost-effective. In the UK, where almost all new-born babies are tested, the money saved is estimated at four times the cost. In 1995, it cost around £800 000 to screen 100 000 babies, but caring for the ones who would have been damaged by excess phenylalanine would have cost over £3 million. The cost saving, of course, goes along with sparing those parents the distress of raising a child with brain damage, but policy-makers like to have both kinds of benefit.

21.2.2   Cystic fibrosis

A different model for the genetic tests of the future is screening for CF. This is a DNA-based test (Section 13.1), which became possible after the gene involved in CF was identified in 1989. CF is a recessive disease, and it should be easy to test to see if prospective parents carry a mutated allele. A simple mouthwash yields enough cells for DNA extraction. If both partners are carriers, they can consider further counselling before conception, and/or prenatal testing of any potentially affected fetus (Sections 19.1 and 19.2).

But even simple disorders are turning out to be not so simple. There are now known to be more than 900 different mutations in the gene for CF (Section 13.1). Many are rare, but even the best (and most expensive) testing currently envisaged would identify only about 85% of couples at risk. Even so, CF screening would probably be cost-effective, too. But the situation is complicated by the fact that the only way to 'prevent' the disorder is for two carriers to avoid having children, or to be prepared for an abortion if a pregnancy turns out to be the one in four that has two mutated copies of the gene for CF. At the same time, treatment for children with CF (Figure 21.3), more and more of whom now live well into adulthood, is getting better, but also more expensive. And prospective parents may, of course, hope that forecasts about gene therapy come true in time to help their child. So once again a potentially straightforward test leads to decisions that are anything but.

21.2.3 Sickle-cell screening

Screening for the DNA mutations that cause sickle cell has been possible for over 20 years, and before that, the direct analysis of the haemoglobin protein had been used as a diagnostic test. Modern day tests are both reliable, inexpensive and in many high-income countries they are routinely used to test or screen high-risk members of those populations through carrier screening and prenatal diagnosis programmes.

Sickle cell disease (SCD) is, of course, one of the commonest genetic diseases to affect countries of sub-Saharan Africa (Section 17.2). If we take Ghana as typical of this region, almost 2% of babies born each year have SCD; when such numbers are extrapolated across sub-Saharan Africa, that equates to almost 0.5 million SCD births per year. In the absence of intensive medical provision typical of high-income countries, less than 5% of SCD newborns would be expected to survive to age 5.

Newborn screening for SCD has been introduced in several African countries, but one of the most successful programmes is in Kumasi in Ghana (Activity 17.1). Since its introduction in 1995, this programme has screened over 225 000 newborns from within Kumasi and in nearby rural communities, demonstrating that screening programmes can be successfully rolled out in sub-Saharan Africa. Similar programmes are in place in The Democratic Republic of Congo and Burkina Faso, with similar success rates. For the Ghanaian programme, early identification of SCD babies has meant that 95% now survive beyond 5 years of age.

The Ghanaian SCD programme sets many precedents but also highlights the important issues that result from introducing genetic screening programmes. For a low-income country, the identification of SCD babies places a huge burden upon the health care system to treat and support these individuals throughout their life. The development of health care worker education for both SCD patient care and genetic testing is now an important priority, as is the establishment of genetic counselling, and carrier and prenatal testing services for a population where as many as 25% of individuals are SCD carriers.

Figure 21.3 A father giving physiotherapy to his son with CF to remove the build-up of mucus from the lungs.

21.2.4   Longer term considerations

Something else to ponder is the effect that screening might have on the longer-term incidence of disease and (not the same thing) on the incidence of gene variants linked to disease. Sometimes, the impact on a disease can be dramatic. Take thalassaemia, a haemoglobin disorder similar to sickle cell disease, in which premature destruction of haemoglobin-containing red blood cells leads to anaemia. It is relatively common in some Mediterranean countries. Like sickle cell disease, it is understood in great detail at the molecular level, but this has produced little in the way of longer-term effective treatment. So screening may be offered to adults to identify carriers. In Cyprus, where there was such a high incidence that the Church endorsed screening before marriage in what are typically close-knit communities, thalassaemia has all but disappeared. In the UK, by contrast, medical services find it harder to reach Cypriot immigrants, as they are scattered among a community of largely low-risk families. As a result, the incidence of thalassemia has only fallen by around 40 per cent.

However, even if marriage avoidance or prenatal diagnosis and abortion were more common, what effect would this have on the frequency of a disease *allele*, as opposed to the incidence of the disease? If the disorder results from a dominant gene, as in HD, then testing and termination tend to eliminate the allele from the population. But then there is no point in mass screening for dominant disorders, such as HD, as families involved already know that the disease is in the family — that is what dominance means. Recall from Section 6.2 that an affected person has an affected parent who in turn had an affected parent. But most of the simple genetic diseases are due to inheritance of two recessive alleles.

■ In recessive disorders, what effect might prenatal diagnosis and selective abortion have on the frequency of the allele in the population?

☐ Not much, since only fetuses with two mutated alleles will be eliminated. Heterozygotes will be spared and, as adults, may pass the mutant allele on to their children.

In fact, the availability of prenatal testing may encourage some couples to have more children than they would have had previously. Similarly, preventing PKU by altering the diet may increase the frequency of the allele concerned, as many of the children who used to be damaged would not have reproduced.

21.3   Scaling up

They may look at dozens of alleles, and involve thousands of people, but existing screening programmes have often been concerned with *individual* genes. But the technologies now being developed will soon permit the recording of hundreds of genes at a time. So-called *gene chips* combine the skills of microchip designers with DNA sequence information to offer rapid, easy-to-read results for an individual covering hundreds of genetic variants. A gene chip is a thin slice of glass about the size of a postage stamp. Stuck to the surface is a grid, each line the width of a human hair and each containing a small sequence of single-stranded DNA, a gene variant. The total DNA can represent either hundreds of gene variants for just one gene, for a number of genes or even a gene set for the entire genome. When a patient's DNA is added to the chip, pieces stick to matching sequences and the rest are washed away. The results are read by means of an electronic scanner and analysed by a computer software program, which identifies the matches within a matter of hours. Gene chips are already in use; for example, the one used for detecting variants in the breast cancer gene *BRCA1* (Section 20.3) can detect any nucleotide change in any position in that gene.

■ If such a DNA chip was developed for CF, what would be the consequences for screening for this disease?

☐ Since at least 900 variants are known, this technology could identify all variants or alleles of the gene (Section 13.1 and 21.2.2) and not just the common ones, making screening much more exact, and eventually foolproof.

When devices like this come into wider medical use, potentially as desktop boxes in the doctor's surgery, then more general DNA profiling of individuals, i.e. identifying variants for many hundreds of genes simultaneously, becomes possible. But what will we do with all this information?

In general, it will not be the kind of information derived from earlier screening programmes, which has been used to choose specific treatments for one known disease, or to offer advice about the chance of a pregnancy producing a child with a particular, usually not very common, disorder. Instead, it is the type of information we obtain from personal genomic profiles (Section 20.4) that add up to a catalogue of individual **susceptibility factors**, or genetic risk factors, or alleles, for the most common, multifactorial diseases — like cancer, heart disease, stroke, diabetes, hypertension or Alzheimer's disease.

And while it may help doctors make predictions, they will be statistical predictions, telling people they are more likely to develop this disease, less likely to develop that, than the population at large. As suggested in Chapter 19 and Section 20.4, this will pose quite different problems of counselling and decision-making than those seen with the single-gene disorders — like CF or HD, for example — which make up the bulk of our experience of genetic testing so far.

The complexities of hereditary influences on breast cancer hint at some of these problems. Spend a few minutes thinking about what might be some of the main problems of counselling and decision-making posed by the discovery of the two genes — *BRCA1* and *BRCA2* — strongly associated with breast cancer, before reading on.

There are a number of features of the link between certain alleles of the two genes and breast cancer that may be hard to convey clearly, to health professionals as well as patients. They include:

• Most breast cancer is *not* associated with either of these two genes — each of which accounts for perhaps 2.5 per cent of the total incidence of the disease.

• Although certain alleles of the genes concerned are associated with an enhanced risk of breast cancer, testing for them does not give a clear-cut result. A positive test does not mean that a woman will definitely get breast cancer. A negative test does not mean that she will definitely not. This is *not* related to inaccuracies in the test — false positive or false negative — it is simply a property of the genetic information. Recall from Chapter 16 that the development of cancer is a multi-step process and involves mutations in at least five or six genes. An individual who inherits a recessive, mutant allele in either the *BRCA1* or *BRCA2* gene is one step nearer to developing cancer than an individual who inherits two normal alleles of both of these genes. The absence of a clear-cut result contrasts testing for a single gene disorder such as HD, where a positive test for a mutant allele means a certainty of developing the disease.

- If a test result is positive, there is no certain route to prevention. Options include so-called prophylactic mastectomy, or breast amputation, along with hysterectomy of womb and ovaries to reduce the risk of ovarian cancer associated with the same genes. Less drastically, regular monitoring may be recommended, but if this is done using X-ray mammography, it may itself increase cancer risks. (Recall from Section 12.3 that X-rays are mutagenic.)

Cancer is a source of particular anxiety to many, so it would probably be wrong to suggest that testing positive increases the numbers of the 'worried well'. They may already have been concerned about breast cancer, especially as many will have seen a high incidence of the disease in their families. What is clear is that publicity about 'cancer genes' increases demand for testing (in contrast with the experience of HD, Section 19.4), and that responsible management of the tests demands a great deal of explanation and counselling. One result has been that some doctors in cancer clinics have had to become genetic counsellors.

This begins to suggest some of the demands that would be produced by more widespread genetic screening that yielded information about health risks and disease probabilities. Another difficulty is that, although more health workers can be trained to help people to deal with information like this, not too much is known about how their customers will respond. We know a certain amount about how people understand probabilities (not too well, on the whole), but much less about how they may react to specific predictions.

■ Can you think of different ways in which people might deal with a genetically-based prediction that they were at high risk, or genetically susceptible, for heart disease in middle age?

□ Research suggests there are two broad classes of reaction: activism and fatalism. Activists try and take control, and strive to minimise their risk by diet, exercise or drugs, and by avoiding smoking. Fatalists, on the other hand, hear the prediction as something they can do little about, and decide they will indulge freely in all the things health-educators say are bad for you — because they are going to get sick anyway.

The trouble is, it is hard to know who will react which way. There are similar uncertainties about other common disorders that are often suggested as candidates for susceptibility, or genetic risk, prediction. If a gene of major effect in the development of schizophrenia is ever identified, for example, some families may feel they are relieved of blame or guilt for the occurrence of the disorder, while others may interpret a test that shows the presence of the gene as showing that they are to blame after all. Again, we do not really know which is more likely.

Activity 21.1   After the genome – Part 2

Now would be a good time to view this video sequence, which requires you to consider some medical benefits arising from knowledge about our genes.

21.4   An example of genetic health care provision: the UK

One way of describing the organisational shift that the advent of predictive medicine would demand is to suggest that genetics would become a general, rather than a specialist service. But it is much easier to say that than to explain how it will happen. For all the publicity about genes, genomes and genetic information, medical genetics is often a very small part of many current health services. As an example of a current system in a high-income country, consider the situation in the UK and how it is facing the task of integrating new genetic technologies and their implications for the existing health care services and regulatory framework.

21.4.1   Genetic testing provision

An indication that a patient or a family has a genetic problem will lead to a referral to one of the regional genetics centres. There are just 25 of them, each catering for a population of between one and five million people. Between them, they dealt with 37 000 amniotic fluid samples from prenatal testing in 1997–98, of which just 4.1% were abnormal. In the same year, a mere 769 DNA tests on adult cells for individual genetic variants, such as those linked with CF or breast cancer, were carried out in UK molecular genetics laboratories. A total of 32 laboratories (including those in the regional centres) are coordinated through the UK Genetic Testing Network (UKGTN) who act to integrate the provision of existing and new services across the UK.

Even at this level, the regional genetics centres are already stretched. Their workload increased by between 50 and 100% between 1991 and 1997, and has gone on increasing since. For example, the number of genetic tests available for use rose from 41 diseases in 1991 to over 350 diseases by 2007. As a specialist service, regional genetics centres are widely regarded as a model of organisation, with specialist doctors typically working alongside counsellors and nurses trained in genetics, and often keeping close links with laboratory researchers.

21.4.2   Newborn screening

Newborn screening is offered to every parent through analysis of a heel-prick bloodspot (Section 21.2.1), although the tests are not compulsory. In all cases, the conditions screened for are those for which a patient would benefit from early intervention. Across the UK in 2010, screening is offered for three disorders that you are familiar with from this course: PKU, CF and SCD. The testing also screens for two other disorders: congenital hypothyroidism (a disorder wherein babies have slow growth and development leading to serious and permanent physical and mental disability that is easily treatable) and a disease called MCADD (a serious disease that prevents babies from digesting fat and which is easily treatable by diet).

Information on these tests is provided to all parents by midwives and health visitors and leaflets are available in over 20 languages common to the UK (Figure 21.4). If a test is positive, follow-up tests are performed and referrals to specialists are arranged and treatment initiated if required. Referrals will likely also be made to discuss options for genetic testing in future pregnancies and for screening of family members.

21.4.3   Health care worker training and education

In the UK, the genetic services have grown up catering for rare disorders such as CF and HD, and not common, multifactorial diseases with a genetic component, which may affect the whole population. So far, policy-makers in the UK have tended to

Figure 21.4   Newborn blood spot screening in the UK: an example of how information can be provided in languages common in the UK population (top) and additional information to help inform those parents when tests have initially been positive (bottom).

assume that the obvious way to bridge this gap is to update health care workers on the new knowledge of human genetics, and get them to advise people about what any new tests might mean. But ask primary health care workers such as doctors and nurse practitioners, and most say they are already much too hard-pressed to take on this work. When you consider that the average consultation with a doctor in the UK lasts a little over five minutes, this is not surprising. Another answer to this problem that is being implemented in the UK is to train more nurses to communicate about genetics, and to integrate genetics with wider health education and public health programmes.

Of course, the latter might simply increase demand for genetic advice, and make it harder for the health services to keep pace. Since 2003, the UK Government has had an ambitious plan to invest heavily in the UK National Health Service (NHS) genetic infrastructure (such as testing centres and new blood screening programmes described above) with a vision to integrate genetic science into NHS practice more fully, both to improve the nation's health and also to create an environment supportive of investment in UK biotechnology firms. Such plans require extensive training of relevant staff in both the application and implications of genetics.

21.4.4   Regulation and consultation

The changes that the UK government are implementing within the NHS are taking place against a backdrop where Government faces demands for stronger regulation of new technologies, both those that pose physical risks and those, like human genetics, that pose what you might call social risks. At the same time, it is trying to respond to calls for more openness in decision-making and advice, and more public consultation about decision-making.

This is affecting the development of new genetic technologies in complex ways. A whole clutch of advisory committees and regulatory bodies have grown up over the last 20 years or so, and their constitutions change quite often. These include the HFEA, which we discussed earlier as the body that approved the first use of BRCA1 testing in PGD (Section 20.2), and the Human Genetics Commission who advise the government on advances in human genetics and how these might impact upon our lives. Several pieces of legislation have been enacted in the UK that restrict access to genetic material and have made genetic testing without consent illegal.

In the UK, the advisory groups are now firmly committed to consulting the public about how far, and how fast, new genetic technologies should be applied, and on what terms. But how much consultation is enough? And what are the best ways to go about it? That, too, is under discussion. There are nearly as many experiments in public consultation under way as there are genetic research programmes.

■ What different ways can you think of to find out what people think about aspects of the new genetics? What might their drawbacks be?

☐ There are lots of ways to try. (i) Opinion poll questions about genetics yield numbers that give a sample of the whole population, but only offer scope for simple answers. (ii) Longer interviews with individuals or groups give much more detail, but may not be representative. (iii) People can be asked to comment on specific proposals, perhaps by writing to the relevant committee, or checking a questionnaire on the internet, but again may not be representative.

Other drawbacks include the difficulty of showing how particular policy decisions relate to what people say, and the problem of making sure they are well-informed about what is at stake. More elaborate exercises, involving lay people cross-examining experts and writing their own recommendations, or having longer discussions before their opinions are recorded, may overcome some of these difficulties.

Research on the public understanding of genes, and the range of responses that application of new knowledge of human genetics is going to require, mean that almost everyone involved in debates about genes and genomes agrees about one thing. There needs to be a big effort to improve public education about genes and what they can do for us — whether it is helping us manage our health or, one day, taking responsibility for future human evolution in the form of designer babies. This course has been one small contribution to that effort.

Question 21.1

(a) What are the differences between genetic testing and genetic screening?

(b) How will future screening for multifactorial disorders differ from the current form of screening for a disorder such as phenylketonuria (PKU)?

21.5   Summary of Chapter 21

When we read about genetics and the future of medicine, we should also think about genetics and the future of health services that have to deliver medical care. The advent of predictive medicine, based on more detailed DNA profiling of individual genotypes using technologies like gene chips, rather than screening for one gene at a time, may shift the relationship between doctor and patient. People will be seeking advice on how to manage their susceptibilities or genetic risks, rather than looking for treatment for an already existing disorder.

This will have implications for how health care is organised — in terms of standardising technologies, informing clients, and training staff. Even in high income countries such as the UK, we know little as yet about how this transition will need to be managed. In low-income countries, even where screening programmes have been established, the ability to extend services will be more limited.

All these changes will occur against a backcloth of public debate and government consultation and decision-making about new genetic technologies. The best ways to involve ordinary citizens in this discussion are still being worked out.

What to do now?

Check Part III of the *Study Guide* for details of what to do next. If you have not already done so, you should also look at the *Assessment Handbook* for advice on when to submit your end-of-course assessment (ECA).

Questions: answers and comments

Question 2.1

Statement (b) is incorrect; the cytosol surrounds the nucleus.

Question 2.2

(a) (i) occurs during the growth phase, and (ii) and (iii) occur during cell division.

(b) The correct order is (i), (iii) and (ii).

Question 2.3

Your answer should include the following essential points, although your wording is likely to be quite different from ours.

'Cell division involves two events: mitosis, in which identical copies of each chromosome are shared out between two progeny cells; and the production of a new cell membrane across the middle of the cell to create two progeny cells from the parent cell.'

We suggest that you continue to write down summaries or definitions of key concepts as you progress through this book.

Question 3.1

(a) Individuals have the same karyotype, although there are slight differences between males and females because of the sex chromosomes. (We will learn about the odd exception later in the course.)

(b) Each individual has a unique genotype (except identical twins) because the combination of alleles is different between individuals.

(c) Each individual has a different phenotype because of their unique genotype and the influence of the environment.

Question 3.2

The incorrect statement is (a); pairs of homologous chromosomes contain the same genes in the same order along the chromosome.

Question 4.1

The ratio is 3 : 2 (i.e. 15 girls to 10 boys); note that we simplified the numbers.

Question 4.2

(a) Meiosis; (b) fertilisation; (c) independent assortment, crossing over; (d) segregation.

Question 4.3

This is because of crossing over, which mixes the genetic material between the members of a homologous pair of chromosomes (as shown in Figure 4.8).

Question 4.4

One possible diagram is shown in Figure 4.9. This is a flow diagram, which clearly shows the order in which the different events occur.

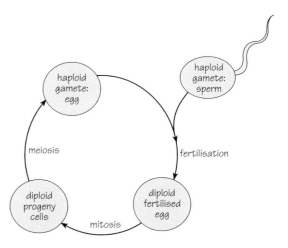

Figure 4.9   A flow diagram showing the events in reproduction.

If you found that drawing this diagram helped you to understand and remember important ideas, remember that you can represent text in the form of diagrams in any notes that you make, even when this is not explicitly suggested as part of a question.

Question 4.5

Cell division involving mitosis results in two progeny cells with identical genetic material, whereas cell division involving meiosis results in gametes with the haploid number of chromosomes that are genetically different from each other because of segregation, independent assortment and crossing over.

Question 4.6

You would not expect any difference in chromosome number. The chromosomes that end up in the egg and sperm that successfully undergo fertilisation arise naturally within gamete-producing cells and will therefore have undergone the normal processes of meiosis. Upon IVF, the resulting chromosome number is restored to the diploid number and the embryo carries a mixture of both parents' genetic material.

Question 5.1

The X chromosomes carry the genes responsible for X-linked characters. A son inherits the Y chromosome from his father and an X chromosome from his mother. The X chromosome of the father will be transmitted to daughters and not to sons.

Question 5.2

The matches between the descriptions and terms are as follows: (a) (iv); (b) (i); (c) (v); (d) (iii); (e) (vi); (f) (ii).

Question 5.3

(a) The mating diagram is shown in Figure 5.4. The children would have either the A phenotype (genotype *A O*) or the B phenotype (genotype *B O*). (Note that the genotypic ratio of this mating again results from the separation of the two copies of a gene to different gametes in equal numbers, and because gametes combine at random at fertilisation.)

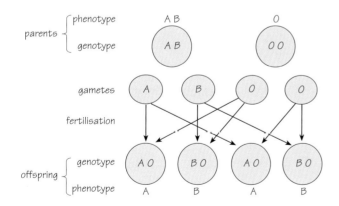

Figure 5.4   A mating diagram for Question 5.3. Note that we have omitted the chromosomes, and you might like to try this in future.

(b) The children have phenotypes that are different from those of both of the parents.

Question 6.1

The mating diagram for this couple is shown in Figure 6.8; you may have drawn yours differently, which is acceptable as long as the genotypes and the relationships between individuals are clear.

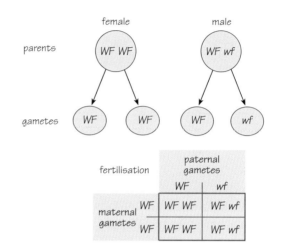

Figure 6.8   A mating diagram that provides the answer to Question 6.1. Note that *WF* represents the dominant allele (white forelock phenotype).

The predicted genotypic ratio of the children is 1 *WF WF* : 1 *WF wf*; and the children will all have the white forelock phenotype, since they all carry at least one dominant *WF* allele.

Question 6.2

(a) The probability is $\frac{1}{2}$, because he will inherit one or other of his father's alleles, only one of which is the Huntington's disease allele.

(b) The probability of his younger sister developing symptoms is the same as his own probability because the outcome of each fertilisation is independent of the first.

Question 6.3

(a) The pattern is characteristic of a dominant disorder in that the two affected parents have an affected child and an unaffected child. If the disorder was recessive, the two affected parents could only have affected children.

(b) Both parents must be heterozygotes since they have a child that is unaffected who must be homozygous recessive.

(If you found this question difficult, try drawing a mating diagram.)

Question 6.4

(a) (i) Tay–Sachs disease is recessive because parents and grandparents are unaffected.

(ii) The genotypes of the individuals, as far as can be determined, are given in Figure 6.9a.

These are the stages we adopted.

1 We used a different layout here by adding the genotypes directly to the pedigree charts.

2 We assigned *t* to the allele for Tay–Sachs disease and *T* to the non-disease allele because it is dominant.

3 We began with the affected individuals, who must be homozygous for the disease allele.

4 The parents of the affected individuals, i.e. 1 and 2, and 9 and 10, must be heterozygous because they are phenotypically normal.

5 All unaffected individuals must have at least one *T* allele.

6 Note that individuals 9 and 10 are cousins; their parents (individual 5 and individual 7) are brother and sister. Hence it is possible that both individuals 5 and 7 are heterozygous *T t* , having inherited the *t* allele from either individual 1 or 2, but we cannot be sure of this.

This pedigree chart shows that a recessive phenotype can skip a generation.

(b) (i) Familial hypercholesterolaemia is dominant because every affected individual has a parent who is also affected. (ii) The genotypes of the individuals, as far as can be determined, are given in Figure 6.9b.

1 We assigned *F* to the disease allele and *f* to the non-disease allele because it is recessive.

2 All unaffected individuals must be homozygous recessive *ff*.

3 All affected individuals must have at least one dominant allele to manifest the disorder.

4 Since affected individuals in generations II and III have one parent who is homozygous recessive they each must have inherited one recessive allele.

5 It is not possible to determine the complete genotype of the mother in generation I; she might be homozygous or heterozygous for the dominant disease allele.

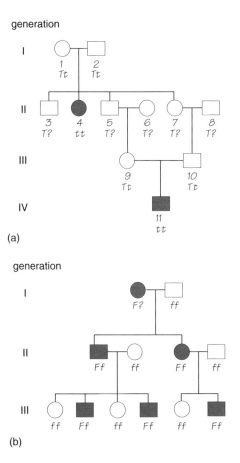

Figure 6.9 Two human pedigrees (a) Tay–Sachs disease and (b) familial hypercholesterolaemia, showing the genotypes of individuals. Answer to Question 6.4.

Question 7.1

(a) The number of men measured is plotted on the vertical axis.

(b) Height is plotted on the horizontal axis, and this is measured in centimetres (cm).

(c) More men had a height less than 175 cm, because if you add together all the numbers represented by all the bars of less than 175 cm they give a higher total than the numbers represented by all the bars of more than 175 cm.

Question 7.2

(a) 35 identical twin-pairs had a height difference of 1 cm.

(b) The majority of identical twin-pairs differ in height by only 1 cm, only two or three twin-pairs differ by as much as 5 cm or 7 cm and the remaining twin-pairs differ by about 3 cm.

(c) Yes, the difference is greater (what matters here is the average difference in height for each twin-pair). For non-identical twins, less than half have a height difference of only 1 cm, and nearly half have a height difference of 5 cm or more, with some as much as 15 cm. Also the *range* of height differences is much greater for non-identical twins than for identical twin-pairs.

Question 7.3

Multiple alleles are alternative forms of the same gene at one locus. Multifactorial inheritance of a character involves a number of genes, each at a different locus and each with a small effect on the phenotype, and has a strong interaction with the environment.

Question 8.1

This is an example of how the maternal nutritional environment affects the development of the fetus. The development of spina bifida may be linked to the deficiency occurring at sensitive periods in development. It could be corrected by giving dietary supplements to pregnant women. For example, in January 2000, the UK Government required the addition of folic acid to bread. However, the fact that not all women with a deficiency give birth to an affected fetus shows that genetic factors might also be involved.

Question 8.2

The correct response is (e). The frequency of club-foot in both twins of a pair is much higher among identical twins (who have identical genes) than non-identical twins (who have only some of their genes in common). This suggests there is some genetic influence on the development of club-foot. However, the fact that in the majority of identical twins, only one twin manifests the character, suggests that environmental factors within the uterus also play a role.

Question 9.1

The incorrect statement is (b). There are 20 amino acids but they may not all occur in a particular protein.

Question 10.1

(a) 100 bases would form 50 complementary base pairs.

(b) Since C always pairs with G, the number of G bases is the same as the number of C bases, i.e. 30.

(c) and (d) Sixty of the 100 bases are either C or G, so the remaining 40 bases are either T or A. As A always pairs with T, then half this number, i.e. 20, are T and 20 are A.

Question 10.2

One student rephrased the idea of semi-conservative replication as follows.

> The two strands of the DNA separate, and two new strands are produced, one that 'matches' (complementary bases) each of the original strands. Thus after replication each DNA double helix has one original strand and one new strand.

There are other ways of rephrasing the idea — this is only one example. The important thing is to *use your own words* so that the meaning is clear to you.

Question 10.3

(a) Figure 10.9 is the completed version of Figure 10.8. Note that the sequences must be the same in the two daughter, or replicating, DNA double helices, so the bases can be deduced from the limited information provided in Figure 10.8. Here is one example. One member of the base pair at the bottom right is C. Since C always pairs with G, the missing base must be G. Because the two replicated double helices are identical, the missing pair at the bottom left must also be C–G.

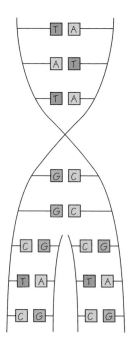

Figure 10.9 Completed Figure 10.8 showing base-pairing in part of a double-stranded DNA molecule during replication.

(b) Since the DNA shown in Figure 10.8 is replicating, the cell must be at the growth stage. This is the stage between two cell divisions during which the DNA, and hence the chromosomes, become replicated (Section 2.2).

Question 11.1

(i) Descriptions (a) and (e) apply to both DNA and RNA.

(ii) Description (c) applies to DNA but not RNA.

(iii) Descriptions (b) and (d) apply to RNA and not DNA.

Question 11.2

The completed sentences are as follows (missing words are shown in italics).

(a) The enzyme *RNA polymerase* copies a stretch of DNA into RNA in a process known as *transcription*.

(b) Only the *template* strand of DNA is 'read' in the process of RNA synthesis.

(c) There are three different types of RNA molecule: *mRNA*, *tRNA* and *rRNA*.

(d) The transfer of information from the mRNA base sequence to the amino acid sequence of a protein is known as *translation*.

(e) The mRNA sequence has a triplet code, and each triplet is known as a *codon*.

(f) *tRNA* binds to both an amino acid and mRNA; it attaches to the latter via its three-base *anticodon*.

Question 11.3

(a) The mRNA sequence will be:

AUG–GAG–CCA–GUA–GGG A…

(b) The amino acid sequence will be:

Met–Glu–Pro–Val–Gly–…

Notice that this is only the start of the amino acid sequence. We cannot say what the last 'A' base might be part of the code for, because two-thirds of the codon is missing.

(c) The DNA sequence of the non-template strand is:

ATG–GAG CCA–GTA–GGG–A….

Notice that mRNA has the same sequence of bases as the non-template strand, except that it contains U in place of T.

Question 12.1

(a) Chromosome mutation; (b) gene mutation; (c) mutagen; (d) gene mutation.

Question 13.1

A heterozygote, with one normal copy of the gene and one mutant copy, makes both proteins — normal CFP and defective CFP. Even with only half the amount of normal CFP, the individual has sufficient normal CFP to ensure transport of salt and accompanying water across cell membranes.

Question 13.2

(a) A DNA test would be useful to confirm whether *cf* mutations are present. The fact that she has a non-standard phenotype does not mean that she has not got CF.

(b) There are a huge number of different *cf* alleles and thus if Jane does not have the usual mutation, she may have other disease alleles, some of which might be difficult to detect.

Question 14.1

The completed sentences are as follows (the inserted words and phrases are italicised).

(a) An *intron* is a non-coding sequence of bases within a split gene.

(b) *Conserved gene sequence* describes the similarity between gene sequences in different types of organism.

(c) *Repetitive DNA* is a DNA sequence that is repeated many times in the genome.

(d) An *exon* is a coding region of bases within a split gene.

Question 14.2

- Speed up the process of isolating human genes.
- To be able to maximise use of 'model' laboratory organisms that are used to study human disease.
- Gain clues about human biology and biological processes in humans.
- Develop and fine-tune the procedures used in the sequencing of the human genome.
- To accelerate study of pathogens that could provide human health benefits.

Question 15.1

Statement (a) is incorrect as the centromere is composed of clustered repetitive DNA. Statement (f) is also incorrect because DNA variants are found scattered across the genome.

Question 16.1

Proto-oncogenes are genes that promote cell growth and cell division; unmutated tumour-suppressor genes block cell growth and division.

Question 16.2

Spontaneous errors occur all the time in cells that are replicating their DNA (Chapter 12), but these errors are normally removed by repair enzymes. If the repair system is defective, errors will go unrepaired and mutations will accumulate. The more frequent the mutations, the more likely that they will occur in proto-oncogenes and tumour-suppressor genes.

Question 16.3

Some people are more susceptible than others to lung cancer because of the particular variants of genes in their genotype. Some individuals convert the chemicals in tobacco into forms that can be excreted from the body, and other individuals convert them into substances that promote cancer.

Question 17.1

There are three main lines of evidence. One is the similarity of the global distributions of the Hb^S allele that causes sickle-cell disease and of malaria, despite the fact that homozygous $Hb^S Hb^S$ individuals die before they reproduce. This suggests that natural selection favours heterozygotes, who pass on both Hb^A and Hb^S alleles to the next generation. A second is the observation that the *Plasmodium* responsible for malaria is not able to survive and reproduce as well in sickle-shaped cells as it does in normal red blood cells. Thus $Hb^A Hb^S$ individuals have a greater resistance to malaria than do $Hb^A Hb^A$ individuals. Finally, the frequency of heterozygotes in black Americans of African descent where there is no malaria, has decreased compared with that in present-day equatorial Africa, because heterozygotes are no longer at an advantage compared with $Hb^A Hb^A$ homozygotes.

(Advice on writing a summary is given in Activity 16.1 in the Study Guide.)

Question 17.2

(a) The high frequency of porphyria in South Africa does not appear to be due to natural selection since there is no survival advantage to the individual who has it. Thus the high frequency is best explained as being due to chance events.

(b) The evidence suggests that the allele involved in thalassaemia is maintained by natural selection in certain regions of the world, particularly those in which malaria is, or was, rife. Thalassaemia seems to work in a similar way to sickle-cell disease, conferring an advantage on carriers in that it gives some resistance to malaria. The process of natural selection preserves the thalassaemia allele in populations exposed to malaria because carriers have a greater reproductive success over both types of homozygote.

Question 19.1

Benefits: susceptibility testing would enable an individual to avoid certain environmental factors such as fatty diets, if implicated (Section 8.2), and change their lifestyle, perhaps by taking more exercise.

Problems: 'genetic pessimism', in that individuals may think that they are going to develop the disease anyway; confidentiality; future employers may discriminate against the individual; possible difficulties with insurance cover; worry of living with the known risk; availability of test because of cost.

Question 19.2

The first three are diagnostic tests carried out on DNA of individuals to determine the presence of disease alleles: pre-natal testing uses fetal tissue; susceptibility testing examines individuals for the presence of a mutation in a gene known to confer a susceptibility to a multifactorial disease; pre-symptomatic testing gives individuals, children or adults, results prior to the onset of symptoms of the disease. Both pre-natal testing and pre-symptomatic testing are predictive, in that they predict a likely outcome, whereas susceptibility testing is not predictive in that it cannot inform people whether they will get the disease or not (it can just indicate whether they might have a higher than average risk of developing the disease). Genetic counselling is the communication of information about the disorder and the consequences of a positive test, without being directive.

Question 20.1

(a) Somatic gene therapy is the transfer of normal copies of genes into the somatic cells of a patient in such a way that the new DNA does not enter the eggs or sperm.

(b) Germline gene therapy is the insertion of normal copies of genes into the gametes so that the new DNA would be present in all the cells of the person so treated.

(c) Pharmacogenetics is the study of genetic variations that control people's reactions to drugs.

Question 20.2

Germline gene therapy carries the risks of accidental introduction of new mutations and an uncertainty of whether or how it would interfere with normal gene functioning; fears about 'designer babies'.

Question 20.3

Drugs usually act on proteins, and individuals have different forms of many proteins because they carry alleles, or variants, of genes.

Question 21.1

(a) Genetic testing is provided for people who are already concerned that they, their children, or fetus, may be at risk of a particular disorder. Screening is the wide-scale search to discover who may be at risk of genetic disease. The test is offered to everyone in a population.

(b) Current screening programmes focus on one gene at a time, or one disease at a time, such as PKU, where a mutated gene poses serious health problems and some form of treatment (such as restricted diet) or prevention can be offered. Screening in the future will be based on DNA profiling, which examines many variants for hundreds of genes, in order to identify susceptibility factors, or genetic risk factors, for common, multifactorial diseases.

Appendix 1
How the human genome was sequenced: molecular cloning and the technique of DNA sequencing

This appendix provides, for those who are interested, an outline of how the DNA fragments from the human genome were isolated and their sequence obtained and an explanation of the technique of DNA sequencing. Study of it is optional.

A1   Subdividing and sequencing the genome

As Section 14.2 revealed, we had a good idea of the content of the genome before the HGP began, but the definitive description will depend on knowing the actual DNA sequence of each chromosome. How is the genome sequence obtained?

The 23 *pairs* of chromosomes (Sections 3.1 and 4.1.1) actually represent two *copies* of the human genome. Thus each cell contains around 6 000 000 000 bp of DNA, packaged into the 23 pairs of chromosomes. Recall from Section 10.1 that the term base pair refers to complementary pairs of bases that sit within the core of the double helix (Figure 10.5).

Each chromosome can be considered as a very long DNA molecule, ranging from over 200 million bp to about 33 million bp arranged in a linear sequence (Figure 10.7).

In this section we examine how researchers handle such large molecules experimentally, how they determine the sequence of base pairs, and, finally, how they store the huge amount of resulting sequence information.

A1.1   Molecular cloning

Handling large DNA molecules such as human chromosomes is made possible by cutting them into small pieces or fragments. A chromosome is reduced to a series of smaller fragments using the technique of molecular cloning (Box A1), by which fragments of a DNA molecule can be isolated and replicated many times. *Molecular clones* are identical DNA sequences that are all produced from the same original fragment. Many copies of a fragment are needed for use in experiments to determine the sequence of bases in the fragment.

The upper limit to the size of DNA fragments that can be cloned in this way is, broadly speaking, between 250 000 and 1 million bp. Thus, the human genome was broken down into many tens of thousands of fragments, of between 100 000 and 500 000 bp, with an average size of about 250 000 bp, which were cloned.

Box A1 Molecular cloning

The term 'cloning' has received much publicity recently in the context of whole organisms. *Molecular cloning*, generally referred to in brief as 'cloning', is a means of copying fragments of DNA to produce a large number of identical copies of one original fragment. The technique relies on the ability to cut large DNA molecules into smaller pieces by means of special proteins that cut double stranded DNA.

After the chromosomes have been cut, a fragment is inserted into a bacterial cell, as shown in Figure A1. The bacterium treats the human DNA just like its own, and copies it each time it divides. *Bacteria* are easy to grow in the laboratory, so large numbers, each containing a copy of the same human DNA fragment, can be obtained. The human DNA can then be extracted from the bacteria in the same way that it is extracted from human cells, ready for further investigation.

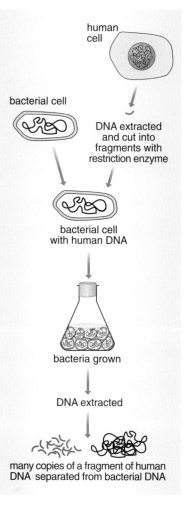

Figure A1   The technique of molecular cloning using bacteria to copy a fragment of human DNA. This process enables large amounts of the human DNA to be extracted for experiments.

Although these fragments vary in size, we will refer to them from now on as 250 000 bp fragments. These fragments were then cut into smaller fragments of about 2000 bp, which were in turn cloned in order to produce a sufficient quantity for sequencing studies (Figure A2).

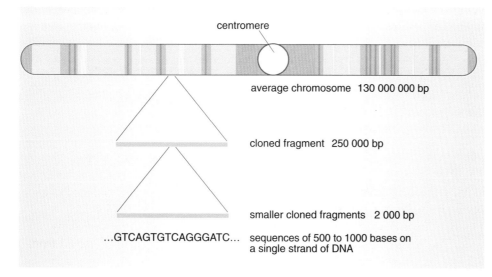

Figure A2   Chromosomes containing many millions of base pairs of DNA are cut into fragments of between 100 000 and 500 000 bp, on average about 250 000 bp. Each of these fragments is further cut into fragments of 2000 bp, which are then sequenced.

A1.2   DNA sequencing

The technique of DNA sequencing is based on the principle that DNA fragments that differ in length by just one base can be separated from one another by gel electrophoresis as you saw in Box 13.1.

The method of sequencing is complicated. However, the details are not so important here as the principle. In order to appreciate how the technique works we need to recall features of DNA structure and the process of DNA replication. In Chapter 10 you learnt how DNA is replicated by successive linkage of nucleotides on a single-stranded template molecule (Figure 10.6).

■   What is the difference between a nucleotide and a base?

☐   A nucleotide consists of phosphate, a sugar and a base, whereas a base (A, G, C and T) is one component of a nucleotide (Figure 10.3).

The starting point is identical copies of a single-stranded DNA fragment, which provides a template for DNA synthesis. This could be from the small cloned DNA fragments (A1.1) or from a PCR reaction (Box 13.1). During replication, the sugar component of one nucleotide links to the phosphate of the next nucleotide in the sequence to form the sugar–phosphate ribbon of the new strand, as shown in Figure A3a. The process of DNA replication can be carried out in a test-tube to which has been added a single-stranded DNA fragment, the four nucleotides (each with the base G, A, T or C) and the enzyme DNA polymerase. If the aim of the replication is to sequence DNA, a small amount of defective nucleotide is also added to the test-tube. The defect lies in the structure of the sugar molecule. DNA polymerase does not discriminate between a normal and a defective nucleotide. Thus the defective nucleotide can be incorporated into the growing complementary strand of DNA in place of a normal nucleotide, but it blocks further growth because it is unable to form a link with the phosphate of the subsequent nucleotide. This is shown in Figure A3b for the nucleotide with

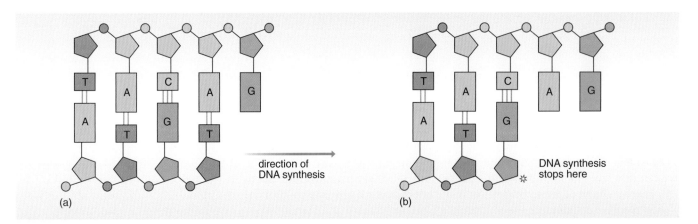

(a)   direction of DNA synthesis   (b)   DNA synthesis stops here

Figure A3   DNA replication. (a) The sugar of one nucleotide links to the phosphate of the next nucleotide added to the growing strand. The phosphate, sugar and base that make up a nucleotide are the same colour in order to show the position of links between individual nucleotides in the sugar–phosphate backbone. (b) Sequencing relies on defective nucleotides in which the sugar component is unable to link with the phosphate of the next nucleotide added. The defective nucleotide here has base G, and the defect lies in the structure of the sugar molecule at the position indicated by an asterisk.

base G. Consequently, the addition of nucleotides occasionally stops at different places along the original fragment.

In a sequencing experiment, such incomplete replications are carried out in four separate test-tubes, each one containing copies of the same fragment of single-stranded DNA, the four normal nucleotides, DNA polymerase and a small amount of defective nucleotide. In one test-tube, a defective nucleotide with base G is added, and in the other tubes defective nucleotides with bases A, T and C, respectively, are added (Figure A4a). In tube G for example, the replication of the strands begins at the same place at one end. But the defective nucleotide

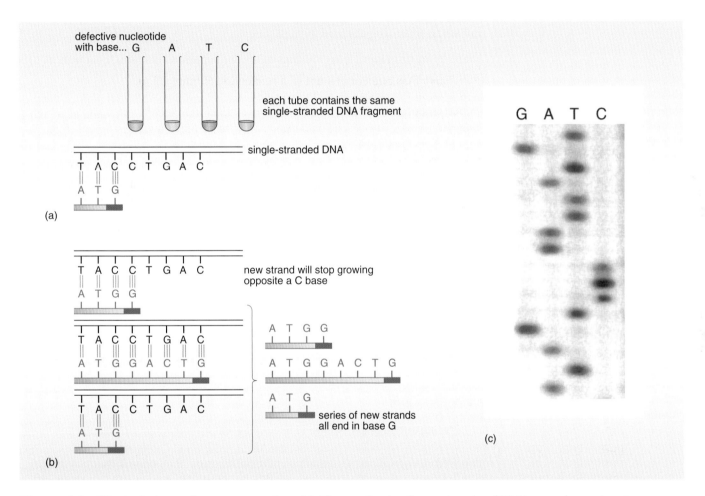

Figure A4 The technique of gene sequencing. (a) The synthesis of new strands of DNA complementary to single-stranded templates. In each of the four tubes, synthesis stops after the addition of a defective nucleotide specifically with base G, A, T or C, respectively. In the example illustrated, replication stops after the addition of a defective nucleotide with base G. (b) A series of fragments of different lengths is produced in each tube, and for any given tube every fragment ends in a nucleotide with the same base. In the example here, replication stops after the addition of a defective nucleotide with base G. (c) The series of DNA fragments generated in each tube are separated into single strands at high temperature. The strands in tube G are placed on one end of a 'lane' of the gel, and those of tubes A, T and C are placed in three adjacent lanes. The strands are separated by gel electrophoresis. Only the newly synthesised strands can be visualised on a piece of X-ray film because the nucleotides are radioactively labelled before being added to each test-tube. Each band is a DNA fragment of a specific number of nucleotides. The sequence is read by noting in which lane each band lies, starting at the bottom and moving band by band upwards.

with base G is occasionally incorporated into the growing DNA strand in place of the normal nucleotide with base G. When this happens, the replication of that strand cannot continue. Since normal nucleotides are present, replication does not always terminate at the first G, for example. In fact, it may continue until several hundred nucleotides have been added before eventually a defective nucleotide is incorporated. This means that in the end there is a mixture of strands of different lengths, and their lengths will depend on the position of the defective nucleotide with base G. In tube A the defective nucleotide with base A is occasionally incorporated, and so on. The result is a series of DNA fragments of different lengths, although for any one tube the fragments all terminate in the same base, G for example, as shown in Figure A4b. In reality, multiple copies of fragments of various lengths are produced in each tube.

These DNA fragments from the four tubes are separated into single strands at high temperature, and analysed by gel electrophoresis. The family of strands generated in the tube containing the defective nucleotide with base G are placed on one end of a 'lane' of the gel, and the families generated in each of the tubes A, T and C are placed at the end of the three adjacent lanes. Recall from Box 13.1 that small fragments move through the gel faster than large ones, and thus reach the far end of the gel quicker. Only the newly synthesised strands can be visualised on a piece of X-ray film because the nucleotides are radioactively labelled before being added to each test-tube. A pattern of bands is produced, as shown in Figure A4c, from which the DNA sequence of the newly synthesised strand can be read. Each band represents a DNA fragment of a specific number of nucleotides. The sequence is read by starting at the bottom of the gel and moving upwards. Notice that each of the four lanes of bands is labelled with the base at which replication stops. The band shown in the first position in Figure A4c, lies in the A lane (i.e. the lane containing the DNA molecules that end in a defective nucleotide with base A), so the first nucleotide in the sequence is A. The next band, corresponding to the DNA molecule that is one nucleotide longer than the first, is in the T lane, so the second nucleotide is T and the sequence so far is AT.

■   What is the sequence of nucleotides that has been run on the gel in Figure A4c?

☐   The sequence reads: ATAGTCCCAATTATGT.

This is the sequence of the newly synthesised strand. The complementary bases in the double helix, of course, can readily be determined from this sequence of bases to give the base pairs of the double helix. Figure A3c shows a sequence of only 16 bases, so you can appreciate the need for the technique to be automated in order to sequence the 3 000 000 000 bp of the human genome. This method uses a different coloured dye for each of the four nucleotides in the DNA and robotic technology. A laser scanner reads the results, which are displayed in colour, as shown in Figure A5.

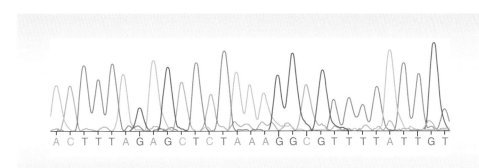

ACTTTAGAGCTCTAAAGGCGTTTTATTGT

Figure A5   Part of a printout from an automated sequencing machine. The sequence is represented by a series of peaks, one for each nucleotide position. The results are displayed in colour, one for each of the four nucleotides, and are read from left to right. In this example, a blue peak is a nucleotide with base G, orange with base A, red with base T and green with base C.

Without the use of automated sequencing machines, workers on the HGP would have taken many more years to determine the sequence of the human genome. By 2010, the technique of sequencing had progressed so that many thousands of such reactions could be analysed at once and robotics meant that the number of sequences that could be obtained was many millions more than was achievable during the sequencing projects that first took place in the HGP. This speed of obtaining a DNA sequence means that obtaining a complete human genome sequence is likely to be routine in the near future.

Acknowledgements

Grateful acknowledgement is made to the following sources for permission to reproduce material in this book:

Cover image

© Lawrence Lawry/Science Photo Library.

Figures

Figures 1.2 and 3.1: CRC Institute of Cancer Studies, University of Birmingham; *Figure 2.2f*: Andrew Syred/Science Photo Library; *Figure 2.5*: Biophoto Associates; *Figure 3.2*: Professor Ferguson-Smith; *Figure 3.3*: Biophoto Associates/Science Photo Library; *Figure 3.4*: Mike Levers; *Figure 4.1a*: Francis LeRoy/Science Photo Library; *Figure 4.1b*: Science Photo Library; *Figure 7.1*: Marc Henrie/Animal Picture Library; *Figure 7.5*: Stern, C. (1973) *Principles of Human Genetics,* W. H. Freeman and Company. The University of Chicago Press; *Figure 8.1* left: Science Photo Library; *Figure 8.1* right: Biophoto Associates/Science Photo Library; *Figure 10.1*: A. Barrington-Brown/Science Photo Library; *Figure 12.1*: From *An introduction to genetic analysis* by A. J. F. Griffiths, J. H. Miller, D. T. Suzuki, R. C. Lewontin, and W. M. Gelbart © 1993 by W. H. Freeman and Company. Used with permission; *Figure 12.3*: Hattie Young/Science Photo Library; *Figure 12.4*: Biophoto Associates/Science Photo Library; *Figure 12.5*: Jones, S. et al. (eds) (1992) *The Cambridge Encyclopaedia of Human Evolution,* © 1992 Cambridge University Press; *Figure 15.2*: From www.ensembl.org/Homosapiens/index.html; *Figure 15.3*: Mark Hirst; *Figure 17.2*: Eye of Science/Science Photo Library; *Figure 21.2*: Science Photo Library; *Figure 21.3*: Camilla Jessel FRPS.

Tables

Table 7.1: Stern, C. (1973), *Principles of Human Genetics,* W. H. Freeman and Company. The University of Chicago Press.

Every effort has been made to contact copyright owners. If any have been inadvertently overlooked, the publishers will be pleased to make the necessary arrangements at the earliest opportunity.

Index

Entries and page numbers in **bold** are glossary terms. Page numbers in *italics* are terms that appear mainly, or wholly, in figures or tables.

A

ABO blood group 38–9, *111,* 145
abortion (termination) 30, 161
 and cystic fibrosis 187
 and prenatal diagnosis 159
 and recessive disorders 188
 spontaneous 100, 160
active gene 91
activism 190
adenine (**A**) **75,** 76, 77, *78*
 in RNA 83–4
adult polycystic kidney disease 162
adult testing 156, 162–4
adverse drug reactions (ADRs) 175, 176
advisory groups 193
aflatoxin 97
Africa
 cystic fibrosis 46
 Huntington's disease 43
 malaria *148*
 porphyria 153
 sickle cell anaemia 147, *148,* 149–50,
  165, 187
 thalassaemia 153
age
 and cancer 136
 late-onset disorders 162, 163–4
 maternal, and Down's syndrome *99,*
  100, 156
AIDS 131, 174
alanine *90*
albinism *128,* 129
alcohol
 and coronary heart disease 65
 during pregnancy 62–3
alleles 17, 28
 in cystic fibrosis 47, 49, 101–5, 145
 dominant and recessive 33–6, 37
 in Huntington's disease 106–8

 multiple 38–9
 susceptible 62, 142, 164
 in sickle cell disease 147, *148, 149,*
  150
 see also DNA mutation; **genes;**
  variants
Alzheimer's disease 123–4
amino acids 70, 72–3
 altered sequence of *95, 96*–7
 codons 89, *90*
 in translation 85–8
 see also **proteins**
amniocentesis 30, 156, 160
amplification, DNA 102–3, 107
anticodon 86
APP gene 123–4, *126*
arginine *90*
arteries, plaque deposits 63, *64*
Asians
 ABO blood group 145
 cystic fibrosis 46
 height 59
 Huntington's disease 43
 Japanese cancer, incidence of 141
 malaria *148*
asparagine *90*
aspartate *90*
atherosclerosis 63, 64
automated sequencing, printout *207*
autosomes 16

B

bacterial cells
 in genetic modification 169, 170
 in molecular cloning *203*
bacterial genome *111,* 117, 118, 119
base-pairing 76–7, *78, 199*
 in DNA replication *199*

 human genome 112
 in transcription *84*
 in translation 86
bases 75–6, 77, *78*
 codons 89, *90*
 gene mutation *95, 96*–7
 in the *OCA2* gene *128*
 in RNA 83–4, 85
 variants 128–9
binding sites 71, 97
biobanks 152
biosociality 166–7
birth weight 56–7, 65
blood clotting 94, 170
blood groups
 ABO 38–9, *111,* 145
 Rhesus 33–5, 41, 55, 93
blood transfusion 33, 38
bone marrow cells 171, 172
bowel (colorectal) cancer 141, 162
bp 112
 see also **base-pairing**
BRCA1/2 gene 165, 173, 180, 189–90
breast cancer 141, 165, 180
 hereditary influences on 189–90

C

CAG codons 106–8
Canavan's disease 166
cancer 135
 environmental factors 141–2
 genetic change and 136–40
 genetic counselling for 190
 somatic mutations 134–6
 susceptibility testing 164
cancer genome *111,* 135
candidate genes 130
carbohydrates *68, 69*

carrier testing 156, **158**

carriers **47,** 48, 49–50, *94*

CCL3L1 gene 131–2

Celera Genomics 112

cell cycle 9–12
and cancer 134–5

cell division *9,* **10**–12, 77
in cancer 136, 137–8
see also **mitosis**

cell growth *9, 10*

cell membrane 7–8, *9, 11,* 69, *70,* 71

cells 2, **7**–9, 154
in cancer 134–8
components of 68–9
gcrmline 20, 93
proteins and genes 91–2
somatic 20, 21, 134, 170
transcription and translation 88

centromere 10, *11, 79, 115*
repetitive DNA and 124, *127*

cf and *CF* alleles 47–49, 101, 103–5

chance 45, 49, 150–1, 152

characters 1, **16**–17
gene inheritance 32–3
and natural selection 146, 150
X-linked 36–7
see also **multifactorial characters**

childhood testing 156, 161–2

cholera 150

cholesterol 64, 65

chorionic villi sampling 160

chromatids 10, *11, 14, 16,* 79

chromosome mutation 93, 98–100
see also DNA mutation; **gene mutation**

chromosomes 2, *7,* **8**
chromosome 1 125, *126*
chromosome 2 127
chromosome 4 106
chromosome 7 101, 103
chromosome 15 128, 129
chromosome 17 131–2
chromosome 21 98–9, 125, *126,* 127
chromosome 22 122, 125, *126*
DNA organisation along 115–16
and DNA replication 79–80

DNA sequence 121, 122–5
during cell division 10–11
gene distribution 125–7
in gametes 20–3, 24–6, 99
gene density 123, *126,* 130
human genome 14–16, 112, 202, *203*
recombination 26–9
repetitive DNA on 127
see also **homologous** chromosomes;
    sex chromosomes

cleft lip/palate 62, 168

clinical effectiveness 184

clinical phenotype 101

clinical trials 176

club-foot *67,* 198

clustered repetitive DNA 115, 116, 124

codeine 175

codominant alleles 38

codon 85–6, *87,* 88, 89, *90,* 91
and gene mutation 96
in Huntington's disease 106–8

colorectal (bowel) cancer 141, 162

colour blindness 36–7, *111*

commercial interest, genetic testing
    164–7

complementary base pairs 76–7, *78,* 84

confidentiality 162

congenital bilateral absence of the vas
    deferens (CBAVD) 179–80

congenital hypothyroidism 191

conserved sequence **119**

consultation, genetic technologies 193–4

continuous variation 55

coronary heart disease 52
environmental risk factors 65–6
genetic susceptibility 63–4
susceptibility testing 164

counselling, genetic 47, 157–8, 189–90

Crick, Francis *74, 75,* 77

crossing over 26, **28**–9

cysteine *90*

cystic fibrosis (CF) 46–52, *111,* 179–80
childhood testing 161
DNA mutation 101–5
gene chips for 189
gene therapy 169, 172

from genotype to phenotype *105*
pedigree charts *158, 163*
population screening 186–7, 191
in populations 144, 145, 150
prenatal diagnosis 158–9

cystic fibrosis gene *47, 103,* 114, 121, 145

cystic fibrosis protein (CFP) 104, 105

cytosine (**C**) **75,** 76, 77, *78*
in RNA 83–4

cytosol *7,* **8,** *11,* 69
translation in 88

D

Darwin, Charles 146

databases 3, 113, 121, 122, 130
biobanks 152
DNA databanks 177–8

deafness 123, 150, 152

deaths, cancer 134, 141

deCODE 152, 177

degenerate genetic code 90

deoxyribonucleic acid
    see **DNA**

deoxyribose 75

designer babies 173–4

designer drug therapy 174–8

diabetes 164, 170

diagnostic therapeutic gap 168

diet 68–9
and cancer 142
and coronary heart disease 65
and phenylketonuria 185, 186
during pregnancy 62, 63, 65

diploid 21, 26

diploid number 21

discontinuous variation 55

diseases *see* human diseases

dispersed repetitive DNA 115, 125

DNA 2, **75**
in cells *68, 69*
chemical structure 74–7
in gene therapy 169, 171, 172
gene visualisation 102–3
genetic information stored in 81–92
and genome organisation 113–16

molecular cloning 202–3
ownership of 166–7
repair enzymes 97, 140
stability of 74, 75
transcription 82–4
variants 117, 188–9
see also repetitive DNA
DNA databanks 177–8
DNA fragments 102–103, 202–203, 205
DNA mutation
in cystic fibrosis 101, 103–5
Huntington's disease 106–8
in populations 145
rate of 97–8
see also **alleles; chromosome mutation; gene mutation**
DNA polymerase 78, 204, 205
DNA probes *127*
DNA repair genes 136, 137, 140
DNA replication 10, 77, **78**–80
and amplification 102–3, 107
errors in *95*, 96, 97, 200
semi-conservative 79, 198
DNA sequences 4, *83*, 204–7
analysing 102–3, 121
chromosome 21 121, 122–5
and genes 113–5
Huntington's disease 106
milestones in research *111*, 112
other 115–16
in populations 145
RAS gene 137–8
variations in 116–7
DNA sequencing 204–7
dominant alleles 33–6
codominant 38
dominant disorders 41, **43**–6, 106
see also Huntington's disease
dominant phenotype **35**
double helix *74, 75*, 76–7, *78, 79, 80*
Down's syndrome 98–100, 122
prenatal diagnosis 156, 158, *160*
draft sequences 2, *3, 111,* 112

Duchenne muscular dystrophy 127
duplication, segmental 131

E

education
and genetic testing 177
health workers 192–3
eggs
fertilised 9, *12,* 24–6
formation 19–24
twin production *57, 58*
elderly *see* age
embryo *12, 21,* 24
genetic alteration 173
Human Fertility and Embryology Authority 173, 193
pre-implantation genetic diagnosis 161
saviour siblings 173
employment and genetic testing 165–6
endoplasmic reticulum *7, 8,* 69
environment 17, 53–**54**
and cancer 141–2
and coronary heart disease 65–6
and genotype 56–9, 60
interplay with genetics *66*
and phenotype 17, 53–60
within the uterus 62–3, 65
enzymes *70,* 71
DNA repair 97, 140
in genetics research *111,* 112
in phenylketonuria 185
Escherichia coli 117
ethics
genetic testing 157
germline therapy 173, 174
pre-implantation testing 161
ethnicity
cystic fibrosis 46, 145, 150
and gene variants 145
human genome 112–13, 117
Huntington's disease 43
and pharmacogenetics 177
and sickle cell disease 147, 149
see also **populations**
eugenics 174

Europeans
cystic fibrosis 46, 145, 150
height 59
PKU screening 186
royal families 93, *94*
see also UK
exons 114, 127
in *OCA2* gene 128–9
eye colour 1, 4, 17, *111,* 121, 145
OCA2 gene and 128–9

F

false positive results 186
familial adenomatous polyposis coli (FAP) 162
familial essential tremor 152
familial hypercholesterolaemia *52, 197*
familial retinoblastoma 139, 140
families
adult testing 163
carrier testing 156, 158–9
characters in 1, 16
childhood testing 162
intermarriage 50, 151
royalty 93–4
saviour siblings 173
variations in 17
see also mothers; twins
family history 32–3, 49, 156
family trees 42
fatalism 190
fats *68,* 69
female
karyotype *14,* 16
maternal age and Down's syndrome *99,* 100, 156
maternal serum screening 160
meiosis in 23–4
fertilisation 19, *22,* 24–6, *34*
and chromosome mutation 99
fertilised egg 9, *12,* 24–6
fetal programming 65
fetoscopy 160
fetus *12*
and the uterine environment 62–3, 65
prenatal diagnosis 156, 158–61

Rhesus system 33
sex of 30
folic acid 63, 142, 178
food *see* diet
frequency
  cystic fibrosis 49–50, 150
  Down's syndrome *99, 100*
  of gene variants 145, 146
  Hb allele *148, 149, 150*
fruit-fly genome *117*

G

gametes 19
  and chromosome mutation 99
  fertilisation 24–6, *34*
  and gene mutation 93
  independent assortment in *27*
  meiosis 20–4, *34*
  Rhesus system gene in 34–35
gel electrophoresis *102,* 103, 107, *205,*
  206
gene chips 188–9
gene density 123, *126,* 130
gene distribution 125–7
gene family 124, 127
gene mutation 93–5
  APP gene 123–4
  protein structure from 95–7
  see also **chromosome mutation;**
    DNA mutation
gene product 91
gene therapy 168–73, 202–3
  germline 172–3
  somatic 170–2
gene variants *see* **variants**
genes 1, **32,** 127
  and cancer 136–40
  causing genetic diseases 130
  chromosome 21 122–4
  in chromosomes 16
  distribution within the genome 125–7
  inheritance 32–9
  milestones in research 4, *111*
  one gene–one protein hypothesis
    81–2
  perspectives for consideration *5*
  and populations 144–53
  proteins and cells 91–2

split 114
  and supporting sequences 113–15
  switched on/off 91, 114, 124, 172
  visualisation in DNA 102–3
  see also **alleles**
genetic citizenship 166–7
genetic code 85–6, **89**–91, *111*
genetic counselling 47, **157**–8, 189–90
genetic disorders 41–52
  genes causing 130
  late-onset multifactorial 162, 164
  late-onset single-gene 162, 163–4
  multifactorial inheritance of 53, 62–7
  population screening 184–8
  prenatal diagnosis *160*
genetic information 59, 157
Genetic Information Discrimination Act
  (GINA) 165
genetic modification 169–70
genetic organisation *see* DNA
  sequences; human genome
genetic ratios *see* **ratios**
genetic risk factors 63–4, 183, 189
genetic testing
  adults 156, 162–4
  children 156, 161–2
  and commercial interest 164–7
  education issues 177
  and health care provision 183
  and personal genomics 178
  prenatal diagnosis 156, 158–61
  susceptibility 164, 178, 179, 201
  in the UK 191
genetics
  environmental interplay *66*
  expectations and prospects 179–81
  media portrayal of 2, *3,* 180–1
  pharmacogenetics 175–7, 183
  tackling problems in 51
Genetics and Insurance Committee
  (GAIC) 165
genetics research *111,* 112
genomes
  and cell division 10–12
  milestones in research *111*
  organisation of 113
  representative organisms 117–19
  see also human genome; **Human**
    Genome Project (HGP)

genomics, personal 178–9, 189
genotype 17, 34, 35
  cystic fibrosis 48, *105*
  and drug effectiveness 175
  and environment 56–9, 60
  Hb alleles *149*
  Huntington's disease 43–4
  to phenotype *105*
  X-linked characters 37
German measles 62
germline cells 20, 21, 93
germline gene therapy 172–3,
  174
Ghana screening programme 187
glutamate *90*
glutamine *90,* 106, 108
glycine *90*
guanine (**G**) **75,** 76, 77, *78*
  in RNA 83–4
Guthrie test *186,* 191, *192*

H

haemoglobin 8, 69, *70*
  disorders of 188
  nucleotide sequence in different
    organisms 119
haemoglobin A 146, 147, 149
haemoglobin S 146, 147, 149
haemophilia 93–4, *111,* 170
haploid 20
Hb allele 147, *148,* 150
  genotypes and phenotypes *149*
health care provision 4, 154, 183–4
  in the UK 191–4
health workers 184, 187
  counselling and decision-making
    189–90
  training and education 192–3
heart disease *see* coronary heart
  disease
heel-prick test *186,* 191, *192*
height 54–6
  around the world 59–60
heritable variation 93
heterozygote 35, *94*
  sickle cell disease 147, 149, 150
heterozygous 35, 38, *44,* 47
  and cystic fibrosis 104, 105

high income countries
    coronary heart disease 63
    genetic testing 156, 177
    health care provision 154, 183
    multifactorial disorders 164
    and pharmacogenetics 176
    population screening 186, 187
    see also Europeans; UK; USA
histidine *90*
HIV/AIDS 131–2, 174
homologous chromosomes **15,** 16, 20
    crossing over 28
    non-separation of 99
homozygote 35
    sickle cell disease 147, *148,* 149
homozygous 35, 38, *44*
    and cystic fibrosis 104, 105
hormones 65
human clotting factor 94, 170
human diseases
    and chromosome 21 123
    classification 41
    continuum of 66
    and the Human Genome Project 119,
    121
    see also **genetic disorders**
Human Fertility and Embryology
    Authority (HFEA) 173, 193
human genome *1,* 2, 154–5
    analysis of 121–33
    chemical structure 74–80
    chromosomal constitution 14–6
    databases 113, 121, 122, 130
    deciphering 110–3
    diversity in 151–2
    duplicated regions in 131–2
    gene distribution within 125–7
    genetic variation in 116–7,
    128–9
    organisation 113–6
    repetitive DNA across 127
    size *117,* 118
    subdividing and sequencing 202–7
Human Genome Consortium 112
Human Genome Project (HGP) 2–4,
    110
    data storage 113, 121
    environment/genetic interplay 142
    establishment and funding 112

gene mapping 115
    human diseases and 119, 121
    media portrayal of 180
    role of other organisms 119
    significant steps in development *111*
human life cycle and chromosome
    number 20, *21,* 24
Huntingtin gene 106
Huntington's disease (HD) 42–6
    adult testing 162, 163
    biosociality 166
    childhood testing 162
    DNA mutation 106–8
    and insurance companies 165
    pedigree chart *42*
hypercholesterolaemia, familial *52,*
    197
hypertension 63–4, 65
hypothyroidism, congenital 191

identical twins 17, 53, 57–9
    club-foot *67,* 198
    height *60,* 198
immune response 172
in-vitro fertilisation (IVF) 24, 161, 172,
    173
incidence, cancer 136, 141, 142
incomplete dominance 147
independent assortment 26, **27**
individual human genome sequences
    112, 116, 129
individuals
    characters in 1, **16**
    growth of 12
    phenotype and genotype 17
infertility 46, 100, 101, 179–80
inheritance
    breast cancer 189–90
    genes 32–9
    genetic disorders 41–52
    heritable variation 93
    multifactorial 53, 62–7
    retinoblastoma 139
    X-linked 36–7, 173
    xeroderma pigmentosum 140
    see also **multifactorial disorders;**
    single-gene inheritance

insulin 170
insurance companies 165–6
intermarriage 50, 151
introns 114, 117, 123, 128
invasive techniques 160
in vitro fertilisation (IVF) 24
isolated populations 150, 151–2
isoleucine *90*

J

Japanese, cancer incidence 141

K

KAP gene 124, *126,* 127
karyotype 14–16
    chromosome 21 122
    and chromosome mutation 98
keratin 124
Koshland, Daniel 180
Kumasi, Ghana 187

L

lactase 71
lactose 71
late-onset multifactorial disorders 162,
    164
late-onset single-gene disorders 163–4
leucine *90,* 96
leukaemia 123, 135, 172
life expectancy, cystic fibrosis 46
liposomes 171
locus 33
locust genome *117,* 118
low birth weight 65
low income countries
    health care provision 154, 183
    population screening 187
    see also Africa; Asians
lung cancer 141
lysine *90*

M

malaria 146, 147, *148,* 149–50, 153
male
    colour blindness 37

karyotype *15, 16*
  meiosis in 23
maternal *see* mothers
mating diagram 24, *25, 26, 27, 34,*
  196
  cystic fibrosis *47*
  Huntingdon's disease *44*
  X chromosome *36*
MCADD 191
media, genetics portrayal in 2, *3,*
  180–1
meiosis 20–4, *34*
  and chromosome mutation 99
  chromosome recombination 26–9
membrane proteins 124, 137
mental retardation 63, 185, 186
messenger RNA *see* mRNA
methionine 85, *86,* 87, 90
migration 151
Ministry of Defence 165
mitochondria *7,* 8, 69
mitosis 10, *11, 14,* 79
  and meiosis 20
model organisms 119
molecular cloning *111,* 202–3
mothers
  age and Down's syndrome *99,* 100,
    156
  Rhesus system 33
  serum screening 160
mouse genome *111, 117,* 118,
  119
mRNA 85–8, 89, *90,* 91
  and gene mutation 96
mucus 46, 101, 104–5, 179, *187*
multifactorial characters 53
  height 54–6
  height around the world 59–60
  twin studies 57–9
multifactorial disorders 62–7
multiple alleles 38–*9*
muscle cells *8,* 9, *70,* 72, 91, 127
muscular dystrophy 127
mutagens 97–8, 141
mutation *see* **chromosome mutation;**
  DNA mutation; **gene mutation;**
  somatic mutation
myoglobin *70,* 71, 72, 73, 91

N

National Health Service (NHS) 193
natural selection 146–50, 152
nature–nurture debate 56
Neanderthal sequence *111,* 112, 113
nerve cells *8, 9*
  in Huntington's disease 106
New Guinea 150
newborn
  birth weight 56–7, 65
  designer babies 173–4
  screening 185–6, 187, 191–2
Newfoundland 152
non-directiveness, in counselling 157
non-identical twins *57, 58, 60, 67*
non-invasive techniques *160*
non-template strand 83, 84, 86
normal distribution 55
normal variation 33
nuclear membrane *7,* 8, 10–11
nucleotides 75–76, 78, 204–6, *207*
  in cystic fibrosis 101, 103
  gene mutation *95,* 96–7
  in the human genome 113
  in RNA 82–4, 85
nucleus 2, *7,* **8**
  transcription in 88
nutrigenomics 178, 181
nutrition *see* diet

O

obesity 65
OCA2 gene 128–9, 145
oncogenes 136, 137–8, 140
one gene–one protein hypothesis 81–2
organisms
  genetic modification 169–70
  genomes of 117–19
ovarian cancer 190
ovaries 19
oxygen transport *70, 71, 72*

P

P450 protein 175
pancreas 46, 101, 104, 105
parent cells 10

parent strands *78, 79*
parents *see* families; inheritance
patents 166
patients' groups 166, 167
pedigree charts 42, *46, 52*
  cystic fibrosis *158*
  haemophilia *94*
  Huntingdon's disease *163*
  recessive genetic disorder *50*
  retinoblastoma *139*
personal genomics 178–9
pharmacogenetics 174, 175–7
pharmacogenomics 178
phenotype 17, 33
  clinical 101–9
  cystic fibrosis 47, 105
  dominant and recessive 35, 37, 105
  environmental factors 17, 53–61
  from genotype *105*
  for *Hb* alleles *149*
  Huntington's disease 45, 106
  pedigree charts 42
  and uterine environment 63
  variations in 39, 55–6
  X-linked characters 37
phenylalanine *90,* 185, 186
phenylketonuria (PKU) 185–6, 191
phosphate 75, 76, 77, 78, 204
plaque deposits, arteries 63, *64*
Plasmodium 149
polycystic kidney disease 162
polymerase chain reaction (PCR) 102–3
population genetics 144
population growth, global *144*
populations 144–53
  chance or random events 150–1
  differences between 144–6
  human genome diversity 151–2
  natural selection 146–50
  screening 184–8, 191–2
  see also ethnicity
porphyria 153
pre-implantation genetic diagnosis
  161, 173
pre-symptomatic testing 162, 163
predicted ratio 49
predictive medicine 183–4
predictive tests 156
  insurance companies and 165
pregnancy
  maternal nutrition 65

prenatal diagnosis 4, 156, 158–61, 188, 191
uterine environment 62–3
prenatal diagnosis (PND) 4, 156, **158**–61, 188, 191
prevalence 146
primary structure 72, 73
probability 45, 49
for two or more separate events 48
progeny cells *9,* 10, 11
in cancer 135
proline 85, *87, 90*
proteins 68, **69**–71
from gene mutation 95–7
from genetic modification 169–70
genes and cells 91–2
information flow from DNA 82
membrane proteins 124, 137
one gene–one protein hypothesis 81–2
from protein to phenotype 101–9
from RNA translation 85–8
from split genes 114
structure 71–3
see also **amino acids;** enzymes
proto-oncogenes 136–7, 138, 140

R

random events 150–1
RAS gene 137–8
ratios 23, 24, 25
deviation from expected 48–52
genetic 44–6, 47
recessive alleles 33–6, 37
recessive disorders 41, **46**–52, 104, 129
prenatal screening 188
see also cystic fibrosis
recessive phenotype **35,** 37, 105
recombination 26–9
red blindness 36–7
red blood cells *8,* 9, 38, 69, *70*
Rhesus system 33–5
in sickle cell disease 146–7, 149
in thalassaemia 188
regional genetics centres 191
regulation, genetic technologies 193–4
repair enzymes 97, 140
repetitive DNA 115, 116, 118

across the genome 127
in chromosome 21 124–5
repetitive strain injury (RSI) 165
reproduction 19, 20, 24, 146
flow diagram *195*
see also **fertilisation; meiosis**
reproductive success 146, 147, 149
restriction enzymes *111*
retinoblastoma
familial 139
gene 138, 140
Rhesus blood group system 33–5, 41, 55, 93
ribonucleic acid 82
see also **RNA**
ribose 82
ribosomal RNA *see* **rRNA**
risk factors 63–4, 183, 189
environmental 65–6
RNA 82
from transcription 82–4
translation 85–8
see also **mRNA, rRNA, tRNA**
RNA polymerase 84
rRNA 88
rubella 62

S

salt
and blood pressure 64
intake 65
transport 46, 101, 104–5, 179
saviour siblings 173
schizophrenia 190
screening 157, 160, **184**–8
newborn 185–6, 187, 191–2
scaling up 188–90
segmental duplications 131, 132
segregation 23
semi-conservative replication 79, 198
serine *90*
sex chromosomes 16
during gamete formation 22–3, 24–6
see also X chromosomes; Y chromosomes
Siamese cats 53, *54*
siblings *see* families; twins

sickle cell disease (SCD) 144, 146–50, 152
gene therapy 172
genetic testing 165
population screening 187, 191
sickle cell trait 147, 150
single-gene inheritance 33–6
disorders 41, 162, 163–4
skin cancer 140
skin cells *8*
skin colour 145
smoking 65, 141, 142
somatic cells 20, 21, 134, 170
somatic gene therapy 170–2
somatic mutation 134–6
sperm
in cell division *9*
cells *8*
formation 19–24
spina bifida 62, 63, 158, *160*
split genes 114
spontaneous abortions 100, 160
sporadic retinoblastoma 139
staining techniques 15, 102
start codon 87, 90
stop codon 88, 89
stress 65
stroke 152
sugar–phosphate backbone 75, 76, 77, *78,* 204
susceptibility factors 189
see also **risk factors**
susceptibility testing 164, 178, 179, 201
susceptible alleles 62, 142, 164
switched on/off gene 91, 114, 124
in gene therapy 172

T

Tay–Sachs disease *52, 197*
template 78
strand 83, 84, 91, *95*
'tentative' pregnancy 159
testes 19
thalassaemia 153, 188
thalidomide 62
threonine *90*

thymine (**T**) **75,** 76, 77, *78*

titin 127

toxigenomics 178

training, health workers 192–3

transcription 82–4

in cells 88

and gene mutation 96

transfer RNA *see* **tRNA**

translation 82, 85–8

in cells 88

and gene mutation 96

transport proteins *70, 71*

triplet repeat 106, *107*

tRNA 86–8

tryptophan *90*

TSH2B gene 127

tumour-suppressor genes 136–7, 138–40

tumours 136, 138–9

pre-symptomatic testing 162

twins 17, 53, 57–9

blood pressure 64

club-foot *67,* 198

height *60,* 198

tyrosine *90,* 185

U

UK

cancer 141

cystic fibrosis 46, 49

genetic disorders 41

genetic testing provision 191

health care worker training and education 192–3

newborn screening 191–2

regulation and consultation policies 193–4

rhesus factor *55*

thalassaemia screening 188

UK Biobank 177

UK Genetic Testing Network 191

UK Human Fertility and Embryology Authority (HFEA) 173, 193

UK Human Genetics Commission 193

UK Insurance industry 165

UK Ministry of Defence 165

UK NHS genetic infrastructure 193

ultrasonography 160

ultraviolet light 98, 140, 141

unit of inheritance 32

uracil (**U**) 83–4, 85, *90*

USA

adverse drug effects 175

cancer 141, 142

cystic fibrosis 46

Genetic Information Discrimination Act (GINA) 165

native Americans 145

PKU screening 186

uterus 62–3, 65

V

valine *90,* 96

variants 17

bases 128–9

DNA *102, 111,* 117, 188–9

environmental factors 141–2

genetic diseases 130

between populations 145–6

see also **alleles**

variation 17, 19, 26, 33, 95

continuous and discontinuous 55

heritable 93

in the human genome 116–17, 128–9

in phenotypes 39, 55–6

Venter, Craig 112, 116

viruses 118, 119, 171

W

Watson, James *74,* 75, 77, 112, 116

Wilkins, Maurice 75

womb 17

world population growth *144*

X

X chromosomes *14,* 16, 22–3, 24–5, 94

X-linked genes 36–7

X-linked inheritance 36–7, 173

X-rays 98

xeroderma pigmentosum 140

Y

Y chromosomes 16, 22–3, 24–5, *126*

yeast genome *111, 117,* 118